MEMOIRS of a
SURREY LABOURER

Also available in 'Country Classics'

The Essential Gilbert White of Selborne
The Gardener's Essential Gertrude Jekyll
Life in a Devon Village by Henry Williamson

A selection of other titles by George Bourne
is available from Caliban Books, 25 Nassington
Road, London NW3 under the name of George Sturt

MEMOIRS OF A SURREY LABOURER

George Bourne

LONDON

Breslich & Foss
43 Museum Street
London WC1A 1LY

First published by Duckworth & Co 1907
Published by Breslich & Foss 1983
Series design: Lawrence & Gerry Design Group

*British Library Cataloguing
in Publication Data*

Bourne, George
     Memoirs of a Surrey Labourer.
     1. Surrey—Social life and customs
     I. Title
     942.2'1081'0924   DA670.596

     ISBN 1-85004-006-0 Pbk.

Printed in Great Britain by
Richard Clay (The Chaucer Press) Ltd,
Bungay, Suffolk

PREFACE

George Bourne (1863-1927) was George Sturt, the owner of a wheelwright business, who took his pen-name from the village where he lived, The Bourne, three miles south of Farnham in Surrey. In 1901 Duckworth & Co published his first book, *The Bettesworth Book*, subtitled 'Talks with a Surrey Peasant' and containing a series of loosely linked conversations with his odd-job man and part-time gardener, an ageing labourer called Frederick Bettesworth. The book was well received by most reviewers and a second impression was made in the following year.

Bourne followed this success with *Memoirs of a Surrey Labourer* in 1907, the subtitle this time being 'A Record of the Last Years of Frederick Bettesworth'. Although Bourne confessed that he was unhappy with the narrative flow of the book, writing that 'the hoped-for sense of progression is too often wanting', it has a strong sense of direction (provided by the approaching death of the old man) which is lacking in the earlier book. It also contains more of Bourne's own words in the form of descriptions of Bettesworth and the passing seasons. Despite the author's modest protestations to the contrary, this is a great advantage, for not only did he possess a gifted ear for dialogue and the nuances of dialect, he was also the master of that clean, uncomplicated prose style that is so well suited to describing the natural world. Henry Williamson, who wrote in a similar manner, introduced a sample of Bourne's work in an anthology with the exclamation, 'There's writing for you'. In many ways *Memoirs of a Surrey Labourer* is a better book than its predecessor. It certainly does not need to be read as a sequel.

Certain points in the introduction to *The Bettesworth Book*, however, may prove valuable to a reader of the *Memoirs*. The first is that Bourne was at pains to emphasise that Fred Bettesworth was 'a type of his class':

> ...it is becoming increasingly plain to me that Bettesworth is as other men, or — what is more to the purpose — that there are thousands of other men who are as Bettesworth is...You see these men about the roads, living their lives unconcernedly and, so far as the book-learned know, obscurely, yet having an unsuspected fame amongst their own people. ...And so, when I hearken to Bettesworth, I feel that it is not to an exceptional man, and still less to an oddity that I am listening; but that in his quiet voice I am privileged to hear the natural, fluent, unconscous talk, as it goes on over the face of the country, of the English Race, rugged, unresting, irresistible.

The next point of note is that in the introduction to *The Bettesworth Book* Bourne described the neighbourhood in which he lived. The unrelenting pressures of the last eighty or so years have altered this area, even as similar pressures were doing in Bourne's own day. It may be helpful to have his description:

...for understanding several points that might otherwise be obscure in Bettesworth's talk, it should be known that we are on the borders of the shaggy waste-land of Surrey. Looking south-wards from our garden we can see it rolling up in long hills, their distant ridges serrated by the multitudinous crests of fir-trees, their slopes brown with heath.

Little else will that waste-land bear, it might be supposed. Yet in truth our valley, green enough in its disordered way, has itself been reclaimed from the waste chiefly during the last half-century. Fifty years ago it was for the most part a common traversed by sand-tracks where now are the hard roads. Then, little by little, the valley was settled; small gardens were enclosed and rough shanties run up by squatters whom none found it worth while to molest. To-day the village, if that name may be applied to so anom-alous a community, lies scattered disorderly, rubbishy-looking, with scarce six houses any-where in a row, for a mile or more on either side of the deep but narrow valley. It is a village without a history, without any central life; and hence the people at one end of it are strangers to those at the other. In the absense of large farms their employment is unsettled, their poverty very great; but, perhaps because of that, one after another they are painfully civilising a very savage tract of English earth.

Bettesworth himself, a native of the place, has done his share towards taming its wildness. This garden of ours owes much to his labour in helping to form it thirty years ago. On the sheltered south-western slope of a spur of hill jutting into the valley, it was still at that time an almost unmanageable sand heap, very steep. Aided by Bettesworth, the owner terraced it up with low walls and grassy banks. "When old Andrew fust come here," Bettesworth has told me, "'twas nothing' but a prighty" (? upright) "hill. He *have* put in some labour here. You'd never find 'n indoors. I've seed'n up on this hill when 'twas cold 'nough to perish a monkey." It is now a brilliant picture of what untiring industry may make out of the most unpromising material.

Bourne also had some interesting comments to make about the way in which he had set down Bettesworth's talk, and since the old Surrey dialect is now virtually extinct, the account of how he preserved it in these pages is worth repeating:

> In reading these conversations it should be remembered that the talk is very rapid as well as very quiet. Without hesitation the words follow one another, every sentence mumbled out as though it were one long polysyllable. Strict phonetic accuracy in the spelling would have made reading almost impossible. I have attempted only to suggest the dialect, not to reproduce it. The items of that farmer's bill for horse hire —
> "Aorsafada, 3s 6d.;

Atakinofunomagen, 6d." —
were set down with phonetic exactness, but they are not easy to understand. Besides, although defective in much besides aspirates (which I have freely supplied where they never occur), Bettesworth's language is a form of English, and deserves to be written as nearly as may be in the normal manner.

It would be unjust to Bourne to omit the reforming note, present in the introduction to *Bettesworth* as in his later books. He felt strongly, as Cobbett had years before him, about the way the English peasant class had been dispossessed by the enclosure of the common land:

> ...in gossiping about his own life Bettesworth is unawares telling of the similar lives, as lived for ages, of a type of Englishmen that may perhaps be hard to meet with in time to come. For it seems as though destiny has decreed that this class of men, by centuries of incalculable struggle and valiant endurance, should prepare England's soil not for themselves, but for the reaping machine and jerry-builder.

Bourne followed the *Memoirs* with *The Ascending Effort* (1910). In 1912 he wrote his most important book from the point of view of the social historian, *Change in the Village* (1912). There he distilled into a sobering and humane document, the feeling and suppressed emotion of the books about Bettesworth, as well as the experience of a lifetime lived as both the employer and friend of the Surrey labourer.

He wrote five more books: *Lucy Bettesworth* (1913), *William Smith, Potter and Farmer* (1920), *A Farmer's Life* (1922), *The Wheelwright's Shop* (1923), and *A Small Boy in the Sixties* (1927), the last two appearing under the name of Sturt. Of these *The Wheelwright's Shop* has often been claimed as his masterpiece, and certainly as a sociological record of a vanishing craft, and indeed the disappearance of a whole way of life, it is magnificent. It lacks, however, the literary quality of the *Memoirs*. This came from three sources: the concentrated prose that derived from striving to record one man, from the strong affection Bourne clearly felt for the old man, and from Fred Bettesworth himself.

The *Memoir* has a lyrical quality. It achieves this more by accident than art, but it is there nonetheless.

One critic, noticing that Bourne wrote no poetry, remarked that he had no poetry in him. To this the only reply is Bourne's own words, 'this old Bettesworth and his kind are not without poetry because they lack verse.'

Nicholas Robinson

INTRODUCTION

BETTESWORTH, the old labouring man, who in the
decline of his strength found employment in my
garden and entertained me with his talk, never
knew that he had been made the subject of a book.
To know it would have pleased him vastly, and
there is something tragical in the reflection that he
had to wear through his last weary months without
the consolation of the little fame he had justly
earned ; and yet it would have been a mistake to
tell him of it. His up-bringing had not fitted him
for publicity. On the contrary, there was so much
danger that self-consciousness would send him
boastfully drinking about the parish, and make him
intolerable to his familiars and useless to any employer, that, instead of confessing to him what I
had done, I took every precaution to keep him in
ignorance of it, and sought by leaving him in
obscurity to preserve him from ruin.

Obscure and unsuspicious he continued his work,
and his pleasant garrulity went on in its accustomed
way. Queer anecdotes came from him as plenti-
fully as ever, and shrewd observations. Now it
would be of his harvesting in Sussex that he told ;
now, of an adventure with a troublesome horse,

or an experience on the scaffolding of a building ; and again he would gossip of his garden, or of his neighbours, or of the old village life, or would discuss some scrap of news picked up at the public-house. And as this went on month after month, although I had no intention of adding to the first book or writing a second on the same lines, still it happened frequently that some fragment or other of Bettesworth's conversation took my fancy and was jotted down in my note-book. But almost until the end no definite purpose informed me what to preserve and what to leave. The notes were made, for the most part, under the influence of whim only.

Towards the end, however, a sort of progression seemed to reveal itself in these haphazard jottings. His age was telling heavily upon Bettesworth, and symptoms of the inevitable change appeared to have been creeping unawares into my careless memoranda of his talk. I do not know when I first noticed this : it probably dawned upon me very slowly ; but that it did dawn is certain, and in that perception I had the first crude vision of the present volume. I might not aim to make another book after the pattern of the first, grouping the materials as it pleased me for an artistic end ; but by repro-ducing the notes in their proper order, and leaving them to tell their own tale, it should be possible to engage as it were the co-operation of Nature herself, my own part being merely that of a scribe, recording at the dictation of events the process of Bettes-worth's decay.

To this idea, formed a year or so before Bettes-

INTRODUCTION

worth's death, I have now tried to give shape. Unfortunately, the scribe's work was not well done. Things that should have been written down prove to have been overlooked ; and although in the first few chapters I have gone back to a much earlier period than was originally intended, and have preserved the chronological order all through, the hoped-for sense of progression is too often wanting. It existed in my mind, in the memories which the notes called up for me, rather than in Bettesworth's recorded conversations. Much explanatory comment, therefore, which I should have preferred to omit, has been introduced in order to give continuity to the narrative.

Bettesworth is spoken of throughout the book as an old man ; and that is what he appeared to be. But in fact he was aged more by wear and tear than by years. When he died, a nephew who arranged the funeral caused the age of seventy-three to be marked on his coffin, but I think this was an exaggeration. The nephew's mother assured me at the time that Bettesworth could have been no more than sixty-six. She was his sister-in-law, having married his elder brother, and so had some right to an opinion ; and yet probably he was a little older than she supposed. It is true that sixty-six is also the age one gets for him, computing it from evidence given in one chapter of this book ; but then there is another chapter which, if it is correct, would make him sixty-seven. Against these estimates a definite statement is to be placed. On the second of October, 1901, Bettesworth told me that it was his birthday, and that he was sixty-four; according to which, at his death, nearly four years later, he must have been close upon sixty-eight. And this, I am inclined to think, was his true age; at any rate I cannot believe that he was younger.

At the same time, it must be allowed that his own evidence was not quite to be trusted. A man in his position, with the workhouse waiting for him, will not make the most of his years to an employer, and I sometimes fancied that Bettesworth wished me to think him younger than he was. But it is quite possible that he was not himself certain of his own age. I have it from his sister-in-law that both his parents died while he was still a child, and that he, with his brothers and sisters, was taken, destitute, to the workhouse. Thence, I suppose, he was rescued by that uncle, who kept a travelling van; and the man who carried the boy to fairs and racecourses, and thrashed him so savagely that at last he ran away to become Farmer Barnes's plough-boy, was not a person likely to instruct him very carefully about his age.

The point, however, is of no real importance. A labourer who has at least the look of being old: thin, grey-eyed, quiet, with bent shoulders and patient though determined expression of face— such is the Bettesworth whose last years are recorded in these chapters; and it does not much matter that we should know exactly how many years it took to reduce him to this state.

MEMOIRS OF A SURREY LABOURER

I

December 7, 1892.—The ground in the upper part of the garden being too hard frozen for Bettesworth to continue this morning the work he was doing there yesterday, I found him some digging to do in a more sheltered corner, where the fork would enter the soil. With snow threatening to come and stop all outdoor work, it was not well that he should stand idle too soon.

"Oh dear!" he said one day, "we don't want no snow! We had enough o' that two winters ago. That was a fair scorcher, that was. There! I couldn't tell anybody how we *did* git through. Still, we *got* through, somehow. But there was some about here as was purty near starved. That poor woman as died over here t'other day. . . ."

Here he broke off, to tell of a labourer's wife who had died in giving birth to twins, one of whom was also dead. Including the other twin, there were seven children living. Bettesworth talked of the husband, too; but presently working round again to the bad winter of 1889-1890, he proceeded :

"' I *knows* they " (this woman and her family)
" was purty near starvin'. *I* give her two or three
half-bushels o' taters. I can't bear to see 'em like
that, 'specially if there's little childern about. I
give away bushels o' taters that winter, 'cause them
as *had* got any had got 'em buried away—couldn't
git at 'em (in the frozen ground). Mine was stowed
away where I could git 'em."

Accordingly, anticipating hard times, I set Bettesworth to work in the sheltered spot where digging
was still possible, and left him. The day proved
sunny on the whole, with a soft winter sunshine,
dimmed now and then by grey fog close down to
the earth, and now and then by large drifts of
foggy cloud passing over from the north. By
mid-day the roads were sticky, where the sunshine
had thawed the surface, but in shady places the
ground was still hard. Here and there was ice,
and odd corners remained white with the sprinkling
of snow which had fallen two nights previously.

Towards sunset I went to see what Bettesworth
had done. He had done very little, and, moreover,
he had disappeared. The air glowed with the yellow
sunset ; the soft dim blue of the upper sky was
changing to hazy grey in the south-east ; in the
west, veiling the sunset, lay a bank of clouds,
crimson shaded to lilac. I turned to ᵣnjoy this as I
climbed the garden to find Bettesworth, where he
was busy at his yesterday's task.

" Well, Bettesworth, how are you getting on ?"

" Oh, *cold*, sir."

Overhead, one or two wisps of smoky-looking cloud were floating southwards. In the sunlight they showed amber against the soft blue, but from their movement and their indistinct and changing form it was plain that they belonged to the system of those larger clouds which had all day been crossing ominously out of the north. I glanced up at them, and remarked that I feared the snow was not far off now.

Bettesworth straightened up from his work.

" Ah, that's what everybody bin sayin'."

" Well, it looks uncommonly like coming."

" Ah, it do. Didn't it look black there, along about nine or ten o'clock this mornin' ? I thought then we was goin' to have some snow, an' no mistake." He chuckled grimly and continued, " I dunno how we shall git on if it comes to that. But there, we've had it before an' got through somehow, and I dessay we shall git through again."

" It's to be hoped so. Anyhow, there seems to be no way of altering it."

" No, sir ; there don't. I 'xpect we shall have to put up with it. Bear it an' grumble—that's what we shall have to do. We've had to do that before now."

It was a blessing, I laughed, that we had the right to grumble ; but we hardly learnt to like the winter the better for being used to it.

" No ; that don't make it none the sweeter, do it ? Still, we can't help that. As my old neighbour, Jack Tower, used to say, ' Puverty en't no *crime*, but 'tis a great ill-convenience.' "   The touch of epigram in Tower's saying seemed to please Bettesworth, and his speech flowed out with a smooth undulating balance as he repeated slowly, tasting the syllables : " No, cert'nly, puverty en't no crime ; but it is a very ill-convenient thing, an' no mistake."

To the same period as the foregoing piece belongs an undated fragment, which tells how news came to Bettesworth of a certain boy's being bitten by a dog. " Have he bit'n *much ?*" was the first eager exclamation, followed by, " These here messin' dawgs ! There's too many of 'em, snappin' and yappin' about. I don't *like* 'em !"

Then he went on, " I don't see what anybody wants to keep dogs for, interferin' with anybody. Why, there's Kesty's dog up there—look at that dog of he's ! Why, that dog of he's, he've bit three or four of 'em. He bit the postman two or three times, till they sent to 'n from the Post Office to tell 'n 'less he mind to keep his dog tied up he'd have to send an' fetch his letters hisself. . . . Nasty sly sort o' dog he is, no mistake. He goes slinkin' an' prowlin' about up there ; he's never tied up. And he don't make no sound, ye know. No, you'll never hear' n make no noise ; but he'll have ye. And he en't partic'lar, neither, about lettin' of ye go by, even if it's on the highroad, onless he've a mind to. He'll come slinkin' round, an goo for ye, 's likely as not."

"Odd," I suggested, "that a man should care to keep a dog like that."

Bettesworth shook his head.

"There's too *many* of 'em about, by half. And I en't partic'lar fond o' dogs, nowhen." He looked up, and a knowing look came into his grey eyes as he continued, "I was workin' one time for Malcolms up here, and they had a dog, and one day he stole a shoulder o' mutton, indoors. Sort of collie, *he* was. And he took this 'ere shoulder o' mutton and run upstairs into one o' the rooms, and he wouldn't come out for nobody. I was at work out in the garden, and the servant she come runnin' out to me, to ast me if I'd come an' get 'n out. 'I dunno s'much about that,' I says; ''ten't a job as I cares about.' I can tell ye, I wa'n't partic'lar about *doin'* of it. 'Oh,' she says, 'do come an' get'n out. We be all afraid. And you can have a stick,' she says. 'No,' I says, 'I won't have no stick '—'cause, what good's a stick, ye know? He'd ha' come for me all the one for that. So I *catches* up a 'and-saw. . . .'"

"A *hand-saw* ?"

"I did. I took this 'ere 'and-saw, and I went upstairs to 'n, and he come for me sure enough. But I give 'n two or three 'cross the nose with this saw, and he didn't like that. He went off downstairs quick sticks."

"H'm ! I shouldn't have relished the job."

"No, sir ; I didn't *like* it. I was afraid of 'n. I

drove 'n out, but I was afraid of 'n all the one for
that."

January 7, 1896.—A task reserved for this winter's
leisure was the making of an arched way of larch-
poles and wire to cover a short flight of steps in the
garden.   Two briars at the top of the steps, one
on each side, had overgrown them, and these were
now to be trained to the new framework, which was
to slant down at the same slope as the steps.

Until we began the work, it seemed simple enough ;
but almost immediately we plunged into bewilder-
ment, owing to the various slopes and slants to be
considered.   The steps go askew between two parts
of a zigzag path, and our archway, therefore, needed
to be several feet longer on one side than on the
other.   The consequence was that the horizontal
ties at the top not only clashed with all the gradients
of the garden, but converged towards one another,
so that, seen from above, they were horrid to behold.
And then the slanting side-rails !   They agreed with
nothing else in all the landscape save the steps
below them.   Of course, when the briars covered
these discrepancies, all would be well ; but just
while Bettesworth and myself were at work upon
this thing, the farther we progressed with it the
more distracted it looked, as though we had gathered
into one spot all the conflicting angles of this most
uneven of gardens, and were tying them up into
one hideous knot.   The work became a nightmare,

and for an hour or two we lost our good spirits, and found it all we could do to keep our temper.

However, we got the framework together some-how, after which the straining of wires over it, being, as we fondly imagined, an easier task, released our thoughts a little. Bettesworth paid out and held the wire while I fastened it.

" Is that tight enough ?" said he.

" That'll do," said I.

" Because," said he, " I can easy tighten it more yet."

" No," said I, " that'll do."

" Well, of course, if that'll *do*," he conceded ; and then, not finishing his sentence, he chattered on. " Only, I don't want to be like ol' Sam Cook. He was 'long o' we chaps at work for Putticks when they was a-buildin' Coswell Church. I was there scaffoldin', an' this here Cook was s'posed to be helpin' of us. But we see as he never pulled, an' so one day we got two ropes and fastened the ends of 'em with jest black cotton. We made it look all like a knot, and he never see what we was up to. An' when it come to pullin', there was he makin' out to be pullin', leanin' back with his arms stretched out a-gruntin' ' Ugh ! . . . Ugh !' and all the time never pullin' a pound. Why, if he'd on'y pulled half a dozen pounds, he'd ha' broke that cotton ; but it never broke. Mr. John Puttick hisself was there, and he says, ' Well, I never see the like o' that in all my time ! Why,' he says, ' you wouldn't pull enough to pull a sausage asunder,' he says.   Ye see, he (Cook) always went by the name o' *Sausage*, 'cause his wife used to make sausages, so Mr. Puttick says to 'n, ' Why, you wouldn't pull a sausage asunder !' he says."

Too soon, unlooked-for difficulties presented themselves in our wire-straining.   We began to agree that we hardly felt as if we had been apprenticed to the work, and Bettesworth muttered,

"/I dunno as I should care much about goin' out to take a job puttin' up wire."

To get the first wire tightly fixed between two posts was easy enough, but, to our dismay, the tightening of a second wire invariably slackened the first.   Bettesworth was jubilating over his second wire.

" There, he's tight, an' *no* mistake !"

" Ah, but look at the first one !"

" What !   He *en't* got loose, is he, sir ?   Oh dear, oh dear !   That *do* look bad !   Never can let 'n go like that, can us, sir ?"   Gradually his memory began harking back to earlier instances of our difficulty.   " 'Tis like when I helped Mr. Franks puttin' wires up for he's ras'berries.   We had just such a bother as this.   Fast 's we got one tight we loosened another.   We did git in a pucker over 'm, an' no mistake.   I remember I told Bill Harris down 'ere what a bother we'd bin 'avin', and he says, ' Ah, I knows you must 've had a job.'   He'd had just such a bother hisself, on'y he had all the proper tools an' everything. He borried Mr. Mills's wire-strainers, and when he got the fust wire up—oh, he thought he was gettin' on capital. He seemed like makin' a reg'lar good job of it. But when he come to put up t'other wire—oh dear, oh dear !—he got in such a hobble. ' There,' he says, ' I was ashamed for anybody to see it, and I come away an' left it.' "

I was in the humour to be glad of other people's perplexities, and I laughed.

" Oh, he came away and left it, did he ?"

" Yes. Don't ye see, 'twas a reg'lar fence, 'tween his garden an' the next. An' he thought for to have it all jest right an' proper. But everybody as come by could see, and he was that put out about it that he come away an' left it."

" Bother the stuff ! I hope we shan't have to go and leave this."

" I dunno how we be to do it. There, 'tis to be done, we knows that, 'cause I've seen it. . . . No, I en't never see 'em a puttin' of it up ; but I've seen the fences after it bin put up, an' very nice they looks wi' the wire all as straight. . . . But how they doos it, I'm sure I don't know."

We finished at last, after a fashion, and Bettesworth went on to train and tie the briars. If work had not been scarce, it would have been cruel to let him undertake such a job. To make up for his defective sight, it was his way to grope out blindly for a thing just before him, and find it by touch ; and in dealing so with this briar, with its terrible thorns, his hands got into a pitiable state. He showed me them on resuming his work the next morning, saying,

"I shan't be sorry when I done wi' this customer. His nails is too sharp for my likin'. When I went 'ome yesterday and washed my hands, goo! didn't they smart wherever the cold water touched one o' they scratches! My ol' gal says to me, 'What be ye hushin' about?' 'So 'd you *hush*,' I says, 'if you'd bin handlin' they roses all the aft'noon, same as me.' I tried with gloves, but they wa'n't no good. You can't git to tie, with gloves on."

March 26, 1896, 10.30 *a.m.*—There are deep cloud-shadows, and rapid sun-glints lighting up the shadows like daffodils shining against grass. And there is the roar of a big wind in the air, and majestic clouds are sailing across, and beyond these the sky is a dazzling blue.

All growing things seem busy. Everywhere on the land men are at work; the swift sunshine glistens on the white of their shirts, and shows them up against the darkness of the new plough-furrows or the freshly dug garden-ground.

Bettesworth was sowing peas. Blustered by the wind, I went to him and complained of the coldness of it. "A good touch of north in it," was a phrase I used.

"Yes, sir; she (the wind) have shifted there since the mornin'. She was due west when I got up—

when that little rain come. She've gone round since then, but she'll git back again to the south, you'll see. I've noticed it many's a time. Right south she was at twelve o'clock when the sun crossed the line o' Saturday (March 21), and that's where she'll keep tackin' back to all through the quarter —till midsummer, that is."

" Well, I don't know that she could do much better."

" No, sir. Strikes me we be goin' to have a very nice, kind spring. I don't say she'll bide there all the time ; but if she gits away, that's where she'll come back to."

Again I expressed my dislike of this strong north wind. It would soon make me sleepy, I said.

" *Would* it, sir ? Oh, I do like to hear the wind ! To lay and listen to it when I be in bed—it makes me feel so comfortable. No matter what 'tis like outside, I feels that *I* be in the warm aw-right."

March 31, 1897.—At six minutes to five this morning Bettesworth was lacing up his boots. The day is the last of March, which, for gardeners in this village, is the middle of the busiest time of the year. The early seeds have been in the ground long ago ; the beans are up two inches ; the first sowing of peas shows well in the rows ; others were put in last week. Shallots are sending up their green spikes ; there are a few potatoes already planted ; and now every effort must be made, and advantage be taken of every opportunity, to get the remainder of the ground ready and the main crops planted at the earliest possible time ; for in this soil, as Bettesworth says, " you can't be much too for'ard."

Late last night he and his old wife planted their potatoes in a few rods of ground he has at the end of my garden. It was seven o'clock, and dark, by the time they had finished ; then they went home and had supper—or, at least, the wife had, whose work had not been arduous until the evening. She scolded her husband.

" There you goes slavin' about, and gets so tired you can't eat."

" It's true," Bettesworth confesses. " The more I works the less I eats. . . . No, nor I don't sleep, neither. If I got anythink on my mind, I can't sleep. I seems to want to be up and at it."

Supper over, he lit his pipe, had one smoke, then kicked off his boots and said,

" Well, I be off to bed. 'Ten't no good settin' here, lookin' at the fireplace."

The wife grumbled again in the morning, urging him to rest.

" But what's the use ?" he said. " It got to be done, and I can't rest ontil 'tis done."

So he got up at the time already mentioned, and came to rake over the potato-ground.

It slopes down to the lane, this ground. Presently the man from the cottage just across the lane came out for his day's work.

" Why, you be for'arder than ever this year, ben't ye, Fred ?"

" No, I dunno as I be. I wants to git it done, though, anyhow."

Then the Vicar's gardener passed. He laughed. " Be you determined on gettin' all your ground planted in March, then, Fred ?"

Bettesworth laughed back. " I don't care whether 'tis March or April. When I be ready it got to go in."

Others, going by, chaffed him. " You bin there all night, then ?"

About a quarter past six he went back home, and met his neighbour Noah.

" Hullo !" says Noah. "What? You bin at work?"

" Ah, and so you ought to ha' bin."

But Noah, who has lived in London, " sits up till eleven or twelve at night readin' the paper. He can't git into the habit of gettin' up early."

Gardening talk is now the staple conversation in the village, and the public-house is the club-room where the discussions take place, the times being Saturday night and Sunday.

". You don't find many there any other time," says Bettesworth. " Cert'nly, after a man bin to work all day, when he gits home he's tired, and wants to go to bed. But Saturday night and Sunday —well, you can't bide indoors solitary, lookin' at the fire. If you do, you never learns nothin'. But to go and have a glass and a pipe where there's others—that sims to enlighten your mind."

The men compare notes, and give and take sage advice. " Where I had that crop o' dwarf peas last year I be goin' to have carrots this," says one. Another answers, " Well, then, if I was you, I should dig that ground up now—rake off the stones " (carrots being " a very tender herbage "). " Then, if it comes rain, that'll settle it a bit. After that, let it bide an' settle for about another fortnight, and then as soon as you gets a shower shove 'em in as fast as you mind."

" Or else," Bettesworth explains in telling me this, " if you don't let it settle the drill sows 'em too deep ; it sinks in. Carrots is a thing you wants to sow as shallow as ever you can."

Somebody informs the company that he had " quarter of a acre o' carrots last year, and he made five pound of 'em." Or was it that he had five tons, and sold them for thirty shillings a ton ? This was it, as Bettesworth at last remembers.

" I 'spose you'll soon be puttin' in some taters, Fred ?"

" I got most o' mine in a'ready."

" *Have* ye ? I en't sowed none yet, but. . . ."

So says Tom Durrant, the landlord.

" But cert'nly," as Bettesworth observes, " down there where he is it do take the frost so—right over there in Moorway's Bottom. Up here, though, we no call to wait. I likes to git taters in. You see, where they lays about they spears so, and then the spears gits knocked off—you *can't* help it ; or, if not, still, where you sees a tater speared so, that must weaken that tater ? About two foot two one way and fifteen inches t'other—that's the distance I gen'ly plants taters. Ten't no good leavin' 'em wider 'tween the rows. But old Steve Blackman, up there by the Forest, I knowed he once plant some three foot both ways. And law, what a crop he did git ! 'Twas a piece o' ground his landlord let 'n have for the breakin' of it up. And he trenched in a lot o' fuzz—old fuzz-bushes as high as you be— and so on. Everything went in. And such a crop o' taters as he had—no, no dressin'. Only this old fuzz-stuff. *Regents*, they was. Oh, that was a splendid tater, too ! But you never hears of 'em now. They sims to be reg'lar gone out. I got some o' these here *Dunbars*, down here. I should like to see half a bushel o' they in this bit o' ground o' yourn. Splendid croppin' tater they be. I ast Tom Durrant if he could spare you half a bushel. He said he didn't hardly know. There's so many bin after 'em—purty near half the parish. They be a splendid croppin' tater, no mistake. He got 'em of some gentleman's gardener to begin with, I reckon. Reg'lar one he is, you know, for gettin' taters an' things, and markin' 'em and keepin' the sorts separate. He had four to start with, an' they produced a peck. Then he got three bushel out o' that peck. And last year he sowed 'em again— three bushel—and he got thirty-nine bushel."

II

May 13, 1896.—The Tom Durrant just mentioned
was frequently spoken of by Bettesworth, and always
in a tone of warm approval. " A wonderful quiet
sort o' man," steadily " putting together the pieces,"
but not assuming any airs, he managed his public-
house well, and with especial attention to the comfort of his older neighbours. " If any of the young
uns come in hollerin' about, 'twas very soon ' Outside !' with Tom. ' There is the door !' he'd say.
' I don't keep my 'ouse open for such as you.' "

So Bettesworth has told me, more than once—
perhaps not exactly in those words.

But sometimes Bettesworth's talk was too thick
with detail to be remembered and written down as
he said it in the time at my disposal ; whence it
happens that I am able only to summarize an anec-
dote about Durrant, which Bettesworth told with
considerable relish. The publican was the owner of
two cottages which were supplied with water from
a good well—a precious thing in this village. These
cottages had lately been overhauled and enlarged—
Bettesworth detailed to me all the improvements,
praising the new sculleries and sheds that had been

added—and then the tenants, as if stricken with madness, found fault with the water-supply, and lodged a complaint with the sanitary inspector. The inspector insisted that the well should be cleaned out. Durrant thereupon examined the water, found it " clear as crystal," cleaned out the well as he was ordered to do, and—gave the tenants notice to pay sixpence a week more for their cottages, or to quit. " So they didn't get much by *that*," said Bettesworth approvingly.

After all, this was but a kind of parenthesis in a talk which, not hurried, but quietly oozing out as we worked side by side in the garden, fairly over-whelmed my memory with variety of subject and vividness of expression. At one time it dealt with a certain road which was to be widened—" all they beautiful trees to be cut down, right from " so-and-so to so-and-so "; at another, it discussed three parcels of building land for sale in the vicinity, estimated their acreage, and related the offers which had been already made for them. From that, working all the while, Bettesworth would wander off to the drought, and I would hear how long this or that neighbour had been without water; how a third (whose new horse, by the way, " was turnin' out well—but there, so do all they that comes from " a certain source, where, however, " they works 'em too hard ")—how a third neighbour was obliged to keep his old horse almost constantly at work fetching water, since he had twenty-two little pigs, besides other live animals whose numbers goodness knows, and so did Bettesworth. At the new schools, again, the water was failing ; and how, and why, and what the caretaker thought, and all about it, Bettesworth was able to explain.

The receptivity of the man's brain was what struck me. One pictured it pinked and patterned over with thousands of unsorted facts—legions of them jostling one another without apparent arrangement. Yet all were available to him ; at will he could summon any one of them into his consciousness. A modern man would have had to stop and sift and compare them, and build theories and systems out of all that wealth of material. Not being modern, Bettesworth did not theorize ; his thoughts were like the dust-atoms seen in a sunbeam. But though he did not " think," still a vast common-sense somehow or other flourished in him, and these manifold facts were its food.

September 26, 1896.—Nor was it only of current topics that he could talk with such fullness of detail. Getting shortly afterwards into the reminiscent vein, he succeeded in paralyzing my memory with the tale of things he had observed many years before in just the same unsystematic yet thorough fashion. My hasty jottings, made afterwards, preserve only a few points, and do not tell how any of them were suggested. The talk was at one time of Basingstoke Fair, " where they goes to hire theirselves for the year." Of " shepherds with a bit o' wool in their hats, carters with a bit o' whipcord, and servant gals," and so on. " I went once," said Bettesworth, " when I was a nipper—went away from Penstead ; but I never got hired. . . . There's the place for games, though ! They carters, when they've jest took their year's money, and be changin' ' racks,' as they calls it. ' You bin an' changed your rack, Bill ?' ' What rack be you got on to ?' ' You got on for old, Farmer So-and-so ?' . . . There they be, hollerin' about. And then they all got their shillin', what bin hired. . . ."

I did not stop then to consider whether this hiring shilling, and the token in the hat, might have any relationship, in the world of old customs, to the " King's shilling " and the bunch of ribbons of the recruit for the army. Bettesworth was talking ; and presently it was about a certain Jack Worthington, of a neighbouring village, who was known as " Cunnin' Jack," and played the concertina at fairs, clubs, and so on : " Newbury Fair, Reading Fair, Basingstoke Fair "—Bettesworth essayed to catalogue them. Cunnin' Jack " learnt it all by hisself, but I've heared a good many—travellin' folk and the like—say as they never heared anybody play the concertina like him. He's the on'y one 's ever I heared play the church bells—chimes, an' fire 'em, and all—wonderful ! *Blue Bells of Scotland*, too— to hear him play that, an' the chimes, jest exact ! No trouble to make out what 'tis. Oh, he's a reg'lar musician ! He've trained all his sons to same thing. One of 'em plays the fiddle ; another of 'em got a thing what he scratches along wi' wires, sounds purty near like a fiddle. . . . 'Ten't no good for 'n in a town, 'less 'tis a fair or summat o' that ; but in any out-o'-the-way place. 'Relse, if he gets to a fair, there'll be three or four landlords about tryin' to get hold of 'n ; and they'll give 'n five shillin's and supper, and his drink an' a bed, an' what he can pick up besides. Very often he'll make as much as five-an'-twenty shillin's in a night (?). And when he comes 'ome, he bring p'r'aps a gallon o' ha'pence along with 'n. Never no silver, o' course. Often, when his wife thought he hadn't got nothing but a pound or so, he'd chuck her five or six pound. Then in the winter he'd go gravel-diggin', onless there come a fair, or anything o' the likes o' that. At these pubs where they dances, too, he'd put round the hat after every dance, an' if there was a good many stood up, p'r'aps he'd pull in half-a-crown or so."

Cunnin' Jack had a contrivance of musical dancing-dolls, about which I did not clearly understand. And I have quite forgotten how Bettesworth spoke of the man's brother, a deaf-mute, who refused to work, and " lived about at Aldershot, along o' the soldiers."

Afterwards another " dummy " was mentioned : " terrible big strong feller. . . . Spiteful. . . . Goes gravel-cartin' with his father." At a difficult place in the gravel-pit the father reached out and struck his son's horse. The "dummy" springs on him, throws him on his back, making a noise "'bu-bu,' like a calf. . . . Sure way to upset 'n—if you was in the gravel pit, touch his hoss. . . ."

Bettesworth had once seen "a dummy, talkin' with a friend of his," in the finger alphabet. "Can't you understand it?" said the friend to Bettesworth. "'No,' I says ; 'how should I?' But, law! to see him! And then write, too! Purty near as fast as you can talk. And all the time his eye 'd be on ye, watchin' ye. But to see him write on his slate—wonderful fast! and then" (here Bettesworth breaks into dramatic action, licking his hand and smudging out slate-writing)—"and then, when he'd rubbed it out, to see him write *again!* Spiteful, though, *he* was. So they all be, I s'pose." There was another dumb man, for instance, who had been apprenticed to a shoemaker. . . .

Unfortunately, I cannot reconstruct this instance. I only remember that the man had become "a wonderful good shoemaker, but didn't sim to care about follerin' it," and had "took to gardenin' now," instead.

May 5, 1898.—On a morning early in May it was raining, quietly, luxuriously, with a continuous soothing shattering-down of warm drops. In the doorway of the little tool-shed I stood listening—listening to the gentle murmur on the roof, on the long fresh grass of a small orchard plot, and on the young leaves of the plum and the blossoming apple which made the daylight greener by half veiling the sky.

Beside and beyond these trees were lilacs, purpling for bloom, small hazels, young elms in a hedge-row—all fair with new greenness ; and farther on, glimpses of cottage roof against the newly dug garden-ground of the steep hillside.   Above the half-diaphanous green tracery of the trees, cool delicious cloud, "dropping fatness," darkened where it sagged nearer to the earth.   The light was nowhere strong, but all tempered moistly, tenderly, to the tenderness of the young greenery.

I ought to have been busy, yet I stood and list-ened ; for the earth seemed busy too, but in a softened way, managing its many businesses beauti-fully.   The air seemed melting into numberless liquid sounds.   Quite near—not three trees off—there was a nightingale nonchalantly babbling ; from the neighbourhood of the cottage came, pene-trating, the bleating of a newly-born goat ; while in the orchard just before me Bettesworth stooped over a zinc pail, which, as he scrubbed it, gave out a low metallic note.   Then there were three under-tones or backgrounds of sound, that of the soft-falling rain being one of them.   Another, which diapered the rain-noise just as the young leaves showed their diaper-work against the clouds, was the all but unnoticed singing of larks, high up in the wet.   Lastly, to give the final note of mellowness, of flavoured richness to the morning, I could hear through the distance which globed and softened it a frequent " Cuckoo, cuckoo." The sound came and died away, as if the rain had dissolved it, and came again, and again was lost.

Framed by all this, Bettesworth stooped over his pail, careless of getting wet. His old earth-brown clothes seemed to belong to the moistened nook of orchard where he was working ; so, too, did his occasional quiet chatter harmonize well with the pattering of the warm rain. And for a time the drift of what he said was so much a part of our quiet country life that I took it as a matter of course, and let it pass by unnoticed.

But presently he raised his head.

" Have ye heared 'bout young Crosby over here ? He's gone clean off his head. They took 'n off to the asylum at Brookwood this mornin'. Got this 'ere religion. I s'pose by all accounts he went right into 't ; and that's what 've come of it."

I suggested that religious mania was often curable.

" Yes. I've knowed a many have it ; and then they gets over it after a time. Get 'em away— that's what it wants. If they can get 'em where they can dummer somethin' else into 'em, then they be all right. Wants to give 'em a change, so 's to get a little more enlightenment into their minds."

He came to join me in the shed doorway, for shelter from a temporary thickening of the rain, and standing there he continued,

" I was up to my sister's at Middlesham o' Sunday. She'd bin to Brookwood to see her sister-in-law. If they hadn't let her " (the sister-in-law) " 'ome too soon that first time, she'd ha' bin all right. Wherefore now she's there again, and jest like a post. If they puts her anywhere, there she bides, and don't try for to do nothing. 'Relse, when she was there afore, they told my sister she'd work as well as e'er a woman in the place. She see several there what she knowed. Fred Baker's wife, what used to be signalman, for one. But what most amused her was a old woman, when they was goin' out two by two for their walk in the grounds, flingin' her arms about and liftin' up her skirts an' dancin'. . . . She was havin' her reels and her capers in highly deglee." The old man pondered a few moments, then concluded pensively, as he stepped out to his work again, " What a shockin' thing, this mind !" His accent on the last word sounded almost resentful.

May 6, 1898.—The next day he reported that the man Crosby was said to have got " religious ammonium, is it ? Some such name as that."

The talk of religion reminded him of a former employer, of the Baptist persuasion, who, when annoyed with him, was wont to say impatiently, " Bother your picture !" So, of a dead pigeon, from whose crop seventy-two peas were taken, " Bother he's picture !" said the Baptist. Another

imprecation of this man's was, " Drabbit it !" at
which, however, Bettesworth used to expostulate,
telling his master, " Look 'ere, you Baptists may
lie, but you mawn't swear ! And so he could
lie, too," he added—"no mistake. And once he
said anything, he'd stick to it."

A month or more passed, and I forgot all about
poor Crosby, until one delicious morning, when
Bettesworth thought fit to tell me that he was no
better. A neighbour had cycled to Brookwood on
Sunday to see him and report about his family,
Crosby's wife being in child-bed. But the information quickened no interest.

" All he kep' on about was the devil. The devil
kep' comin' and botherin' of 'n. 'Tis a bad job. I
s'pose he went right into it—studyin' about these
here places nobody ever bin to an' come back again
to tell we. Nobody don't know nothin' about it.
'Ten't as if they come back to tell ye. There's my
father, what bin dead this forty year. What a
crool man he must be not to 've come back in all
that time, if he was able, an' tell me about it.
That's what I said to Colonel Sadler. ' Oh,' he
says, ' you better talk to the Vicar.' ' Vicar ?' I
says. ' He won't talk to me.' Besides, what do
he know about it more 'n anybody else ?"

Early in the summer of 1896 Bettesworth had
been immensely proud of his peas, which were ready
for picking quite a week before other people had

any. The fame of these peas had got abroad in
the parish ; it had reached a youth—a new curate
fresh from a theological college—and had appealed
to his fancy so strongly that he sent a servant to
buy threepennyworth of the precious crop. And
Bettesworth had chuckled.

" I bin a-laughin' to myself all the mornin'. . . .
Three penn-'oth o' peas ! I never heared talk o'
such a thing ! I told the gal to go back and tell
'n to save his money till they was cheaper."

June 13, 1899.—But three years later Bettesworth
seems to have changed his policy. On June 13
once more he had peas to boast of, and already for
some days his wife was itching to be at them.

" Look, there's a nice pea, and there," she would
say, handling the dangling pods.

But Bettesworth would answer, " Yes, they be ;
and you let 'em bide."

" For the sake of a shillin' now," he explained to
me, " I en't a-goin' to have that haulm spoilt, and
lose two or three shillin's later on."

His brother-in-law agreed that he was right. It
was all reported to me in Bettesworth's own words.

" ' I thinks you be right, Fred,' he says. ' You
better get along without that shillin' now, and have
two or three later on.' "

Old Mrs. Skinner, too, commended him. She
told of a neighbour who had picked a few peas very
early, and ruined his crop ; for in the hot weather

the juicy haulm was sure to wither soon if bruised by handling.

The weather was glorious just then, yet ill for our sandy gardens.

" As blue as a whetstone," said Bettesworth, in forecast of what the cabbage crop would be, should rain not soon come. " And en't the grass slippery and dry ! *'Twas* a hot day yest'day, no mistake ! I was up in my garden when Mrs. Skinner come up lookin' at my peas. She reg'lar laughed at me. ' Well, Fred, you *be* a purty picture !' There was the sweat all trinklin' down my arms, an' the dust caked on. . . . But she did admire they peas. Still, she reckoned I was right leavin' 'em. So I says to my old gal, ' You let 'em bide.' So she'll have to, too. 'Tis for me to give the word."

III

October 7, 1899.—I have mentioned Bettesworth's neighbour Noah, the young man who used to sit up too late at night reading the paper. Notwithstanding this bad habit, he and Bettesworth had been on excellent terms of friendship. It was to Noah that Bettesworth had turned, for example, when I lent him those copies of the *Daily Chronicle* in which the first particulars of Nansen's voyage in the *Fram* were published. Unable to read himself (" I can't see well enough," he said, " or else I be scholard enough "), he invited Noah and Noah's wife to come on the Sunday and read to him the explorer's narrative.

" We started," said he, " about two o'clock, and there they was, turn and turn about, as hard as ever they could read up to half-past five." The evening was spent in raising the envy of other neighbours. " They wanted to borry the papers, but I says, ' No, they ben't mine to lend.' "

The readers themselves seem to have conceived an intense admiration for Nansen, whose bed of stones especially excited Bettesworth's imagination.

" *I*'ve had some hard lay-downs in my time," he

exclaimed, " but *that!* Gawd! what they poor fellers must ha' suffered!"

Not long afterwards, Noah was called in again to help enjoy a seedsman's catalogue. It was read through from cover to cover.

Yet Noah proved to be a treacherous friend, after all. I have no record of the occurrence, but I think it must have been in the summer of 1897 that he began to covet Bettesworth's pleasant cottage, and by offering the owner a higher rent succeeded in getting possession of it. Bettesworth was obliged to quit. He took a cottage in a little row at three-and-sixpence a week, where he was comfortable enough for about a couple of years. At the end of that period, however, certain difficulties over the water-supply became acute—a laundress next door was pumping the well dry—and other discomforts arising, he began in the autumn of 1899 to look out for another home.

It is a singular place, this parish. The narrow valley it occupies is that of a small water-course commonly known as " The Lake," which in summer is a dry bed of sand, but in winter becomes a respectable brook of yellow waters which grow quite turbulent at times of flood. In their turbulence through long ages they have cut deep into the northern side of the valley, and now for some two miles that northern side, all warm and sunny, slopes down towards the stream, and there breaks off in precipitous sand-banks which in most places over-

hang the stream and make it inaccessible. But not
in all places. There are various gaps in the sand-
banks, where the rains and storms of centuries have
scooped out the upper slope into tiny gorges and
warm secluded hollows, down which footpaths wind
steeply, or narrow bumpy lanes, to some plank
bridge or other thrown across the stream. In these
hollows the cottages cluster thickest; there they
form little hamlets whose inhabitants sometimes
hardly know the other villagers. Such, indeed, is
my own case : hundreds of my fellow-parish-
ioners half a mile away are practically strangers to
me. Hundreds, for it is a large parish. The bluffs
which separate the hollows are not unpeopled ; they
have their cottages and gardens dotted over them
without order at the caprice of former peasant
owners. All sorts of footpaths and tracks connect
these habitations, but there are few roads, and
those are deep in sand. For the labouring people
do not interchange visits and pay calls ; they just
go to work and come home again, each to his own
place. At home, they look out upon their own
particular hollow, and upon little besides ; or, living
high up on a bluff, they get outlook upon the other
side of the main valley, which is lower, tamer,
smoother than this. It begins—that other side—
in narrow meadow or plough land at the bottom,
and so rises gently to a ridge fringed with cottages.
In addition to these dwellings, there are a few
hovels down by the stream itself, with their backs

stuck into the sand-cliffs, and with gardens between cliff and stream so narrow that a man might almost jump across them. A second jump would take him over the stream into the meadow-land just mentioned.

With a rapidly increasing population empty cottages are scarce, as Bettesworth now found. Moreover, his choice was restricted. There were reasons against his going to the upper end of the valley. It was more newly peopled by labourers from the town, who had never known, or else had lost, the older peasant traditions which Beltesworth could still cherish—in memory, at least—here in the more ancient part of the village. Of course, that was not how he explained his distaste ; he only expressed a dislike for the society of the upper valley. " They be a roughish lot up there," he would say. The fact was, he did not know many of them intimately, from which it may be seen how curiously our parish society is disintegrated.

Besides, he wanted a cottage not a mile away, but near to his work, so that he might go home to dinner and see how his wife was getting on. If he was growing old, she was older ; and what was worse, she was subject to epileptic fits. There were days when he worried about her all the time while he was at work, and went home uneasily, dreading to find her fallen down in a fit. It was necessary, therefore, that if he moved it should be not far away. His last move had been in the wrong direction—from the adjoining bluff to a hollow further down stream—and now he desired to get back.

One of the steep and narrow lanes mentioned above is that which runs down beside this garden, where Bettesworth's work lay. It is picturesque enough, beneath its deep banks and hedgerows and over-hung by my garden trees ; but that is of no moment here. Within Bettesworth's memory it afforded access even for a waggon right down to " the Lake," and so over into the meadow opposite ; but the last hundred yards of it, from Mrs. Skinner's cottage downwards, have long been washed out into a mere foot-track, deeply sunk between its banks, swooping down precipitously to the stream-level, and scarce two feet wide. So you emerge from the sand cliffs, and the valley is before you. Then the footpath winds along to the left (eastwards), having the cliff on one hand and the stream on the other, to a wider stretch, until with this for its best approach you come to a little hovel of three rooms and a lean-to shed, standing with its back walls close in against the sandy cliff.

At the period we are dealing with, this cottage had a poverty-stricken appearance, upon which Bettes-worth himself had been wont to comment severely, though the place was in reality no worse than others beyond it and elsewhere in the parish. But it had suffered from utter neglect under the previous tenant, a thriftless Irishman, while, after the Irishman left, it stood empty for a time, and looked

like falling quite derelict. Then, however, the landlord had a few repairs done, and at the end of September, to my amazement, I heard from Bettesworth that he had taken it. He would save eighteen-
pence a week by the change : the new rent was only
two shillings.

Ought I to have expostulated ? Perhaps I should
have done so, but for the queer expression in the old
man's face when telling me his intention. There
was some shame, but more of dogged defiance.
" You think what you like," so I interpreted it—
" that's the place I'm going to." He was armed,
too, with testimony in favour of the cottage.

" Skinner " (the bricklayer) " says he don't see
why it shouldn't make a very nice little place for
two. He done up the roof there t'other week, and
he ought to know." Later, the old man repeated
Skinner's opinion, and added, " I think *I* can make
it comfortable. Ye see, there en't bin nobody to
try before."

This was true enough. The Irishman's tenancy
had not in any sense improved the cottage. The
place could not be worse used, and it might con-
ceivably be fairly habitable in more careful hands.

During the first week in October Bettesworth
effected his removal. It was an inauspicious time.
He had been counting upon the stream-bed for a
roadway along which to cart his things, so as to
avoid scrambling up and down the devious path-
ways and tracks that led to the cottage, but, unfor-

tunately, the stream this week was in flood. A
cart might, indeed, have struggled along it, and
one was, in fact, bespoken—Jack Crawte's, to wit ;
but at the appointed time the cart failed to arrive,
and upon Bettesworth's going to inquire for it, he
discovered that the Crawtes were all gone into the
town to the fair.

Next day they promised to come " by-and-by."
Bettesworth accepted the promise, but he also
chartered two donkey-carts, which were really more
suitable for getting out from the first cottage into
one lane, and then round and about, up and down,
to the head of the gully by Mrs. Skinner's. Farther
than that even donkey-carts were useless. For the
last and worst hundred yards nothing but a wheelbarrow or a strong back could be of any use.

Fortunately (in these circumstances), poor old
Bettesworth's household goods were not many, nor
yet magnificent ; yet still they were enough for him
to manage. The main of them were shifted on the
Thursday, and I should not like to say how many
times that day the old man slaved down the gorge
with loaded wheelbarrow and up with it empty ;
but Mrs. Skinner witnessed his doings, and compli-
mented him.

" Why, Freddy," she said—" why, Freddy, you'd
kill half the young uns *now*, old as you be."

There should have been a helper—one Moses
Cook, familiarly known as " Little Moser "; but
little Moser was not a success. On the Wednes-

day, promising to lend a hand " in five minutes,"
he delayed coming until he had found time to get
drunk and then arrived with the proposal that
Bettesworth should give him a pint to start with.
" *Git* out o' my way !" was Bettesworth's reply.
The next day the little man was willing, but useless.

" Couldn't even git up there by ol' Dame Skinner's
with a empty barrer ! I says to 'n, ' Git in an' let
me wheel ye up !' I says. Made me that wild !
Why, I'd lifted a chest into the barrer all by myself—and *he* must ha' weighed a hundred and a
quarter, with what there was in 'n, ye know—and
wheeled 'n down. And then to see this little feller.
' You be in my way,' I says. ' You better go 'ome
and sit down, and then p'raps we shall be able to
git something done !' I *was* wild. I told 'n, ' They
says Gawd made man in His own image—you must
be a bloomin' counterfeit !' "

At one time there was a threat of rain, and
Bettesworth " whacked all the beddin' he could
on to the barrer, and down and in with it." Fortunately, the rain held off.

Towards night the cart came into action. It
brought a load or two of firewood—not along the
stream itself, but beside it, through the flooded
meadow. The wood was tipped out on to the
raised bank across the stream, just opposite Bettesworth's new home, there to remain for the night.
But the old man could not rest with it there.

" I got all that across," he said, " and into the

dry. Crawte couldn't hardly believe it when I told 'n this mornin'. But I *did*. Fetched it across in the dark." It was an almost incredible feat, for the night was of the blackest, and the stream four or five feet wide. " And then, when I got in, I had to put up the bedstead, with only the ol' gal to help me. An' if you told her one thing, it only seemed to make her forget to do something else. Talk about *tired !* I never had nothin' all that time—not even half a pint o' beer. Ye see, there wa'n't nobody I could send, an' I couldn't spare time to go myself, 'relse I *should* ha' liked a glass o' beer. But I never had nothin' not afore I'd done. Then I had some tea, but I was too tired to eat. P'r'aps, if I'd ha' been able to have half a pint earlier, I might ha' bin able to eat ; but, as 'twas, I couldn't eat. And now this mornin' my back and shoulders aches— with wheelin' down that gully, ye know."

As it is not mentioned elsewhere, I may as well say here that Bettesworth's endeavours to make this little place habitable and respectable were for a time fairly successful. As it should have been explained, after emerging from the gully the public footpath runs close in front of the doorway of the place, leaving some eight feet of garden between itself and the stream. Of old, in the Irishman's time, this garden was an entanglement of weeds and stunted cabbages, while the footpath was unswept, disgusting, and often blocked with a pail of ashes or other household refuse. But now a spirit

of order had appeared on the scene. The cabbage-
plot became comely; in due season old-fashioned
cottage flowers—pinks and nasturtiums—appeared
in two tiny borders under the windows on either side
of the door, and the mean doorway itself was
beautified by a rough but sufficient arbour of larch-
posts before it, up which "canary-creeper" found
its way. Accordingly, I heard from time to time,
but neglected to set down, how this and that way-
farer had praised the old man's improvements. Did
not the Vicar himself say (I seem to remember Bettesworth's telling me so with much gratification) that
he would never have believed the place could be
made to look so well? Of the inside, perhaps, not
so much could be said; but even this was passable
at first, before the old wife's breakdown spoilt all.
For several years, in fact, Bettesworth was, I believe,
very happy in this cottage. At any rate, it gave
him scope for labour, and he always liked that.
He had hardly been in possession a week before he
was talking of an improvement much to his mind.

"There's a rare lot o' capital soil in the lake
under they withies just against my garden," he
said; and he proposed taking it out to enrich his
garden.

"It'll be good for the lake, too," I suggested.

"Yes," he replied, "it wants clearin' out. Why,
in some places there en't no lake, and half the water
that comes down got to overflow and make floods."

IV

AND now, Bettesworth being settled in this hovel, his story begins at last to move forwards. For a while, indeed, little, if any, change in the man himself will be discernible. We shall be aware only of the quiet lapse of time as the seasons steal over him, and leave him older, or as the progress of public events is dimly reflected in occasional scraps of his conversation. And even of public events not much will be heard. Such things, which had never greatly concerned Bettesworth, were less likely than ever to attract his attention now. For five days in the week he rarely got farther from home than the lower half of the lane, where it degenerates into the gully between my garden and his cottage. On Saturday afternoons he journeyed into the town to get a shave and do his shopping ; on Sunday evenings he generally went to the public-house ; and as this was all he saw of the world, it is no matter for surprise if his interests remained extremely parochial.

And yet his ignorance of what was happening did sometimes surprise me. Of course, I know that what was wanting was the opportunity of enlightenment, and that he was not naturally deficient in the instincts that make for it. His appreciation of Nansen's adventures may be cited as a proof that he was ready and even eager to be informed. But for all that, it is true that the affairs which excited the rest of the world usually left him undisturbed, and the public noise needed to be a great one to reach his ears. Mr. Chamberlain's protectionist propaganda was not loud enough, incredible though that may seem. As a peasant, Bettesworth had a theory which I have often heard him affirm, that, for farmers to prosper, " bread never ought to be no less than a shillin' a gallon," so that I expected to hear him at least talk of " fiscal reform." But he never did. The proposal was months old when I at last broached the subject to him, and all he said was, " Oh dear ! we don't want no taxes on food !" as if he had never heard that such a thing was projected. And it is my firm belief that to the day of his death he knew only what little I told him about it, and would hardly have been able to say where he had heard the name of Chamberlain. His home was down there by the stream bed ; his work was half-way up the lane. Walking to it, he might hear Mrs. Skinner talking to her pigs ; walking back, he could see Crawte's cows turned out in the meadow at the bottom of the valley. He never read a newspaper, and how should he have learnt anything about the political ferment which was spreading through the towns of all

England, and engaging the attention of the whole world ?

At the end of 1899, however, he had not long been in his new dwelling before his attention was effectually arrested by the war in South Africa ; and my next note is a remark of his on this subject, which shows him taking not quite a parochial view of the situation. He did not approve of war. Several years previously, at the outbreak of the Spanish-American affair, he had spoken uneasily of the consequent rise in the price of bread, and his concern now may therefore be imagined. Still, there was one bright spot.

" There's one thing I be glad of," he said : " all they reserves called out. There never no business to be none o' they in the country."

His reason was that in time of peace the reserves, with their retaining pay, had been wont to undersell the civilian workman in the labour market, and that such competition was unfair.

This, of course, was soon forgotten in the interest of the war itself. Our parish, so near to Aldershot, sent out perhaps a disproportionate number of its young men to the front, men whom Bettesworth knew, whose fathers and mothers were his good friends, and at whose deaths, now and then announced, he would grimly shut his lips. Morning after morning he asked, " Any news of the war, sir ?" and listened gravely to what could be told. But he did not so much think as feel about it all. He

knew nothing, cared nothing, about the policy
which had led up to hostilities ; he was too ill-in-
formed to be infected by the raw imperialism of
the day ; his attitude was simply "national."
" Our country "—that was his expression—was in
difficulties, and he longed to see the difficulties over-
come. Such was his simple instinctive position,
and it excused in him some feelings which would
have been less pardonable in a more enlightened
man. At the close he would have liked to shoot
without pity President Kruger and the Boer
Generals, as the enemies of " our country."

But how ignorant of the facts he was at the beginning of the war ! Of our many talks on the subject
I seem to have preserved only one, but that is so
strange that now I can hardly believe in its accuracy.

December 16, 1899.—Dated the 16th of December,
1899, it states that Bettesworth had heard the
week's disastrous news from the seat of war, and was
letting off his dismay in exclamatory fashion.
" Six hundred missin' ! Look at that. What do
that *missin'* mean ?" His tone implied that he knew
only too well.

I said, " Most likely it means that they are
prisoners."

And then he said, " Ah, prisoners—or else
burnt."

It was my turn to exclaim. " Burnt ? No, no !
They are prisoners."

" But they burns 'em, some says."

Heaven only knows where he could have picked up such an idea. As the war proceeded, he kept himself fairly up to date with its main events by listening to other men's talk. He used, as we know, to go to the public-house on Sunday evenings " to get enlightenment to the mind ;" and there is mention in the next fragment of another source of information which he valued. To reach that, however, we have to enter another year—the year 1900.

V

February 13, 1900.—The winter was passing by,
with the war, indeed, to make it memorable to us,
but uneventfully at home. January, like December, had been mild—too mild, some people said, of
whom, however, Bettesworth was not one. February set in with more severity of weather. On the
third we had snow, and in the succeeding days frost
followed, and the roads grew slippery.

These things no doubt provided Bettesworth with
topics for many little chats I must have enjoyed with
him, although I saved no reminder of any of them.
But about the middle of the month a circumstance
came to my knowledge which made his good-tempered gossip seem rather remarkable. I could not
but admire that a man so situated should be able to
talk with such urbanity.

He had been at the barber's the previous evening,
where another man was discoursing at large about
the war. And said Bettesworth :

" I *do* like to hear anything like that. Or if
they'll read a newspaper. There I could 'bide lis-
tenin' all night. And if anybody else was to open
their mouths, I should be like enough to tell 'em to

43

shut up. Because, if you goes to hear anything, *hear* it. Same as at church or chapel or a entertainment : *you* goes to listen, an' then p'r'aps four or five behind ye gets to talkin'. I always says, if you goes anywhere, go and be quiet. You en't obliged to go, but when you do go, behave yourself."

The talkers, I might have reminded Bettesworth, are not always " behind ye " ; there are those who take front seats who might profit by his little homily on good manners. But he only meant that the discourtesy is the more disturbing, because it is the more audible, when it comes from behind.

He passed easily on to a discussion of the weather, and again his superlative good sense was to the fore. On Sunday, he said, he had tried to persuade his neighbours — working - men, like himself, only younger—to bring their shovels and scatter sand on the path down the gully, which was coated with ice. Already he had done a longish piece of it himself, but much remained to do. Several men had " went up reg'lar busters," and " children and young gals " on their way to church had fallen down. It would be a public service to besprinkle the path with sand. So Bettesworth made his suggestion to his neighbours—" four or five of 'em. They was hangin' about : hadn't got nothin' to do." But no. They shrugged their shoulders and walked away. It was no business of theirs. They even laughed at the old man for the trouble he had already taken, for which no one would pay him. And now, in telling me about it, it was his neighbours' want of public spirit that annoyed him. They had not come up to his standard of the behaviour meet for a labouring man.

Who would have imagined that, while he was telling me this, and for days previously, he was in a state of severe mental distress, aggravated by bodily fatigue ? I had no suspicion of it, and was surprised enough when told by a third person. But it was true—too true. He admitted it readily when I asked him. His wife was ill again, worse than she had been for three years, since the time when she fell down in an epileptic fit and broke her wrist. She had had many minor attacks during the interval, but this was serious now.

As I have already told the poor old woman's story, or at least this part of it, in another place, I may not repeat it here ; but for the sake of continuity the episode must be summarized. Three years earlier Bettesworth had obtained an order for his wife's admission to the workhouse infirmary. Hateful though the merest suspicion of benefiting by parish aid was to him, there had been no other course open at that time ; for what could he do for an old woman with a broken limb, and a malady that made her for the time half-witted ? And yet, owing to over-crowding at the infirmary, amazed and indignant he had brought her home again on the fourth day, because she had been lodged and treated as a common pauper. Consequently I knew that he must be at extremities now, when it came out that he was deciding again to send the old lady to the infirmary. But he was at his wits' end what to do for her. He could not afford to stay at home from work ; yet while he was away she was alone, since her condition and temper made neighbours reluctant to help. Sometimes the fear haunted him that she would meet a violent death, falling in a fit on to the fire, perhaps ; sometimes he dreaded that he would have to put her finally away into an asylum. What he endured in the long agonizing nights when her fits were upon her, in the silent winter evenings when he sat for hours watching her pain and wondering what to do, no one will ever know. As best he could, he used at such times to wash her and dress her himself—he with his fumbling fingers and dim eyes ; and wanting sleep, wanting the food that neither of them could prepare, alone and unknown, he struggled to keep in order his miserable cottage. Almost a week must have passed like this before I heard of the trouble, and asked him about it. Then he laid his difficulties before me, and asked for my advice.

To men in Bettesworth's position it is always an embarrassment to comply with the formalities of official business. They do not see the reason, and they feel keenly the wearisomeness, of the steps which must be taken to gain their end. Bettesworth now seemed paralyzed ; he had forgotten how to go on ; moreover, he could not be satisfied—although there was a new infirmary—that his wife would be more decently treated there than in the old one. If only he could be sure of that! But of course he was not important enough to approach, himself, anyone so important as a guardian; and, accordingly, I undertook to make inquiries for him.

It is indeed a tedious business—I experienced it afterwards too—that of getting a sick person from this village into the local infirmary. It seemed that Bettesworth must lose at least a day's work in arranging for the removal of his wife. She could not be admitted to the house without a certificate from the parish doctor, who lived in the town, a mile and a half away. But the doctor might only attend upon Bettesworth's presenting an order to be obtained from the relieving officer, two miles away in the exactly opposite direction. The medical man would then come as soon as he found convenient, and Bettesworth would be provided with a certificate for his wife's removal to the infirmary. But he might not act upon that alone. With that in his possession, he would have to wait again upon the relieving officer, to get an order upon the workhouse master to admit the patient, and to arrange for a conveyance to take her away.

We talked it over, he and I, that afternoon, not cheered by the wild weather that was hourly worsening. If all went well on the morrow, Bettesworth would have some twelve miles of walking to do; but it was most likely that, between relieving officer and doctor, two or even three days would elapse before the desired relief would be accomplished. However, the immediate thing to do was clear enough : he must make his first visit to the relieving officer as soon as possible.

I forget on what grounds, but we agreed that it was useless to attempt anything that night ; and since the officer would be off at eight in the morning for his day's duty in other places, Bettesworth proposed to be up betimes, and catch him at his office before he started. It would be just possible then, by hurrying, to get back over the three or four miles to the town, and find the doctor before he too should leave for the day. Otherwise there would be a sickening delay.

The whole thing was sickening already, in its inevitable mechanical clumsiness. Still, there was no help for it. The weather meanwhile was threatening hindrance. A small driving snow had set in in the afternoon, and was inclined to freeze as it fell ; and for some time before dark the opposite side of the valley had become all but invisible, blotted out by the dreary whiteness of the storm. At nightfall, the weather seemed to turn wicked. Hours afterwards, as I sat listening to the howling gusts of wind, which puffed the smoke from out of my fire, and brought the snow with a crisp bristling sound against my window, I could not get out of my head the thought of Bettesworth, alone with his crazy wife down there in that cottage, or the fear that deep snow might prevent his morning's journey. And then it was that recollection of his recent quiet conversations came over me. So to have talked, keeping all this trouble to himself, while he listened to the war news, and did his best to make the footways passable—there was surely a touch of greatness in it.

And it makes no difference to my estimate of him that, after all, he did not go to the relieving officer the next morning. On the further progress of Mrs. Bettesworth's illness at this time my notebook is silent ; but, as I recall now, she took a turn for the better that night, and by the morning was so improved that thought of the infirmary was given up.

VI

FOR eight months after this the account of Bettesworth's sayings and doings is all but a blank. There
was one summer—and perhaps it was this one of
the year 1900—when he joined an excursion for his
annual day's holiday, and made a long trip to Weymouth. Need it be said that he enjoyed the outing
immensely ? He came back to work the next day
overflowing with the humour and interest of what he
had seen and done. Had not old Bill Brixton lost
his hat out of the train ? And some other old chap
sat down on a seat on Weymouth front, and stayed
there all day and seen nothing ? Bettesworth, too,
had sat down, and had a most enjoyable conversation with a native of the place ; but he had also taken
steamer to Portland, and there got a drive to the
prison and seen the convicts, and had a joke and a
laugh with the driver of the brake, and a drink with
a party of excursionists from Birmingham, who
appreciated his society, and called him " uncle,"
and whose unfamiliar speech he imitated well enough
to make me laugh. And then he had persuaded a
seaman to take him out to the fleet and show him
over a man-of-war ; and finally had enlivened the
homeward journey by chaffing old Bill, and sharing

with him " a quarten o' whisky," which he carried in a medicine bottle.

This, I am inclined to believe, was an event of 1900, but I cannot verify it, and in any case it accounts for but one day. The dimness of the remainder of those eight months is but faintly illuminated—and that, it may be, for me only—by two memoranda mentioning Bettesworth as present at certain affairs, and by one all too short scrap of his own talk. He was speaking of Irishmen, no doubt in reference to some gallant deed or other in South Africa, and this is what he said:

" Ye see, they makes as brave soldiers as any. . . . All I got to say about Irishmen is, when you be at work with 'em, you got to think yourself as good as they, or a little better. 'Relse if they thinks you be givin' way they'll trample on ye. 'Xcept for that, I'd as lief work with Irishmen as Englishmen. . . . I remember once when I was at work on a buildin' for Knight, a Irishman come for me with his shovel like this." Bettesworth turned his shovel edgeways, raising it high. " He'd ha' split me if he'd ha' hit me ; and as soon as he'd missed me I downed 'n. Little Georgie Knight come down off the scaffold to stop us ; I'd got the feller down, an' was payin' of 'n. '*I'll* give 'n 'Ome Rule !' I says ; and so I did, too. He'd ha' killed me if he'd hit me. I s'pose I'd said somethin' he didn't like."

A March note, this last. As there is nothing else, I take it that the daily conversation was of the usual kind, about being forward in sowing seeds, and allowing enough room for potatoes, and so on.

June 10.—A note of June names Bettesworth among other interested spectators of an event no less singular than the death of a donkey. To me, the name of him on the page of my journal, coupled with one of his dry remarks, brings back vividly the whole scene : the glowing Sunday afternoon, the blue loveliness of the distant hills, the look`of the grass, and all the tingling sense of the far-spread summer life surrounding the dying animal. But the narrative has little to do with Bettesworth, and would be out of place here. It just serves as a reminder that one more summer was passing over him ; that, among the strong men who felt the heat in this valley that season, he was still one.

Carry that impression on, through the harvest time, and yet on and on until the end of September, and you may see him (or I, at least, may) one dark night, entering, all dazzled by the naked lamp, a little room where the Liberals have summoned an " important meeting of Liberal workers." He has come, like the present writer, in the expectation of hearing some " spouting," as he said afterwards. But though he is disappointed, and finds himself, —he, the least fanatic of men—the witness only of excited efforts to arrange for canvassing the district in readiness for the approaching election, still, conforming to his own rule of " behaving," he sits respectfully silent, though looking disconsolate and " sold," and his grey head, the home of such steady thoughts, has a pathetic dignity in its dark corner, and surrounded by the noisy politicians.

VII

So cramped-in as it was between sandbank and stream, Bettesworth's garden had no place for a pigsty ; and as his wife could not be happy without " something to feed," he had bought her a few fowls to amuse her. With stakes and wire netting he made a diminutive " run " for them, which really seemed to adorn the end of the cottage, being stuck into the corner made by the whitewashed wall and the yellow sand-cliff. The fowls, it is true, had not room to thrive ; but if Bettesworth made but little profit of them, they afforded him much contentment ; and the afternoon sunshine used to fall very pleasantly on the little fowl-pen.

Needless to say, he was not exempt from the common troubles of the poultry-keeper. I remember smiling to myself once at his gravity in mentioning that one of the hens had begun to crow. He did not, indeed, own to thinking it a sign of bad luck, but his looks seemed to suggest that he was uneasy. As everyone knows, a crowing hen, if it does not portend death, is neither fit for gods nor men ; so Bettesworth realized that he must kill the ill-omened bird, " as soon as he could find out which of 'em

53

'twas." Another time there were some little chicks, and his cat became troublesome ; and, worse still, there came a rat, which had to be ferreted out.

And were there marauders besides these ? I have stated that beyond Bettesworth's own cottage there were others of the same class, one of which was inhabited for a little while by a family whose honesty was not above suspicion. Would these people interfere with his fowls ? It was a point to be considered.

He considered it—it was on a day in October, 1900—and so strayed off into a rambling talk of many things. The ill-conditioned neighbours (he comforted himself by thinking) would leave his fowls alone, because depredations of that kind were an unheard-of thing in our parish.

" There, I will say that," he observed, " you never no fear o' *losin'* anything here. If a man leaves his tool—a spud or anything—in the ground, there 'tis. Nobody don't touch it. Up there at (he named a near village) they say 'tis different. But here, I should think there never was a better place for that !"

For a certain reason I took up this point, and hinted that Flamborough in Yorkshire must be an equally honest place. The Flamborough people, I had been told, never lock their doors at night, for fear of locking out the spirits of relatives drowned at sea.

Would Bettesworth take the bait, and tell me anything he might know about ghosts ? Not he. The interruption changed the course, but not the character, of his talk. He looked rather shocked at these benighted Yorkshiremen, and commented severely, " Weak-minded, *I* calls it." Then, after a momentary silence, he was off on a new track, with reminiscences of Selsey fishermen whom he used to see when he went harvesting into Sussex ; who go about, " any time o' night, accordin' to the tides," and whose thick boots can be heard " clumpin' along the street " in the dark. All men at Selsey, he said, were fishermen. The only regular hands employed by the neighbouring farmers were shepherds and carters.

He had got quite away from the point in my mind. But as I had long wondered whether Bettesworth had any ghost stories, I harked back now to the Flamborough people, egging him on to be communicative. It was all in vain, however. He shook his head. The subject seemed foreign to him.

" As I often says, I bin about all times o' the night, an' I never met nothin' worse than myself. Only time as ever I was froughtened was when I was carter chap at Penstead. Our farm was down away from t'other, 'cause Mr. Barnes had two farms— 't least, he had three—and ourn was away from t'other, and I was sent late at night to git out the waggon—no, the pole-carriage. I set up on the front on the shafts, with a truss o' hay behind me ; and all of a sudden she " (the mare, I suppose he meant) " snarked an' begun to turn round in the road. The chap 'long with me—no, he wa'n't 'long with me, 'cause he'd gone on to open the gate, and so there was I alone.   And all 'twas, was a old donkey rollin' in the road.   She'd smelt 'n, ye know ; an' the nearer we got, the more froughtened she was, till she turned right round there in the road.   'Twas a nasty thing for me ; they hosses with their legs over the traces, and all that, and me down atween 'em."

He was fairly off now.   A tale followed of stumbling over a drunken man, who lay all across the road one dark night.

" Wonder's 't hadn't broke his ribs, me kickin' up again' him like that.   I went all asprawl ; barked me hands too.   But when he hollered out, I knowed who 'twas then.   'Twas old . . ."

Well, it doesn't matter who it was.   There were no ghost stories to be had, so I related a schoolday adventure, of a glow-worm picked up, and worn in a cap for a little way, and then missed ; of a glimmer seen in the ditch, which might be the glow-worm ; of a groping towards the glimmer, and a terrified leap back, upon hearing from behind it a gruff "Hullo, mate !"

Bettesworth did not find this silly, like my Flamborough story.   It opened another vista of reminiscence, down which he could at least look.   Unhesitatingly he took the chance, commenting,

" Ah ! porchers, very likely, lurkin' about there for a meetin, p'r'aps.   They do like that, sometimes. I remember once, when Mellish was keeper at Culverley, there was some chaps in there at The Horse one night with their dogs, talkin' about what they was goin' to do. Mellish, he slips out, to send the word round, 'cause all the men at Culverley was s'posed to go out at such a job, if need be. So he sends round the message to 'em—Bromley, an' Dick Harris, an' Knight, an' several more, to meet 'n at a certain place, where he'd heard these chaps say they was goin' to work. And so they (the poachers) set in there talkin' about what they was goin' to do ; and at last, when they come away, they went right off into the town. While they'd bin keepin' the keeper there a-watchin' 'em, another gang had bin' an' purty well cleared the place out. *Bags*-full, they must ha' had. Mellish told me so hisself. While he was expectin' to have they, they was havin' him. He never was so sold, he said. But a clever trick, I calls it."

VIII

October 17, 1900.—Two words of Bettesworth's,
noted down for their strangeness at the time, restore
for me the October daylight, the October air. He
was discussing the scarlet-runner beans (I can picture
now their warm tints of decay), and he estimated our
chances of getting another picking from them. The
chances were good, he thought, because in the sheltered corner where the beans stood, uplifted as it was
above the mists that chilled the bottom of the valley,
" these little snibblin' frostis that we gets o'
mornin's " would not be felt. " Snibblin' " was a
new word to me, and now I find it associated in my
mind with the earliest approaches of our English
winter.

Near the beans there were brussels sprouts, their
large leaves soaked with colour out of the clouded
day. Little grey swarms of " white fly " flitted out
as I walked between them ; and, again, Bettesworth's name for that form of blight—" they little
minners "—brings back the scene : the quiet vegetable garden, the sad rich autumn tints, the over-
cast sky, the moist motionless air.

To this undertone of peace—the peace you can

best absorb at labours like his—he was able to discourse dispassionately of things not peaceful. In a cottage higher up the valley there was trouble this October. I may not give details of it ; but, in rough summary, an old woman had died, her last days rendered unhappy by the misbehaviour of her son— a young labourer. Talk of his " carrying on," his late hours, his frantic drinking, and subsequent delirium, crept stealthily up and down the lanes. He was " a low blackguard," " a scamp," and so forth. The comments were excited, generally breathless, once or twice shrill. But Bettesworth kept his head. An indignant matron said spitefully,

" 'Ten't every young feller gets such a good home as that left to 'n."

" Well, and who got a better right to 't ?" was Bettesworth's calm rejoinder.

November 10.—A month later a ripple of excitement from the outside world found its way down the lane. Saturday, November 10, was the day when General Buller, recalled from the war, arrived at Aldershot, and for miles around the occasion was made the excuse for a holiday by the working people. It was a point of honour with them not to desert their favourite under a cloud. They left off work early, and flocked to Aldershot station by hundreds, if not thousands, to make sure that he had a welcome. On the following Monday Bettesworth, full of enthusiasm, gave me an account of the affair as he had had it from numerous eyewitnesses. For, in truth, it had been " all the talk yesterday "—on the Sunday, namely. Young Bill Skinner, in particular, had been voluble, with such exclamations, such staring of excited eyes, that Bettesworth was reminded not without concern of the sunstroke which had threatened Skinner's reason two summers previously. Nevertheless, the tale was worth Bettesworth's hearing and repeating ; " there never was a man in England so much respected " as Buller, Skinner supposed. On alighting from the train, the General's first act had been to shake hands with his old coachman—a deed that touched the hearts of all these working folk.

" And there was never a sign o' soldiers ; 'twas all townspeople—civilians, that is ; and the cheerin'—there ! Skinner said he hollered till he was hoarse. He ast me " (Bettesworth) " how 'twas I didn't go over ; but I said, ' Naw . . .' Not but what I *likes* the old feller !"

Bettesworth made no answer but that expressive " No " of disinclination, but I can amplify it. He was not now a young man, to go tearing off enthusiastically for an eight-mile walk, which was sure to end in a good deal of drinking and excitement. His days for that were gone by for ever. Prudence warned him that he was best off pottering about in his regular way, here at home.

There was another reason, too, to restrain him. It brings us swiftly back for a moment from war incidents and the public excitement to the very interior of that hovel down by the " Lake," to learn that poor old Lucy Bettesworth was once more ill at this time. Her brother calling, and exhibiting an unwonted kindliness, had thrown her into sudden hysteria ending in epileptic fits. Even had Bettesworth felt inclined, he could not have left her. He told me the circumstances, and much, too, of her life history—the most of which has been already published, and may be omitted here. The illness, however, was not so severe as to engage all Bettesworth's thoughts. It allowed him to take interest in Buller's return, and on the same day to discourse of other outside matters too, in which all our valley was interested through these months.

Word had reached him somehow of the proposals just then announced for the higher training of our soldiers ; and he foresaw increased difficulties in recruiting on these terms. There was too much work to be had, and it was too well paid, to make young men eager to join the army ; and the service certainly did not need to be rendered less attractive than it was. Bettesworth, it seemed, had already been discussing this very point with his neighbours. As to the disturbance of the labour market consequent upon the war, he viewed it with no favour. The inflated prices of labour seemed to him unwholesome ; they were having an injurious effect upon young men, giving them an exaggerated opinion of their true worth as labourers. And this was particularly true,

since the building of the new camp at Bordon had
begun. " Old Tom Rawson," he reported, had
" never seen the likes of the young fellers that was
callin' theirselves carpenters an' bricklayers now.
Any young chap only got to take a trowel over to
Woolmer (by Bordon), and he'd be put on as a
bricklayer, at sixpence a hour. And you mawn't
stop to show 'em nothing. If the clurk o' the works
or the inspector come round, 't 'd be, ' What's that
man doin', showin' the others ?' Tom said he
wa'n't *goin'* to show 'em, neither. Why, at one time
nobody ever thought of employin' a man, onless he
could show his indentures. But now—'tis anybody." " The foreman " had lately come to Tom
Rawson " askin' him jest to give an eye to some
young chaps," and promising him another halfpenny
an hour. And Bettesworth commented, " But
dessay he (the foreman) was gettin' his bite out o'
the youngsters."

Not Bettesworth, not even that hardened old Tom
Rawson, would have countenanced such things had
they been appealed to ; but tales of this kind only
filtered down into Bettesworth's obscure nook, to
provide him with a subject for five minutes' thought,
and then leave him again to his homely occupations.
What had he to do with the War Office and in-
efficiency in high places ? From this very talk, it
is recorded, he turned appreciatively to watch the cat
purring round my legs, and by her fond softness
was reminded of his rabbits—six young ones—which

the mother had not allowed him to see until yesterday. And he spoke wonderingly of her mother-instinct. The old rabbit was " purty near naked," having " almost stripped herself " to make a bed for these young ones, so that the bed was " all white fluff before they come," and now she " kep' 'em covered up." " Everything," said Bettesworth, " has their *nature*, ye see."

In this fashion, with these trivial interests, the year drew on to its close in our valley. December gives glimpses of trouble in another household—that of the Skinners, Bettesworth being cognizant of all, but saying little. It did not disturb the peacefulness of his own existence. Events might come or delay, he was content ; he was hardly in the world of events, but in a world where things did not so much " happen " as go placidly on. He worked, and rested, and I do not believe that he was often dull.

IX

January, 1901.—The winter, which so far had been
mild and open, began to assume its natural character
with the new year ; and on the first Monday of
January—it was the 7th—we had snow, followed by
hard frost. The snow was not unexpected. Saturday—a day of white haze suffused with sunlight—
had provided a warning of it in the shape of frozen
rime, clinging like serried rows of penknife blades to
the eastern edges of all things, and noticeably to the
telegraph-wires, which with that additional weight
kept up all day a shiver of vibration dazzling to
look at against the misty blue of the sky. Then the
snow came, and the frost on top of that, and by
Tuesday it was bad travelling on all roads.

Bettesworth grumbled, of course ; but I believe
that really he rather liked the touch of winter. At
any rate, it was with a sort of gloating satisfaction
that he remarked :

" I hunted out my old gaiters this morning. They
en't much, but they keeps your legs dry. And I do
think that is so nice, to feel the bottoms of your
trousers dry."

I suppose it is, when one thinks of it, though it

had never struck me before.   But then, I had never
had the experience which had shown Bettesworth
the true inwardness of this philosophy of his.

" I've knowed what it is," he said, " to have my
trousers soppin' wet all round the bottoms, and then
it have come on an' freezed 'em as stiff as boards all
round."

That was years ago, during a short spell of piece-
work in a gravel-pit.   Now, secure in his gaiters
and in his easier employment, he could look back
with amusement to the hardships he had lived
through.   One of a similar kind was hinted at presently.   For the roughness of the roads, under this
frozen snow, naturally suggested such topics.

" What d'ye think of our neighbour Mardon ?"
he exclaimed.   " Bin an' chucked up his job, and 's
goin' back to Aldershot blacksmithin' again.   He
must be in want of a walk !"

" Regular as clockwork," Mardon, be it explained,
had walked daily to his work at Aldershot, and then
back at night, for upwards of twenty years.   The
day's walk was about ten miles.   Then suddenly he
left, and now for six months had been working as
bricklayer's labourer, at a job about an equal distance away in another direction, to which he walked
as before every day, wet or fine.   This was the job
he had " chucked," to return to his old trade in the
old place.   He might well give it up !   Said Bettesworth,

" How many miles d'ye think he walked last week,

to put in forty-five hours at work ? Fifty-four !
Four and a half miles there, and four and a half
back. Fifty-four miles for forty-five hours. There's
walkin' for ye ! And through that enclosure, too !"

The " enclosure " is a division of Alice Holt Forest
—perhaps two miles of it—on Mardon's way to his
now abandoned job. And Bettesworth recalled the
discomforts of this walk.

" I knows what it is, all through them woods in
the dark, 'cause I used to go that way myself when
I was workin' for Whittingham. 'Specially if the
fox-hounds bin that way. Then 'tis mud enough to
smother ye. There was a fancy sort o' bloke—a
carpenter—used to go 'long with us, with his shirt-
cuffs, and his trousers turned up, and his shoes
cleaned. We did use to have some games with 'n,
no mistake. He'd go tip-toein' an' skippin' to get
over the mud ; an' then, jest as we was passin' a
puddle, we'd plump one of our feet down into 't, an'
send the mud *all over* 'n. An' with his tip-toein' an'
skippin' he got it wuss than we did, without that.
An' when we come to the Royal Oak, 'cause we
gen'ly used to turn in there on our way home, he'd
be lookin' at hisself up an' down and grumblin'—
' Tha bluhmin' mud !' (this in fair imitation of
Cockney speech)—' tha bluhmin' mud ! Who can
stick it !' Same in the mornin' when he got there.
He'd be brushin' his coat, an' scrapin' of it off his
trousers with his knife, an' gettin' a bundle o'
shavin's to wipe his boots.

" But a very good carpenter ! Whittingham used to say he couldn't wish for a better man. But he'd bin used to bench-work all his life, an' didn't know what to make of it. An' we used to have some games with 'n. If there was any job wanted doin' out o' doors, they'd send for he sooner 'n one o' t'others, jest to see how he'd go on. And handlin' the dirty timber, an' lookin' where to put his saw— oh, we did give 'n a doin'. But 'twas winter, ye know, and I fancy he didn't know hardly where to go. We had some pantomimes with 'n, though, no mistake.

" There used to be another ol' feller—a plumber— when I was at work for Grange in Church Street ; Ben Crawte went 'long with 'n as plumber's labourer. Ben had some pantomimes with he too. He'd git the handles of his tools all over dirt, for he to take hold of when he come to use 'em. Oldish man he was—old as I be, I dessay. And he'd pay anybody to give 'n a lift any time, sooner 'n he'd walk through the mud. We never knowed the goin' of 'n, at last. . . ."

I, for my part, do not remember " the goin' " of these queer reminiscences. They are like the snows of the past—like the snow which actually lay white in our valley while Bettesworth talked.

As to his heartless treatment of this unhappy carpenter, those who would condemn it may yet consider how that gang of men could have endured their miserable journeys, if they had admitted that anyone had the least right to be distressed. Among labourers there is such peril in effeminacy that to yield to it is a kind of treason. Bettesworth had nothing but contempt for it. I more than once heard his scorn of " tip-toeing," and shall be able to give another instance by-and-by.

X

DURING this year 1901, until the last month or two, not much additional matter relating to Bettesworth was recorded ; it just suffices to show his life quietly passing on in company with the passing seasons.

February 1, 1901.—We have already had a glimpse of the winter. And now, although it is only February, there comes, as in February there often will, a day truly springlike, and Bettesworth's talk matches it. The first morning of February was clear and shimmering, the roads being hard with frost, the air crisp, the trees hung with the dazzling drops into which the sunshine had converted the rime of the dawn. Most of these drops appeared blinding white, but now and again there would come from them a sparkle of flame-red or a glisten of emerald, or, best of all, a flash of earnest burning blue, as if the morning sky itself were liquefying on the bare branches. The grass, although under it the ground was frozen, had a brilliancy of colour which certainly was no winter tint. It suggested where, if one looked, one would find the green spear-points of crocuses and daffodils already inch-high out of the

soil. The spring, in fact, was in the air, and the
earth was stirring with it.

In Bettesworth's mood, too, was a hint of spring.
All through the winter many hours which would
otherwise have been lonely for him in this garden
had been cheered by the companionship of a robin.
How often he remarked, " You may do anything
you mind to with 'n, but you mawn't handle 'im " !
For the bird seemed to know him, and he used to call
it his " mate," because it worked with him wherever
he was turning up the soil.

And now on this gay morning, as we crossed the
lawn together, he said, " Little Bob bin 'long with
me again this mornin', hoppin' about just in front o'
my shovel, and twiddlin' and talkin' to me. . . .
Look at 'n ! There he is now !" on the low bough
of a young beech-tree at the edge of the grass. And
as we stood to admire, " *There's* a little chap !" he
exclaimed exultantly. Then he took up his shovel
to resume work near the tree, and " Little Bob "
hopped down, every minute picking up something to
swallow. I could not see what tiny morsels the bird
was finding, and, confessing as much, felt snubbed
by Bettesworth's immediate reply, " Ah, *he* got
sharp eyes." Presently, however, the robin found
a large centipede, and suddenly—it was gone alive
and wriggling down the small throat. " He must
ha' got a good bellyful," said Bettesworth.

At intervals Bob would pause, look straight at us,
and " twiddle " a little song in an undertone which,

for all one could hear to the contrary, might have come from some distance behind or beside us, and could only be identified as proceeding from the robin by the accompanying movements of his ruddy throat.

" Sweet little birds, I calls 'em," said Bettesworth, using an epithet rare with him. " And it's a funny thing," he continued, " wherever a man's at work there's sure to be a robin find him out. *I*'ve noticed it often. If I bin at work in the woods, a robin 'd come, or in the harvest-field, jest the same. . . . Hark at 'n twiddlin' ! And by-'n-by when his crop's full he'll get up in a tree and *sing*. . . ."

The old man did a stroke or two with his shovel, and then : " I don't hear no starlin's about. 'Relse, don't ye mind last year they had a nest up in the shed ?"

I hinted that my two cats might have something to do with the absence of the starlings, and Bettesworth's talk flitted easily to the new subject.

" Ah, that young cat—*she* wouldn't care " how many starlings she caught. " *She's* goin' to be my cat " (the cat for his favour). " Every mornin', as soon as the servant opens the door, she " (the cat) " is out, prowlin' all round. And she don't mind the cold ; you see, she liked the snow—played with it. Now, our old Tab, as soon as I be out o' my nest she's in it. Very often she'll come up on to our bed, heavin' and tuckin' about, to get into the warm.".

What a gift of expression the old man had got! But almost without a pause he went on, " The postman tells me he brought word this mornin' to all the pubs, tellin' 'em they was to close to-morrow " (Saturday, the day of Queen Victoria's funeral), " out of respect to our Queen's memory. 'T least, they're requested to—en't forced to. But so they ought to show her respect. Go where you will, you can't hear anybody with a word to say against her. 'Tis to be hoped the new King 'll be as worthy of respect."

Again, without transition : " How that little tree do grow !" He placed his hand on the stem of a young lime. " Gettin' quite a body. So-and-so tells me he put them in overnight Mr. Watson's forty-five years ago, and look what trees they be now ! They terrible wanted to cut 'em down when they made that alteration to the road down there, but Watson said he wouldn't have 'em moved for any money. . . . I likes a lime ; 'tis such a bower."

So the pleasant chatter oozed out of him, as he worked with leisurely stroke, enjoying the morning. With his robins and his bowers, he was in the most cheerful spirits. At one time there was talk of the doctor, whom he had seen going down the lane on a bicycle, and had warned against trying to cross the stream, which the coming of the mild weather had flooded ; and of the doctor's thanks, since he disliked wading ; and of Bettesworth's own suggestion, laughingly assented to, that the doctor's " horse " was not partial to water.

It was all so spontaneous, this chatter, so innocent

of endeavour to get the effect it produced, that a
quite incongruous subject was powerless to mar its
quality. He told me that, two days ago, he had
bespoken at the butcher's shop a bullock's head,
and that when he went to get it on this same glistening morning the butcher commended him for coming
early, because " people was reg'lar runnin' after him
for 'em." So early was he that the bullock had not
been killed an hour, and he had to wait while they
skinned the head and " took the eyes out," Bettesworth no doubt looking on with interest. And he
had brought this thing home with him—was going
to put it in brine at night, " and then to-morrer into
the pot it goes, and that 'll make me some rare nice
soup."

March 1, 1901.—I am reminded, however, that
this was not real spring, but only a foretaste of it.
As yet the birds were not pairing, and before their
day came (according to Bettesworth, St. Valentine's
is the day when the birds begin to pair) there was
more snow. But observe the advance the spring
has made when March comes in. On the first
afternoon of March I noticed Bettesworth's " mate "
with him again, " twiddlin'," as usual ; but I fancied
and said that he looked larger than before, and
Bettesworth suggested that perhaps he was living
better—getting more food. Then I thought that
the robin's crest seemed more feathery, and was
told at once, " That shows the time o' year. Won-

derful how tame he is !" exclaimed the old man. He added, shaking his head, " But he goes away courtin' at times. He loses a lot o' time " (from his work with Bettesworth). " Then he comes back, and sets up on the fence an' *sings* to me. . . . But he loses a lot o' time. I tells 'n I shall 'ave to 'ave done with 'n."

April 19.—Six weeks go by, during which the lawn grass has been growing, and by the middle of April Bettesworth is busy with the lawn-mower. There was a neglected grass plot, never mown before save with the scythe, over which he tried this spring to run the machine. But failing, and explaining why, he used an old word so oddly that I noted it, whereby it happens that I get now this minute reminder of an April occupation.

" She," he said, meaning the machine, would certainly refuse to cut some of the coarser tussocks of this grass. " Why, even down there where I bin cuttin', see how she took they cuds in her mouth and spet 'em out—like a old feller with a chew o' baccer—he'll bite and spet. . . ."

The " cuds " to which he referred were little tufts of grass, which only persistent rolling would reduce to a level meet for a lawn-mower.

June 22.—Omitting one short reference to somebody else's family history, and one yet shorter observation on horses and their eyesight, we skip right over May, nor stop again till we come to the longest days. Here the record alights for a moment, just long enough to show a wet mid-June, and Bettesworth keenly alive to the duties of husbandmen in it. He glanced down towards the meadow in the bottom of the valley. An unfinished rick of hay stood there, waiting for the remaining grass, which lay about on the ground, and was losing colour. And Bettesworth said,

" Bill Crawte 'll play about wi' that little bit o' hay down there till 'tis all spoilt."

In truth, it should have been taken up the previous day, as I ventured to suggest. Then Bettesworth, contemptuously,

" He told me he heared it rainin' this mornin' at three o'clock, and got up to cover his rick over. *He'd heared* it *rainin'*. Why, he might ha' bin asleep, an' then that rain would ha' gone down into that rick two foot or more."

That is all. There is no more to tell of the old man's summer, nothing for July and August. But in September we get a glance back to the past harvest, a glance round at the earliest autumn prospects, and a strange suggestion of the first-class importance of these things in the life of country labouring folk. In brief compass, the talk runs rapidly over many points of interest.

September 6.—For if " the fly " was not on our seedling cabbage, as we were inclined to fear, it had certainly ruined sundry sowings of turnips, both in this garden and down there where Bettesworth lived.

" We can't help it," so he philosophized, " and I don't care if we get enough for ourselves, though I should ha' liked to have more." But " Hammond says *he's* turnips be all spiled, and Porter's brother what lives over here at this cot " (the brother, that is, of Porter, who lives over here), " he bin down to Sussex harvestin' for the same man I worked for so many years. Seven weeks. But then he bin hoein'. . . . He was tellin' me his master down there sowed hunderd an' twenty acres o' swedes, and never saved twenty of 'em. Fly took 'em all, and he had to drill again with turnips. Swedes, and same with the mangol'.

" He says they've had it as hot down there as we have here. But, straw ! There was some straw, by all accounts. Young Collison what lives over opposite me was 'long with 'n. Seven weeks he " (which ?) " was away, but it seems he had a bit of a miff with his wife, and went off unbeknownst to her. She went to the relievin' officer, and he told her *they'd* find 'n, if she'd go into the union. He was off harvestin'. He told me o' Sunday he thought 't 'd do her good."

" Who was she ?"

" Gal from Reading. He was up that way somewhere for 'leven year, in a brick-works. And she thought very likely as he was gone off into some brick-works again ; but he was down in Sussex, harvestin'."

September 21.—Though only two weeks later, there is distinct autumn in the next fragment, and yet perhaps for me only, because of the picture it calls up. I remember a very still Saturday afternoon, a sky curtained by quiet cloud, the air motionless, a grey mist stealing into the lane that leads down into the heart of the valley. Certainly it was an autumn day.

As he always did on Saturdays, Bettesworth had swept up the garden paths with extra care, and on this afternoon had taken the sweepings into the lane, to fill up a rut there. Upon my going out to see him, he chuckled.

" You'd ha' laughed if you'd ha' bin out here wi' me at dinner-time. A lady come up the lane, wantin' to know who you was. ' Who lives here ?' she says." He mimicked a high-pitched and affected voice. " ' Mister Bourne,' I says. ' Iss he a gentil-man ?' she says. ' You don't s'pose he's a lady, do ye ?' I says. ' What a beastlie road !' she says, and went off, tip-toein' an' twistin' herself about—dunno how to walk nor talk neither."

I asked who the lady was.

" I dunno. Strangers—she and a man with her. ' Iss he a gentilman ?' she says. I can't *bear* for people to be inquisitive. What should she want to know all about you for ? Might ha' knowed you wasn't a lady. There, I was *bound* to give her closure, askin' me such a silly question !"

" What were they doing down here ?"

" They was down here hookin' down blackberries
with a stick.   And then come askin' me a silly question like that !   *Silly* questions !   I don't see what
people wants to ast 'em for.   She went off 'long o'
the man, huggin' up close to him, an' twistin' herself about.   Dunno how to walk nor yet talk !   ' Iss
he a gentilman !' "

November 10, 1901.—Two odd words—one of them
perhaps newly coined for the occasion, the other
misused—were the reason for my preserving a short
note which brings us to November, and shows us
Bettesworth proposing to himself a task appropriate
to the season.   The sap was dying down in the trees ;
the fruit bushes had lost their leaves, and stood
ready for winter, and their arrangement offended
Bettesworth's taste.   He would have had the garden
formal and orderly, if he had been able.

" I thought I'd take up them currant bushes," he
said, " and put 'em in again in rotation "—in a
straight row, he meant, as he went on to explain.
" They'd look better than all jaggled about, same
as they be now."

And so the currant-bushes, which until then were
" jaggled," or zig-zagged about, were duly moved,
and stand to this day in a line.   At that time he
could still see a currant-bush, and criticize its
position.

November 22.—Towards fallen leaves, it is recorded
a little later, he preserved a constant animosity.

His patient sweepings and grumblings were one of the notes of early winter for me—" the slovenliest time of all the year," he used to say.

He even doubted that leaves made a good manure, and he quoted authorities in support of his own opinion. Had not a gardener in the town said that he, for his part, always burnt the leaves, as soon as they were dry enough to burn, because " they be reg'lar poison to the ground " ? Or, " if you opens a hole and puts in a bushel or two to form mould, they got to bide three years, an' *then* you got to mix other earth with 'em." As litter for pigs, he admitted, dead leaves were useful ; yet should the cleanings of the pigsty be afterwards heaped up and allowed to dry, the first wind would " purl the leaves about all over the place. . . . And that makes me think there en't much *in* 'em," or surely they would rot ?

But unquestionably leaves make good dry litter. " My old gal " (so the discourse proceeded)—" my old gal used to go out an' get 'em," so that the pig might have a dry bed ; in which care the " old gal " contrasted nobly with " Will Crawte down 'ere," who had little pigs at this time " up to their belly in slurry." They could not thrive—Bettesworth was satisfied of that. His wife, in the days of her strength, would " go out on to the common, tearin' up moth or rowatt with her hands—her hands was harder 'n mine—and she'd tear up moth or rowatt or anything," to make a clean bed for the pig.

I suppose that by " moth " he meant moss.
" Rowatt " is old grass which has never been cut,
but has run to seed and turned yellow. With
regard to rowatt, it makes a good litter and a toler-
able manure, said Bettesworth ; with this drawback,
however, that " if you gets it wi' the seed on," however much it may have been trampled in the pigsty,
" 'tis bound to come up when you spreads the manure
on the ground."

XI

A TIMELY reminder occurs here, that with all its rustic attractiveness—its genial labours in this picturesque valley, its sensitive response to the slow changes of the year—Bettesworth's life could not be an idyllic one. For that, he needed a wife who could make him comfortable, and encourage him by the practice of old-fashioned cottage economies ; but Fate had denied him that help. From time to time I heard of old Lucy's having fits, but I paid little heed, and cannot tell why I noted the attack by which she was prostrated at the end of this November, unless that again it was borne in upon me how Bettesworth himself must suffer on such occasions.

November 24, 1901.—On Sunday, November 24, the trouble was taking its ordinary course. There had been the long night, disturbed by successive seizures, in one of which the old woman could not be saved from falling out of bed " flump on the floor " ; there was the helpless day in which Bettesworth must cook his own dinner or go without ; there were the dreadful suggestions from the neighbours that he ought to put his wife away in an asylum ;

there was his own tight-lipped resolve to do nothing of the sort, but to remember always how good to him she had been. It was merely the usual thing; and if we remember how it kept recurring and was a part almost of Bettesworth's daily life, that is enough, without further detail.

To get a clear impression of his contemporary circumstances is necessary, lest the narrative be confused by his frequent references to old times. Tending his wife, working unadventurously in my garden, loving the succession of crops, humbly subservient to the weather or gladdening at its glories, as he went about he spilt anecdotes of other years and different scenes, which must be picked up as we go. But the day-to-day existence must be kept in mind meanwhile. He gossipped at haphazard, but the telling of any one of those narratives which so often interrupt the course of this book was only the most trivial and momentary incident in his contemporary history. He spoke for a few minutes, and had finished, and his day's work went on as before.

November 26.—Thus, around the next glimpse of an exciting moment forty odd years ago, one has to imagine the November forenoon, raw, grey with pale fog, in which Bettesworth was at some pottering job or other, slow enough to make me ask if he were not cold; and so the talk gets started. No, he was not cold; he felt "*nice* and warm. . . . But yes-

terday, crawlin' about among that shrubbery after
the dead leaves," his hands were very cold.   Yesterday, I remembered then, had been a day of hard rimy
frost, so that it had surprised me, I said, to see " one
of Pearson's carmen " driving without gloves.
Bettesworth looked serious.

"You'd have thought he'd have had gloves for
drivin'," he said.   Then, meditatively, " I don't
think old *Wells* drives for Pearsons much now, do
he ?   You very often sees somebody else out with
his horse.   He bin with 'em a smart many years.
He went there same time as I lef' Brown's.   That
was in 1860.   Pearsons sent across the street for me
to go on for they, but I'd agreed with Cooper the
builder, you know."

From amidst a confusion of details that followed,
about Cooper's business, and where he got his harness, and so on, the fact emerged that the builder
had the use of a stable in Brown's premises, which
explains how Bettesworth's former master makes
his appearance on the scene presently.   For Bettesworth had still to work at this stable, though for a
new employer.

"Cooper had a little cob when I went on for 'n.
His father give it to 'n—or no, 'twas the harness
his father give 'n.   One o' these little Welsh rigs.
Spiteful little card he was.   I knocked 'n down wi'
the prong seven times one mornin'.   When I went
in to the stable he kicked up, and the manure an'
litter went in here, what he'd kicked up.   In here."

Bettesworth thrust forward his old stubbly chin, and pointed into the neck-band of his shirt.

I said, " There would have been no talks for me with Bettesworth if he had touched you !"

" No. He'd have killed me. I ketched up the ^fust thing I could see, an' that was the prong, and 't last I was afraid *I'd* killed *he*. A bad-tempered little card he was, though. They be *worse* than an intire 'orse. . . . They be worse than an intire *'orse*."

He was dropping into meditation, standing limply with drooping arms, and fixing an absent-minded look upon his job. For his memory was straying among the circumstances of forty years ago. Then suddenly he straightened up again and continued,

" While I'd got the prong, Brown heard the scufflin', and come runnin' down. ' What the plague's up now ?' he says. ' I dunno,' I says ; ' I shall either kill 'n or conquer 'n.' . . . But he *was* a bad-tempered one. He wouldn't let ye go into the stable to do 'n. I had to get 'n out and tie his head to a ring in the wall, high up, an' then I could pay 'n as I mind to. Brown says at last, ' That's enough ;' he says, ' I won't have it.' But Cooper says, ' You let 'n do as he likes.' And I says, ' If I don't have my own way with 'n, you'll have to do 'n yourself.' But a *good* little thing on the road, ye know. Quiet ! And wouldn't touch no vittles nor drink away from home, drive 'n where you mind. Never was a better little thing to go. I think Cooper give eighteen or twenty pound for 'n. But a *nasty* little customer—

wouldn't let ye go near 'n in the stable. They jockeys thought *they* was goin' to have 'n. They all said they thought he'd be a rum 'n, and so he was, too.

" One time Mrs. Cooper come into the yard with a green silk dress on, and he put his head round and grabbed it " (near the waist, to judge by Bettesworth's gesture), " and tore out a great piece—a yard or more. Do what I would, I couldn't help laughin', though she was a testy sort o' woman. And she did fly about, the servant said, when she went indoors.

" But I thought I'd killed 'n that time with the prong. Sweat, he did, and bellered like a bull ; and 't last I give 'n one on the head. I made sure I'd killed 'n. *I* was afraid, then. I thought I'd hit too hard. And I sweat as much as he did then."

XII

December 2, 1901.—In view of the hatred in which Bettesworth had previously held the workhouse infirmary, and which he was destined to renew later, it is interesting to observe how favourably the place impressed him about this time, when he visited a friend there.

The friend, whom I will rename " Tom Loveland," had been taken to the infirmary in October, suffering with the temporary increase of some obscure chronic disorder which to this day cripples him. Bettesworth had gone to see him on Sunday afternoon, December 1, in company with Harriett Loveland, the man's wife.

The patient still lay there, " on his back," I heard on the Monday.

" On Saturday they took off the poultices. Seven weeks they bin poulticin' of 'n ; but Saturday the doctor thought there was ' a slight change.' But, law !" Bettesworth continued, in scorn of the doctor's opinion, " they abscesses 'll keep comin'.

" There was two more died, up there in that same room where he is, o' Saturday." This made six deaths since Loveland's admission. " One of 'em was a man I used to know very well—that 'ere Jack Grey that used to do " so-and-so at where-is-it. " They sent for his wife, an' she got there jest two minutes afore he died. Loveland says, ' I tucked my head down under the blankets when I see 'em bring in the box ' (the coffin) ' for 'n.' ' What, did ye think he was for you, Tom ?' I says. But he always was a meek-hearted feller : never had no nerve."

But it was in the appointments of the place where Loveland lay that Bettesworth was chiefly interested. He was almost enthusiastic over the whiteness of the sheets, the beeswaxed floor (" like glass to walk on. I says to Harriet, ' You must take care you don't slip up ' "), the little cupboards (" lockers, they calls 'em ") beside each bed ; the nurse, who " seemed to be a pleasant woman ;" the daily attendance of the medical men ; and other advantages. All these things persuaded Bettesworth that the patients were " better off up there than what they would be at home." And out in the grounds, " You'd meet two old women, perhaps, walkin' along together ; and then, a little further on, some old men," which all appeared to be very satisfactory.

Were there any circumstances to give offence ? Yes : " There's that Gunner, what used to live up the lane, struttin' about there, like Lord Muck, in his fine slippers. He's a wardsman. And Bill Lucas, too." (This latter is a man who lost good work and a pension by giving way to drink.) " *He* books ye in an' books ye out. 'I s'pose this is your *estate ?*' I says to 'n." In fact, Bettesworth would seem to have been publicly sarcastic at this man's expense ; and other visitors, I gathered, laughed at hearing him. "' You be better able to work than what I be,' I says ; ' and yet we got to keep ye. It never ought to be allowed.' "

To those in the infirmary " You may take anything you mind to, except spirits or beer. Tea, or anything like that, they may have brought." And so Bettesworth, having gone unprepared, gave Loveland a shilling, " to get anything he fancied."

XIII

As yet Bettesworth's cottage by the stream still suited him fairly well, but he had not lived there for two years without finding out that it had disadvantages. Of these perhaps the worst was that the owner was himself only a cottager—an old impoverished man who never came near the place, and was unable to spend any money on repairing it. Difficulties were therefore arising, as I learnt one Monday morning. The reader will observe the day of the week.

December 9, 1901.—" Didn't it rain about four o'clock this mornin' !" Bettesworth began, with an emphasis which provoked me to question whether the rainfall had amounted to a great deal, after all. But he insisted : " There must ha' bin a smartish lot somewhere. The lake's full o' water, down as far as Mrs. Skinner's. When the gal come after the rent yesterday . . ."

This day being Monday, I exclaimed at his " yesterday." Did he mean it ?

" Yes, they always comes Sundays. She says, ' Gran'father told me I was to look to see whether you'd cleaned out the lake in front of the cottage.' "

In fact, a fortnight previously a message from the owner had reached Bettesworth requesting him to do this. The answer given then was repeated now : " You tell your gran'father he may come an' do it hisself. I shan't."

" ' Oh,' she says " (I continue in Bettesworth's words), " ' Mr. Mardon ' " (the tenant of the next cottage) " ' said he'd do some.'

" ' He may come and do this if he mind to,' I says. ' 'Twon't flood *me*.' " Mardon's cottage was certainly in danger of flooding, should there come prolonged rain.

" Then I said to her, ' How about our well, then ? We en't had no water ever since I spoke to you 'bout it before.'

" ' Oh,' she says, ' they come an' looked at the well Saturday. But gran'father says 't 'll cost too much. 'T 'll want a lot o' bricks an' things. If he has it done, he says he'll have to put up your rent— yours and Mr. Mardon's—'cause you be the only two as pays anything. En't it a shame ?' she says. ' There's that old Mileham—he earns good money every week, and never pays a ha'penny.' "

At this point I foolishly interrupted, and being told how Mileham " won't pay, and poor old Mrs. Connor, she en't *got* it to pay," I interrupted again, not understanding.

" Hasn't *got* it to pay ? How do you mean ?"

" Why, what *have* she got, sir ? All the time her husband was alive, drawin' his pension, the rent was paid up every pension day. But now she en't got nothin' comin' in, and that lout of a boy of hers don't do nothin'. So there's only me and Mardon pays any rent."

I laughed. " It's a fine encouragement to you to be asked to pay more."

" Yes. I says to her, ' Then we two got to pay for four ? You tell your gran'father he may put it up, but I shan't pay no more for this old hutch. And I shan't pay what I do, as soon as I can find another place to go to. If he mind to let we get the well done, and we take it out o' the rent,' I says, ' I'll agree to that. Not pay no more rent till we've took it all out.' But she wouldn't say nothin' to that. Or else generally she got plenty o' gab."

" Who is she ?" I asked.

" He's grand-daughter. . . . That young Mackenzie was her father. She've got plenty o' gab. ' You 'alf-bred Scotch people,' I says to her sometimes, ' talks too much.' I tells her of it sometimes. She don't like me."

It seemed unlikely that Bettesworth would long continue to be a tenant under such a landlord. The change, however, was not to come yet.

As yet, indeed, difficulties like these were but trivial incidents of the life in which Bettesworth continued to take an interest as virile as ever. He had dealt with landlords before, and had no qualms now. It might be that the great strength of his prime was gone, but his health seemed unimpaired, and I believe he still felt master of his fate as he went quietly about his daily work.

It is true that my very next note of him contains evidence of a digestive weakness which, having not much troubled him hitherto, though he had always been subject to it, was growing upon him, and beginning to undermine his forces. But it was for another reason—because of a curious word he used —that I then recorded what he told me.

The entry in my journal, bearing still the date December 9, is to the effect that " on Friday afternoon " a horrid pain took him right through the midriff, from front to back. " I begun to think I was goin' to croak," he said afterwards, when telling me about it. " And I reached, and the sheer-water run out o' my eyes an' mouth. I didn't know where to go for an hour or more, I was in that pain. I 'xpect 'twas stoopin' down over my work brought it on. I'd had a hot dinner, ye see—bit o' pickled pork an' pa'snips. And then stoopin' down. . . . But that sheer-water—you knows what I means—run out o' my mouth." I did not know what he meant, until the next day, when I asked how he felt. He was " all right," but, repeating the story, said, " and the water run out o' my mouth, jest like boilin' water."

During the last year or two of his life I think he seldom went a week without a recurrence of this pain of indigestion, the disorder being doubtless aggravated by the breakdown of his domestic arrangements. But this is looking too far ahead. At the period which now concerns us, he was far from thinking of himself as an invalid. He could joke about his passing indispositions as he could defy his landlord. This particular attack, unless I am much mistaken, was the subject of a flippancy I remember his repeating to me. A neighbour looking in upon him and seeing his serious condition said genially, " You ben't goin' to die, be ye, Freddy ?" And he answered, " I dunno. Shouldn't care if I do. 'Tis a poor feller as can't make up his mind to die once. If we had to die two or three times, then there might be something to fret about." In relating this to me, he added more seriously, " But nobody dunno *when*, that's the best of it."

Knowing now how his attitude changed towards death when it was really near, I can see in this sturdy defiance the evidence of the physical vigour he was still enjoying. There was no real cause for fretting about himself, any more than about his affairs ; and so he went through this winter, garrulous and good-tempered, even happy in his way.

Accordingly, taking my notes in their due order, they bring before my mind, as I read them again now, pleasant pictures of the old man. I can see him at work, or taking his wages, or starting for the town ; often the very weather and daylight around him come back to me ; and the chief loss is in his voice-tones, which I cannot by any effort of memory recover.

December 10, 1901.—One such mind-picture dates from December 10. The short winter afternoon was already closing in, with a mist—the forerunner of rain—enveloping the garden between the bare-limbed trees. Over our heads sounded the roar of wind in a little fir-wood ; but down under the oak-trees by the well, where Bettesworth was digging, there was shelter and stillness, or only the slight trembling of a few leaves not yet fallen. It was " nice and warm," he assured me, and then paused— himself a dusky-looking old figure in the oncoming dusk—to ask, whom did I think he had seen go down the lane just now ? It was no other than his former neighbour, " old Jack Morris's widow."

And once again his talk shows how far he was, that afternoon, from thinking of himself as an infirm person, or an object of pity. I am struck by the contrast between his later view of things and this which he professed, when still in good health. For, speaking appreciatively of Widow Morris as " the *cleanest* old soul as ever lived," he went on to say that, though he did not know what she was doing at that time, she had been in the workhouse. It puzzled him how she lived, and others like her. And when I said, " She ought to be in the work-house," he echoed the opinion emphatically. " *Better* off there than what they be at home, sir." So with Mrs. Connor. " It's a mystery how she lives. And there's that son of hers, mungs about with a short pipe stuck in his mouth," and by sheer idleness had lost several jobs, at which he might have been earning eleven shillings a week. "And that poor gal, he's sister, got to starve herself to keep her mother and that lout. Cert'nly, she ought to keep her mother," but, for the lout, Bettesworth's politer vocabulary was insufficient.

So we talked in the gathering winter dusk, able, both of us, in the assurance of the comfortable evening before us, to consider the workhouse as a refuge with which neither of us would ever make personal acquaintance. If I was unimaginative and therefore callous, so was Bettesworth. It was he who said, " I reckons that's what they places be for—old people past work, and little helpless children." But as to the able-bodied, " That stone-yard's the place for they. *I*'d put it on to 'em, so's it 'd give 'em sore hearts, if it didn't sore hands."

And then he told of a tramp—a carpenter—who had earned his tenpence an hour, and now was using workhouses to lodge in at night, while all day he was "munging about" (or " doing a mung "), cadging a few halfpence for beer.

" And that 'ere bloke down near we, he's another of 'em. Earns eightpence-halfpenny, and his son sixpence. But they gets it all down 'em." They had not paid Mrs. Skinner for the pork obtained from her the previous week ; indeed, they paid no-body. " Never got nothing, and yet there's only they two and the old woman."

What a contrast were these wasters—that was the idea of Bettesworth's talk—with those two poor old widow women, whom he could afford to pity in his strength and comfort !

December 24.—The next note brings us to Christmas Eve. The weather on the preceding day had changed from rimy frost to tempestuous rain, which at nightfall began to be mingled with snow. By his own account Bettesworth went to bed soon after seven, although even his wife urged that it was too early, and that he would never lie till morning. He had heard the tempest, and the touch of the snow against his bedroom window, and so had his wife. It excited her. " Ben't ye goin' to look out at it ?" she said. And he, " That won't do me no good, to look at it. We got a good fire in here."

Such was his own chuckling account of his attitude towards the storm when I stood by him the next morning high up in the garden, and watched him sweeping the path. He discussed the prospects for the day, rejoiced that the snow had not lain, and, looking keenly to the south, where a dun-coloured watery cloud was travelling eastwards, its edges melting into luminous mist and just hiding the sun, he thought we might expect storms. The old man's spirits were elated ; and then it was, when the western end of the valley suddenly lit up as with a laugh of spring sunlight, and the radiance came sweeping on and broke all round us—then it was that Bettesworth, as I have elsewhere* related, stood up to give the sunshine his glad welcome.

A narrative followed which helps to explain his good spirits, or at least discovers the powers of endurance on which they rested. I said, " We have passed the shortest day—that's a comfort." He stopped sweeping again, to answer happily, " Yes. And now in about four or five weeks we shall begin to see the difference. And that's when we gets the bad weather, lately."

He stood up, the watery sunshine upon him, and leaning on his broom, he continued, " I remember one winter, after I was married, we did have some weather. Eighteen inches and two foot o' snow there was—three foot, in some places. I'd bin out o' work—there was plenty o' work to do, but we was froze out. For five weeks I 'adn't earnt tuppence. When Christmas Day come, we *had* somethin' for dinner, but 'twa'n't much ; and we had a smartish few bottles o' home-made wine.

" Christmas mornin' some o' the chaps I'd bin at work with come round. ' What about that wine ?' they says. So we had two or three cupfuls o' wine ; and then they says, ' Ben't ye comin' 'long o' we ?' ' No,' I says, ' not 's mornin'.' " Here he shut his mouth, in remembered resignation, as if still regarding these tempters. " ' What's

* Author's note. "The Bettesworth Book" (second impression).

up then ?' they says. '*Come* on !' 'No,' I says,
' not to-day.' 'Why not ?' 'Cause 'I en't got no
money,' I says. 'Gawd's truth !' they says, ' if
that's it. . . .' and I raked in six shillin's from
amongst 'em. I give four to the old gal, and I kep'
two myself, and then I was right for the day.'

He made as if to resume sweeping, but desisted,
to explain, " Ye see, they was my mates on the
same job as me ; and they knowed I'd ha' done
the same for e'er a one o' they, more 'n once.

" My old mother-in-law was alive then, over here "
(he looked across the hollow to the old house),
" and they wanted we to go and 'ave the day with
they. But my temper wouldn't have that. I
says to the old gal, ' None o' their 'elp. We'll bide
away, or else p'r'aps by-'n-by they'll twit us.' I'd
sooner ha' gone without vittles, than for they to
help and then twit us with it afterwards, talkin'
about what they'd done for us at Christmas."

XIV

ONE of Bettesworth's swift short tales about his neighbours interested me considerably at this time, as illustrating the half-sordid, half-barbarous state of the people amongst whom he had to hold his own when not at work. I did not suspect that the same tale would put me on the track of a curious discovery relative to his own past history.

January 23, 1902.—It was a quiet, windless morning, and the sound of the knell reached us through the still air. Bettesworth said, " I s'pose old Jerry's gone at last, then."

" Old Jerry ?" I asked.

" Ah, old Jerry Penfold. We always called 'n Old Jerry. He bin dead several times—or, 't least, they thought so. Rare ructions there bin over there, no mistake. They got to sharin' out his kit. One come an' took away his clock, and another his chest o' drawers, and some of his sons even come an' took away his tools. But the oldest son got the lawyer an' made 'em bring it all back."

" Rare ructions "—yes : but Bettesworth used the word " rare " as we should use " great," and did not mean that the affair was very unusual. He was not scandalized so much as amused by it. For my part, knowing nothing of the family, who dwelt in another quarter of the parish, I sought only to identify Old Jerry. Some years previously an old man who walked along the road with me one night had interested me with a tale of his shepherding and other labours on a certain farm. I had never learnt his name, nor had seen the man since ; but now it occurred to me that perhaps he was old Penfold. I asked Bettesworth.

Bettesworth decided in the negative. Old Penfold had never been a shepherd, or worked for the farmer I named.

Yet another old man then came into my mind : a diminutive man, upwards of eighty, who was still creeping honourably about at work. Frequently I met him ; but he seemed so shut up in himself that I had never cared to intrude upon him with more than a " Good-day " when we met. But now I named him to Bettesworth : old Dicky Martin. Could the missing shepherd have been he ?

Bettesworth shook his head emphatically. It turned out that he and old Dicky were chums in their way : they knew all about one another, and with mutual respect. " Couldn't ha' bin old Dicky," said Bettesworth. " He never worked anywhere else about here 'xcept in builders' yards. Forty-four year ago he started for Coopers, and bin on there ever since. He was a sailor before that. He come out o' the navy when he come here."

Out of the navy! And to think I had been ignorant of such a thing as that! I had not found my shepherd; but to have discovered a sailor was something. Scenting romance, in the foolish superficial way of outsiders, I resolved to improve my acquaintance with old Dicky, little dreaming that the sailor was going to show me a soldier too; little supposing that Bettesworth's information about this old man would be capped by information from him, quite as surprising, about Bettesworth.

How I fell in with old Martin, early in February, is of no moment here. He talked very much in Bettesworth's manner, and especially about cruising in the Mediterranean sixty years ago· But when I said at last, believing it true, " I don't suppose there is another man in our parish has travelled so far as you," his reply startled me.

" No, I dessay not—without 'tis your man, Fred Bettesworth."

" He? He never was out of England."

" Yes he was. He bin as fur as Russia and the Black Sea, at any rate."

" You must be wrong. I should have heard of it if he had."

" I dunno about that. P'raps he don't care to talk about it, but 'tis right enough. I fancy he did get into some trouble. He was a soldier though, in the Crimea."

Old Dicky was so convinced that I held my
peace, though far from convinced myself. A vague
sensation crept over me of having heard some faint
rumour of the same tale, years ago ; but what
might have been credible then seemed hardly
credible now. I thought that now I knew all there
was to know about Bettesworth's life ; and I could
not see where, among so many episodes, this of
soldiering was to find room. Besides, how was it
possible that, in ten years or so, during which
Bettesworth had prattled carelessly of anything
that came uppermost in his mind, no hint of this
had escaped him ? It would have slipped out
unawares, one would have supposed ; by some
inadvertence or other I should have learnt it. But,
save for that forgotten rumour, nothing had come
until now. Now, however, the man who spoke of
it spoke as from his own personal knowledge. It
was very strange.

One thing was clear. If there were truth in this
tale after all, Bettesworth's silence on the subject
must have been intentional. Was there something
about it of which he was ashamed ? What was that
" trouble " to which old Dicky so darkly alluded ?
Eager as I was to question Bettesworth, I was most
reluctant to hear anything to his discredit. And
the reluctance prevailed over my curiosity. Feeling
that I had no right to force a confidence from him,
I tried to dismiss the subject from my mind ; and
for a time I succeeded.

XV

April 17, 1902.—We pass on to April, when bird-notes were sounding through all the gardens.

" Hark at those starlings !" I said to Bettesworth. And he, " Yes—I dunno who 'twas I was talkin' to this mornin', sayin' how he liked to hear 'em. ' So do our guv'nor,' I says. I likes 'em best when there's two of 'em gibberin' to one another—jest like 's if they was talkin'. An' they lifts up their feet, an' flaps up their wings, an' they nods." The old man's words ran rhythmically to suit the action he was describing ; and then, dropping the rhythm, " I likes to hear 'em very well. And I don't think they be mischieful birds neither, like these 'ere sparrers and caffeys " (chaffinches). " They beggars, I shouldn't care so much if when they picked out the peas from the ground they'd eat 'em. But they jest nips the little green top off and leaves it. Sims as if they does it reg'lar for mischief."

April 28.—This sunny, objective side of Bettes-worth's temperament may be remembered in con-nexion with some other remarks of his on a very different subject. There was at that time a man living near us whose mere presence tried his

patience. The man belonged to one of the stricter
Nonconformist sects, and had the reputation of
being miserly. " Looks as miserable, he do "
(so Bettesworth chanced to describe him), " as
miserable as—as sin. I never see such a feller."

At this I laughed, admitting that our neighbour certainly did not look as if he knew how to enjoy himself.

" He *don't*. Don't sim to have no pleasure,
nor 'sociate with anybody. There ! I'd as lief
not have a life at all, as have one like his. I'd do
without, if I couldn't do no better'n that."

Bettesworth's judgment was possibly in error ;
for there is no telling what mystical joys, what
dreams of another world, may have illuminated
this man's inner life, and made him suspicious of
people like Bettesworth and me. But if there were
such compensation, Bettesworth's temperament
was incapable of recognizing it, and the point is
instructive. His own indomitable cheerfulness was
of the objective pagan order. The field of his
emotions and fancies had never been cultivated.
His thoughts did not stray beyond this world.
From such deep sources of physical sanity his
optimism welled up, that he really needed, or at any
rate craved for, no spiritual consolation. Like his
remote ancestors who first invaded this island, he
had the habit of taking things as they came, and
of enjoying them greatly on the whole. He half
enjoyed, even while he was irritated by it, the odd
figure presented by this Nonconformist.

May 7.—A week afterwards he exhibited the same sort of aloof interest, annoyed and yet amused, in a jibbing horse. A horse had brought a ton of coal a part of the way down the lane, and then refused to budge farther ; and Bettesworth could not forget the incident. It tickles me still to recall with what a queer look on his face he spoke of the noble animal. The expression was the result of his trying to say his word for *horse* (not *'oss,* but *'awss*), while a facetious smile was twitching at the corners of his mouth. This was several days after the event. At the time of its occurrence, someone had remarked that the horse had no pluck, and Bettesworth had rejoined indignantly, " *I'd* see about his pluck, if I had the drivin' of 'n !" But after a day or two his indignation turned to quiet gaiety. " Won't back," he said, " and he won't draw."

I suggested, " Not bad at standing still."

Then came the queer expression on Bettesworth's face, with " ' Good 'awss to *eat,*' the man said." Truly it was odd to see how Bettesworth's lips, grim enough as a rule, arched out sarcastically over the word *'awss.*

And it was in a temper not very dissimilar that he commonly regarded our Nonconformist neighbour. The man amused him.

A pagan of the antique English kind, ready to poke fun at a bad horse, or sneer at a fanatic, or be happy in listening to the April talk of the starlings, Bettesworth had quite his share too of the pugnacity

of his race. Years ago he had said that a fight
used to be " just his clip," as a young man ; not
many years ago he had promptly knocked down in
the road a baker who had got down out of his cart
to make Bettesworth move his wheelbarrow out of
the way (I remember that when the old man told me
of this I advised him not to get into trouble, and he
pleaded that it " seemed to do him good ") ; and now
during this spring—I cannot say exactly when—the
fighting spirit suddenly woke up in him once more.

The circumstance takes us out again from the
peace of the garden to the crude struggle for life
in the village. Looking back to that time, I can
see our valley as it were sombrely streaked with the
progress of two or three miserable family embroil-
ments, squalid, weltering, poisoning the atmosphere,
incapable of solution. And though Bettesworth
was no more implicated in these than myself, but
like me was a mere onlooker, he was not, like me,
an outsider. He was down on the very edge of
these troubles, and it was the momentary overflow
of one of them in his direction one night that
suddenly started him fighting, in spite of his years.

I may not go into details of the affair. It is
enough that during this April and May our end of
the parish was looking on, scandalized, at the
blackguard behaviour of a certain labourer towards
his family and especially his own mother. Of
powerful build, the man had been long known for
a bully ; and if report went true, he had received

several thrashings in his time. But just now he was surpassing his own record. He was also presuming upon the forbearance of better men than himself, and could not keep his tongue from flouts and gibes at them. Speaking of him to me, Bettesworth expressed his disapproval and no more. Others, however, were less reticent ; and there came a day when I heard of a quarrel this man had tried to fix upon Bettesworth at the public-house one evening. He was summarily ejected, my informant said ; and something—I have forgotten what—caused me to suspect that the " chucker out " was old Bettesworth. That was not explicitly stated, however. Nor did Bettesworth himself tell me at the time any more than that there had been a disturbance in the taproom, the man being turned out, after insulting him.

May 15.—But, alluding to the affair some time afterwards, he placidly continued the story. " I cut 'n heels over head, an' when he got up, and made for the doorway and the open road, I went for 'n again. They got round me, or I should ha' knocked 'n heels over head again. I broke my way through four or five of 'em. ' If I was twenty years younger,' I says to 'n, ' I'd jump the in'ards out of ye.' Some of 'em says, if he dares touch the old man they'd go for 'n theirself. ' All right !' I says, ' you no call to worry about me. I can manage he.' And they told 'n, ' You got hold o' the wrong one this time, Sammy.' "

XVI

DURING these months, the story of Bettesworth's having been a soldier in the Crimea remained unverified. I was watching for hints of it from him, and he gave not the slightest ; for opportunities of asking him about it without offence, and not one occurred. And slowly the tale receded from my mind, and my belief in it dwindled away.

By what chance, or in what circumstances, the mystery suddenly recurred to me is more than I can tell now. But one rainy May afternoon—I remember that much—the old man was in the wood-shed, sitting astraddle on one block of wood, and chopping firewood on another block between his knees. He looked careless enough, comfortable enough, sitting there in the dry, with the sound of rain entering through the open shed door. What was it he said, or I, to give me an opening ? I shall never know ; but presently I found myself challenging him to confess the truth of what was reported of him.

And I remember well how at once his careless expression changed, as if he had been taxed with a fault, and how for some seconds he sat looking fixedly before him in a shamefaced, embarrassed way, like a schoolboy who has been " found out." For some seconds the silence lasted ; then he said reluctantly, " It's true. So I was." And the circumstantial talk that followed left me without any further doubt on the point.

It was at the Rose and Crown—a well-known tavern in the neighbouring town—that he 'listed. His " chum " (I don't know who his chum was) had already enlisted at Alton, and " everybody thought," as Bettesworth said, that he too had done so at the same time, for he had the soldier's belt on, there in the Alton inn. But he had not taken the shilling there. He returned home to his brother Jim, " what was up there at Middlesham, same job as old Stubby got now—seventeen year he had 'long with the charcoal-burners up there "—and Jim urged him to " go to work." Bettesworth, how-ever, was obstinate. " No," he said, " I shall go to Camden Fair." " Better by half go to work." " No, I shall git about." " And I come down to the town " (so his tale continued), " and there I see my chum what had 'listed at Alton day before. ' Come on,' he says ; ' make up your mind to go with we.' ' 'Greed,' I says. And I went up 'long with 'n to the Rose and Crown. . . ."

" How old were you then ? It must have been before you were married ?"

" Yes ; I was sixteen. I served a year and eight months."

" Ah." I looked out at the May foliage and the kindly rain, and thought of the Crimean winter.

" You saw some cold weather, then ?"

" No mistake. Two winters and one summer." He was, in fact, before Sebastopol, and now that the secret was out, he hurried on to tell familiarly of Kertch, the Black Sea, the Dardanelles, so glibly that my memory was unable to take it all in. What was most strange was to hear these places, whose names to stay-at-home people like myself have come to have an epic sound, spoken of as the scene of merely trivial incidents. As it was only of what he observed himself that Bettesworth told, this could hardly have been otherwise ; yet it is odd to think that Tolstoi, writing his marvellous descriptions of the siege, may have set eyes on him. To this harum-scarum English plough-boy, ignorant, rollicking, reckless, it was not the great events, on a large scale, that were prominent, but the queer things, the little haphazard details upon which he happened to stumble. Through the narrative his own personality was to the fore ; just the same dogged personality that I was to know afterwards, but not yet chastened and made wise by experience.

It was here in the Crimea that, carrying that letter to post to his brother, as already told in " The Bettesworth Book," he met his " mate," and, opening the letter, took out the " dollar " it contained, and spent it on a bottle of rum, tossing the letter away. " In those days," said he, " I could drink as much

rum as I can beer now. We had rum twice a day :
rum and limejuice. That was to keep off the scurvy.
Never had no cups nor nothing. We had knives,
same as that old clasp-knife I got now, and used to
knock off the necks o' the bottles with they."

He remembered well the hard times, and the
privations our troops endured. " Sixteen of us in
one o' they little tents. We had a blanket and a
waterproof sheet—not the fust winter, though ; and
boots that come up to your thigh, big enough to get
into with your shoes on. There was one little chap
named Tickle, he got into his boots with his shoes
on, and couldn't git 'em off again. He was put
under stoppages for 'em. Fifty shillin's for a pair
o' they boots. You got into 'em—they was never
made to fit no man—and bid in 'em for a month
together—freezed on to ye."

Again, " It was starvation done for so many of our
chaps out there. Cold an' starvation. I've bin
out on duty forty-eight hours at a stretch ; then
march back three mile to camp ; and then some of
us 'd have to march another seven mile to fetch
biscuit from the sea. And *then* you only got your
share, same as the rest. . . . Sometimes the biscuit
was dry ; and then again you'd on'y git some as had
bin trod to death by mules or camels. . . . That
was the way to git a appetite. . . . But there was
plenty o' rum ; good rum too ; better 'n what you
gits about here." The system of pay, or rather the
want of system, appears to have made this abun-

dance of rum a more than usually doubtful blessing. The men went sometimes " weeks together without gettin' any pay ; and then when we got it, it was very soon all gone." Sixpence a day—four and two-pence a week—(Bettesworth figured it out)—a very handy sum was this week's pay, I gathered, for buy-ing rum by the bottle. The price of a bottle of stout was half a crown.

Reverting to the terrible weather, Bettesworth told how he had seen "strong men, smoking their pipe," and four hours afterwards beheld them carried by on a stretcher, to be buried. Ill-fed, I inferred, they succumbed thus suddenly to the fearful cold. Green coffee was provided, and the men had to hunt about for roots to make a fire for cooking it. And then, just as they had got their coffee into their mess-tins, they would be called out, perhaps, to stand on duty for eight hours together.

The dead were buried " in their kit," with their clothes on. Sometimes, Bettesworth hinted, money would be found on them and appropriated from their pockets, but " we wan't allowed no plunder," he added. As for the graves, " I've see 'em chucked into graves eighteen inches or two foot deep, perhaps —just a little earth put over 'em ; and when you go by a fortnight or so after, you might see their toes stickin' out o' the ground. You never see no coffin." The only coffin that Bettesworth saw was Lord Raglan's. " That was a funeral ! Seven miles long. . . ."

At the close of the war Bettesworth came home
" among the reductions," yet not for several months,
during which he was employed on " fatigue parties "
in collecting old metal—guns, ammunition cases,
and so forth—for ballast to the ships in Balaclava
Harbour. He described the Harbour : it was " like
comin' in at that door ; an' then, when you gets
inside, it all spreads out. . . ." Storm in the Black
Sea overtook the troop-ship, where were " seventeen
hunderd of us. Three hunderd was ship's company. . . . And some down on their knees prayin',
some cursin', some laughin' an' drinkin', some
dancin'. . . . And the troop-ship we come home
in—might 's well ha' come in a hog-tub. She'd
bin all through the war, and he " (the captain)
" reckoned 'twas great honour to bring her home, and
he wouldn't have no tugs. Forty-nine days we was,
comin' home. And she leaked, an' then 'twas ' all
hands to the pumps.' . . . Great pumps. . . ."

Yes, of course he remembered the pumps. It was
Bettesworth all over, to take a vivid and intelligent
practical interest in anything of the kind that there
was to be seen. He had had no observation lessons
at school, and had never heard of " object studies ";
he simply observed for the pleasure of observing,
instinctively as a cat examines a new piece of furniture, and if not with any cultivated sense of proportion, still with a great evenness of judgment. On
one other occasion, and one only in my hearing, he
reverted to his Crimean experiences ; and as will be

seen in its proper place, the narrative again showed him observing with the same balanced mind, never enthusiastic, but also never satiated, never bored.

But what of the " trouble " into which he was alleged to have fallen ? I may as well tell all I know, and have done with it. From Bettesworth himself no breath of trouble ever reached me. But his avoidance of this period as a topic of conversation often struck me as a suspicious circumstance ; so that I was not quite unprepared for a statement old Dicky Martin volunteered when Bettesworth had been some three weeks dead. He had been " rackety," and had been punished : that was the substance of the tale. " He got into trouble for goin' into the French lines after some rum—him an' two or three more. They never stopped, he told me, to ask 'n no questions, but strapped 'n up and give 'n two or three dozen for 't."

XVII

I suppose that Bettesworth's Crimean reminiscences occupied in narration to me something less than fifteen minutes of his life, so that obviously the space they take up in this volume is out of all proportion to their importance. For my theme is not this or that recollection of his, but the way in which the old man lived out these last of his years, while the memories passed across his mind. It is of small consequence what he remembered. Had he recalled the Indian Mutiny instead of the Crimea, it would have been all one, by that wet afternoon of May, 1902. He would have sat on his block dandling the chopper just the same, and the raindrops from trees outside would have come slanting into the shed doorway and splashed on my hand as I listened to him.

And as they are disproportionately long, these day-dreams of Bettesworth, so also they become too solid on the printed page, side by side with the reality which encompassed them then, and is my subject now. They provoke us to forget the old man, alive and talking. They take us back fifty years too far. From the hardships of the Crimean War it is a wrench to return to the reality—the shed in this valley, the patter of the rain, the old gossipping voice. But all this, so impossible to restore now that it too has become only a reminiscence, being then the commonplace of my life as well as of Bettesworth's, was allowed to pass by almost unnoticed. I let slip what I really liked, took for granted the strong life that alone made me care for the conversation, and saved only some dead litter of observation which was let fall by the living man and seemed to me odd.

Need I explain how of this too I was gradually saving less and less ? The oddness was wearing off ; only the more exceptional things seemed now worth taking care of. Unless there was something as surprising to hear as this talk of the Crimean War— and such exceptions of course appeared with increasing rareness—I hardly took the trouble, at this period, to set down in writing any of Bettesworth's daily gossip. The naturalist, having noted in his diary the first two swallows that do not after all make a summer, has no record save in his brain of the subsequent curvings and interlacings in the summer sky ; and I, similarly, find myself with little besides a vague memory of Bettesworth's doings in this summer of 1902. In fact, it is not even a memory that I have. There is only an inference that day by day he must have done his work in the warm weather, and I must have talked to him. But I am unable to restore this for a reader's benefit. " Imagine him going on as usual," shall I say ? Why, it is more than I can do myself. A row of asterisks would serve the purpose equally well.

So there is a void for two months—nay, with one exception, for more than three, from the middle of May to the end of August ; in which one surmises that the summer flies buzzed in the garden, and Bettesworth did his hoeing and grass-cutting, and was companionable. The one exception, fortunately, has the very life in it which I am regretting. It is but a short sentence of six words, yet they are as if spoken within the hour, and are the clearer for the void around them.

On the afternoon of July 15, the grape vine on the wall near my window was being attended to by the pruner. He stood on a ladder, which was held steady by Bettesworth at the foot ; and presently through the open window the old man's voice reached me, complaining of the recent blighty weather : " There en't nothin' 'ardly looks *kind*."

" No ; not to say *kind*," the pruner assented.

That is all. But precisely because there is nothing in it, because it is a piece of normal instead of exceptional talk, it has the accent of the season. Bettesworth's voice reaches me ; the light falls warm through the vine-leaves ; the lost summer seems to come back with all the accompanying scene, almost as distinctly as if I had but just written the words down.

August 28, 1902.—The harvest, of course, could not go by without remark from him. From the garden we could see, beyond the meadow in the bottom of the valley, a little two-acre cornfield, which had stood for several days half reaped—the upper side uncut, the lower side prosperous-looking with its rows of sheaves. Then there came a morning when it was all in sheaves, and Bettesworth said,

" Old Ben " (meaning Ben Turner) " done it for 'n " (the owner) " last night. Made a dark job of it."

I realized that in his cottage down by the lake, Bettesworth, going to bed, had been able to hear the reaping in the dark, across the meadow.

He proceeded, " Ben took his hoss and cart down into Sussex a week or two ago, to see if he could get a job harvestin'. Was only gone three days, though : him an' four or five more. But I reckon they only went off for a booze—I don't believe they made e'er a try to get a job. . . .

" Our Will " (his brother-in-law) " says down there at Cowhatch they had a wonderful crop of oats. But he reckons they've wasted enough with the machine to ha' paid for reapin' it by hand. Stands to reason —where them great things comes whoppin' into it over and over, it shatters out a lot. Will says where they've took up the sheaves you can see the ground half covered with what they've wasted."

Not knowing what to say, I hesitated, and at last muttered simultaneously with Bettesworth, " 'T seems a pity."

" It's what I calls ' pound wise,' " added he, mis-
quoting a proverb which possibly was not invented
by his class, and was foreign to him.

September 20, 1902.—I turn over the page in my
note-book, but come to a new date three weeks later.
Quiet autumn sunshine, the entry says, had marked
the last few days, breaking through with a limpid
splash in the mornings, after the mist had gone.
Amidst this, under the softened tree-shadows,
Bettesworth was cutting grass with his fag-hook.

And " Ah," he said, " it's purty near all up with
charcoal-burnin' now."

This was in allusion to the indifferent crop of hops
just being picked and the consequently small demand for charcoal ; but it was a digression too. We
had begun talking of a wasp sting. From that to
gnats, and from gnats to a certain tank where they
bred, was an obvious transition.

And now the tank suggested charcoal. For,
according to Bettesworth, a little knob of charcoal
put into a tank is better than an equal quantity of
lime, for keeping the water sweet. Further, " If
you got a bit o' meat that's goin' anyways wrong,
you put a little bit o' charcoal on to that, and you
won't taste anything bad. I've heared ever so
many charcoal-burners say that. And meat is a
thing as won't keep—not butcher's meat ; partic'lar
in the summer when you sims to want it most—
something with a little taste to 't." So, charcoal is

useful; but "Ah! it's purty near all up with char-coal-burnin' now."

A good deal that followed, about the technicalities of charcoal-burning, has been printed in another place, and is omitted here. One point, however, may now be taken up. It is the curious fact that all the charcoal-burners of the neighbourhood are congregated in one district, and the numerous families of them rejoice in one name—that of Parratt.

"I never knowed anybody but Parratts do it about here," Bettesworth said; and the name re-minded him of a story, as follows :

"My old brother-in-law Snip was down at Devizes one time—him what used to travel with a van—*Snip* they always called 'n. And there was a feller come into the fair with one of these vans all hung round with bird-cages, ye know—poll-parrots and all kinds o' birds. So old Snip says to 'n, 'Parrots?' he says, 'what's the use o' you talkin' about parrots? Why, where I come from,' he says, 'we got Parratts as 'll burn charcoal, let alone talk. Talk better 'n any o' yourn,' he says. 'You give 'em some beer and *they'll* talk—or dig hop-ground, or anything.' Lor'! how that feller did go on at 'n, old Snip said!"

Bettesworth knew something of charcoal-burning by experience, but he owned himself ignorant of its inner technical niceties. Moreover, he felt it right to respect a trade "mystery," explaining, "'Tis no use to be a trade, if everybody can do it. 'Relse we should have poor livin' then."

October 31, 1902.—A memorandum of October 31 gives just a foretaste of the approaching winter, and just a momentary searching back into the experience gained when Bettesworth worked at a farm. For there must have been hoar-frost lingering on the lawn that last morning in October, to evoke the old man's opinion, " the less you goes about on grass while there's a frost on it the better " for the grass. " If anybody goes over a bit o' clover-lay with the white frost on it you can tell for a month after what course they took."

November 11.—Amid some personalities which it would be difficult to disguise and which had better be omitted, I find in November another reference to the harsh social life of the village, and it is in connexion with that same bully whom Bettesworth had previously chastised. As before, details must be suppressed ; I only suggest that in these dark November nights the labourers in want of company of course sought it at the public-house. There, I surmise, the bully was boasting, until Bettesworth shut him up with a retort brutally direct. Even as it was repeated to me his expression is not printable. Bettesworth was no angel. He seemed rather, at times, a hard-grained old sinner ; but he always took the manly side, whether with fists or coarse tongue. In this instance his fitting rebuke won a laugh of approval from the company, and even " a pint " for himself from one who was a relative, but no friend, of the offender.

December 16.—One dry, cloudy day in December Bettesworth used his tongue forcibly again, but in how much pleasanter a connexion ! A little tree in the garden had to be transplanted to a new position, on the edge of a bed occupied by old sprouting stumps of kale. One of these stumps was exactly in the place destined for the tree, and Bettesworth ruthlessly pulled it up, talking to it :

" You come out of it. There's plenty more like you. If you complains, we'll chuck ye in the bottom o' the hole for the tree to feed on !"

XVIII

THE Old Year, so far as my notes show it, had run to
its close without event for Bettesworth, just as the
New Year was to do, excepting for one big trouble.
Yet he was not quite the man at the opening of
1903 that he had been at the opening of 1902. The
twelve uneventful months had, in fact, been leaving
their marks upon him—marks almost imperceptible
as each occurred, yet progressive, cumulative in
their effect. On this day or on that, none could have
pointed to a change in the old man, or alleged that
he was not so the day before ; but as the seasons
swung round it was impossible not to perceive how
he was aging. It is well, therefore, to pause and see
what he had become by this time before we enter
upon another year of his life.

There was one silent witness to the increasing
decay of his powers that could not be overlooked.
The garden gave him away. People coming to visit
me and it were embarrassed to know what to say,
or they even hinted that it would be an economy
to allow Bettesworth a small pension and hire a
younger man, who would do as much work, and do
it better, in half the time. As if I needed to be told

that ! But then they were not witnesses, with me, of the pluck—better worth preserving than any garden—with which Bettesworth sought to make amends for his vanished youth. His tenacity deepened my regard for him, even while its poor results almost wore out my patience. He who had once moved with such vigour was getting slow; and the time was coming, if it had not come, when I had to wait and dawdle while he dragged along behind me from one part of the garden to another. A more serious matter was that with greater effort on his part the garden ground was less well worked. I don't believe he knew that. He used a favourite old spade, worn down like himself, and never realized that " two spits deep " with this tool were little better than one spit with a proper one ; and he could not make out why the carrots forked, and the peas failed early.

But the worst trial of all was due to another and more pitiful cause. I could reconcile myself to indifferent crops—after all, I had enough—but exasperation was daily renewed by the little daily failures in routine work, owing to his defective sight, which grew worse and worse. There were the garden paths. With what care the old man drew his broom along them, working by faith and not sight, blindly feeling for the rubbish he could not see, and getting it all save from some corner or other of which his theories had forgotten to take account ! Little nests of disorder collected in this way, to-day here,

to-morrow somewhere else, surprising, offensive to
the eye. Again, at the lawn-mowing, never man
worked harder than Bettesworth, or more conscien-
tiously ; but he could not see the track of his
machine, and seams of uncut grass often disfigured
the smoothness of the turf even after he had gone
twice over it to make sure of perfection. It was
alarming to see him go near a flower border. He
would avoid treading on any plant of whose existence
he knew, by an act of memory ; but he could not
know all, and I had to limit his labours strictly to
that part of the garden he planted or tended himself.

What made the situation so difficult to deal with
was that his intentions were so good. He was himself hardly aware that he failed, and I rather sought
to keep him in ignorance of the fact than otherwise.
I felt instinctively that, once it was admitted, all
would be over for Bettesworth ; because he was
incapable of mending, and open complaints from me
must in the end have led to his dismissal. For
that I was not prepared. He would never get
another employment ; to cut him off from this
would be like saying that the world had no more use
for him and he might as well die out of the way.
But I had no courage to condemn him to death
because my lawn was ill cut. With one exception,
when I sent him to an oculist to see if spectacles
would help him (the oculist reported to me that
there was " practically no sight left "), we kept up

the fiction that he could see to do his work. And his patient, silent struggles to do well were not without an element of greatness.

But though the drawbacks to employing the old man were many, and such as to set me oftentimes wondering how long I should be able to endure them, it must not be thought that he was altogether useless. If he was slow, he was still strong ; if he was half blind, he was wholly efficient at heavy straightforward work. During this winter, in making some radical changes which involved a good deal of excavating work, Bettesworth was like a first-rate navvy, and eagerly put all his experience at my disposal. There was a trench to be opened for laying a water-pipe. With a young man to help him, he dug it out and filled it in again, in about half the time that the job would have taken if it had been entrusted to a contractor. In one place a little pocket of bright red gravel was found. This, of his own initiative, he put aside for use on the paths which he was too blind to sweep clean. But, in truth, a sort of sympathy with my desires and a keen eye to my interests frequently inspired him to do the right thing in this kind of way. He had identified himself with the place ; was proud of it ; boasted to his friends of " our " successes ; and like a miser over his hoard, never spared himself where the good of the garden was concerned, but with aching limbs —his ankle where he had once broken it pained him cruelly at times—went slaving on for his own satisfaction, when I would have suggested to him to take things easily.

I have said that there were those who considered him too expensive a protégé for me. There were others, I am sure, to whom he appeared no better than a tedious old man, opinionated, gossiping, not over clean. Pretty often—especially in bad weather, when there was not much he could be doing—he went on errands for me to the town, to fetch home groceries and take vegetables to my friends, and all that sort of thing. At my friends' he liked calling ; they owed to him rather than to me not a few cookings of cabbage and sticks of celery, for which they would reward him with praise, and perhaps a glass of beer or the price of it. Afterwards I would hear lamentings from them how long he had stayed talking. Once or twice—hardly oftener in all these years—I had to speak to him in sharp reprimand for being such a prodigious long time gone ; for the glass of beer and the gossip where he delivered his cabbages did not always satisfy his cravings for society and comfort : he would turn into a public-house—" Dan Vickery's " for choice—and come back too late and too talkative. It was a fault, if you like ; but the wonder to me is, not that he sometimes drank two glasses where one was enough, but that, with his wit and delight in good company, he did not oftener fall from grace. Those two or three occasions when he earned my sharp reproofs, and for half a day afterwards lost his sense of comfort in me as a friend, were probably times when his home had grown too dreary, his outlook too hopeless, even for his fortitude. Some readers, no doubt, will be offended by his taste for beer. I hope there will be some to give him credit for the months and years in which, with these few exceptions, he controlled the appetite. Remember, he had no religious convictions, nor did the peasant traditions by which he lived afford him much guidance. Alone, of his own inborn instinct for being a decent man, he strove through all his life, not to be rich, but to live upright and unashamed. Fumbling, tiresome, garrulous, unprofitable, lean and grim and dirty in outward appearance, the grey old life was full of fight for its idea of being a man ; full of fight and patience and stubborn resolve not to give in to anything which it had learnt to regard as weakness. I remember looking down, after I had upbraided a failure, at the old limbs bending over the soil in such humility, and I could hardly bear the thought that very likely they were tired and aching. This enfeebled body—dead now and mouldering in the churchyard—was alive in those days, and felt pain. Do but think of that, and then think of the patient, resolute spirit in it, which almost never indulged its weaknesses, but had its self-respect, its half - savage instincts toward righteousness, its smothered tastes, its untold affections and its tenderness. That was the old man, gaunt-limbed, but good-tempered, partially blind and fumbling, but experienced, whom we have to imagine now indomitably facing yet another year of his life, and a prospect in which there is little for him to hope for. Nay, there was much for him to dread, had he known. A separate chapter, however, must be given to the severe trouble which, as already hinted, overtook him in the early weeks of 1903.

XIX

WHILE the advance of time was affecting Bettesworth himself, another influence had begun to play havoc with his environment. A glance in retrospect at this nook of our parish during this same winter of 1902-3 shows the advent of new circumstances, of a kind full of menace to men like him. Things and persons of the twentieth century had begun to invade our valley, where men and women so far had lived as if the nineteenth were not half through.

The coming of the new influence was perhaps too subtle for Bettesworth to be conscious of it. Perhaps he marked only the normal crumbling away of the old-fashioned life, by death or departure of his former associates, and failed to notice that these were no longer being replaced, as they would have been in former times, by others like them. Of our old friends close around us four or five were by this time dead, and others had moved farther afield. We missed especially old Mrs. Skinner. Since her husband's death in 1901 her domestic arrangements had not been happy, and in the autumn just past she had disposed of her little property, and was gone to

live across the valley. But note the circumstances.
Only some ten years previously her husband had
bought this property—the cottage and nearly an
acre of ground—for about £70. He may have
subsequently added £50 to its value. Now, however, his widow was able to sell it for something like
£220. The increase shows what a significant change
was overtaking us.

I shall revert to this presently. For the moment
I stop to gather up some stray sentences of Bettesworth's which, perhaps, indicate how unlikely he
was to accommodate himself to new circumstances.

The purchaser of Mrs. Skinner's cottage was a
man named Kelway—a curious, nondescript person, as to whose " derivings " we speculated in
vain. What had he been before he came here ?
No one ever discovered that, but his behaviour was
that of an artisan from near London—a plasterer or
a builder's carpenter—who had come into a little
money. I remember his telling me jauntily on one
occasion that he should not feel settled until he had
brought home his American organ (I was heartily
glad that it never came !), and on another that he
had made " hundreds of wheelbarrows " in his time,
which I thought unlikely ; and I cannot forget—for
there are signs of it to this day—how ruthlessly he
destroyed the natural contours of his garden with
ill-devised " improvements." He pulled out the
interior partitions of the cottage, too, wearing while
at the work the correct garb of a plasterer ; and it

was in this costume that he annoyed Bettesworth
by his patronizing familiarity. " He says to me "
(thus Bettesworth), " ' I suppose you don't know
who I am in my dirty dishabille ?' ' No,' I says,
' and if I tells the truth, I don't care nuther.' *He's
dirty dishabille !* . . . He got too much old buck for
me ! " Shortly afterwards he asked Bettesworth to
direct him to a good plumber. " ' I can do everything else,' he says, ' but plumbing is a thing I
never had any knowledge of.' So I says, ' If I was
you I should sleep with a plumber two or three
nights.' "

January 27, 1903.—Again, in the end of January,
Bettesworth reported : " That man down here ast
me about peas—what sort we gets, an' so on."
(Remember that he had nearly an acre of ground.)
" So I told 'n, and he says, ' What do they run to
for price ?' ' Oh, about a shillin' a quart,' I says ;
and that's what they *do* run to. ' I must have
half a pint,' he says. I bust out laughin' at 'n. An'
he says he must have a load o' manure, too ! He
must mind he don't overdo it ! I was *obliged* to
laugh at 'n."

Of course, such a neighbour would in no circumstances have pleased Bettesworth. I believe the
man had many estimable qualities, but they were
dwarfed beside his own appreciation of them ; and
his subsequent disappointments, which ultimately
led to his withdrawal from the neighbourhood, were

not of the kind to engage Bettesworth's sympathy. Indeed, he had no chance of approval in
that quarter, coming in the place of old Mrs. Skinner,
with her peasant lore and her pigs.

But if this egregious man was personally offensive
to Bettesworth, he was not intrinsically more strange
to the old man than those who followed him or than
others who were settling in the parish. There were
to be no more Mrs. Skinners. Wherever one of the
old country sort of people dropped out from our
midst, people of urban habits took their place.
These were of two classes : either wealthy people of
leisure, seeking residences, and bringing their own
gardeners who wanted homes, or else mechanics
from the neighbouring town, ready to pay high rents
for the cottages whose value was so swiftly rising.
The stealthiness of the process blinded us, however,
to what was happening. When Bettesworth began,
as he did now, to feel the pressure of civilization
pushing him out, neither he nor I understood the
situation.

Right and left, property was changing hands. A
big house in the next hollow, but with its grounds
overpeering this, had been bought by a wealthy
resident, and was under repair, already let to some
friends of his. There went with it in the same
estate the hill-side opposite this garden, with two
or three cottages visible from here ; and everybody
rejoiced when the disreputable tenants of one of
these cottages had notice to quit. It was hoped

that the new owner was sensible of the duties as well as the rights attaching to property.

Meanwhile, Bettesworth's hovel, too, was in the market, the landlord of it being lately dead; and in the market it remained, while Bettesworth clamoured in vain for repairs. At last he gave up hope. By the beginning of 1903 he had resolved to quit his old cottage as soon as he could find another to go into.

He waited still some weeks, however—property was valuable, cottages were eagerly sought after—and then what seemed a golden opportunity arose. The cottage with the disreputable tenants has been mentioned, adjoining the grounds of the big house. It must have been early in February when the whisper that it was to be vacant reached Bettesworth, who forthwith announced to me his intention of applying for it. Too big, perhaps too good, for him and his wife I may have thought the place; but there was no other in the neighbourhood to be heard of, and it was not only for its pleasantness that the old man coveted it. With his wife there he would be able to keep watch over her while he was at work here, and there would be almost an end to those anxieties about her fits, which often made him half afraid to go home. I remember the secrecy of his talk. He wanted no one to forestall him. The thing was urgent; and I had no hesitation in writing a recommendation of him as a desirable tenant, which he forthwith took to the owner. Why, indeed, should I have hesitated ? Between Bettesworth's punctiliousness on such matters and my own intention of helping him if need be, there was no fear as to the payment of the rent. And the improvements he had made to that place down by the stream argued well for the care he would take of this better cottage.

My recommendation did its work. Bettesworth was duly accepted as tenant ; he gave notice to leave the other place, and began preparations for moving ; and then, too late, it dawned upon me that perhaps I had made a mistake. I had forgotten old Mrs. Bettesworth. I had not set eyes on her for months ; for much longer I had not been inside her dwelling, to see the state it was in. I only knew that outside the walls were whitewashed, the garden and paths orderly.

The first doubts visited me when I saw that repairs to the new abode were being done on a scale too extravagant to fit the Bettesworths. The next resulted from an inspection I made of the cottage at Bettesworth's desire. He was beyond measure proud to have a place into which he could invite me without shame ; and he took me all over it, and described to me his plans for improving the garden, without suspicion of anything amiss. Probably his eyes were too dim to see what I saw. Some of his furniture, already heaped on the floor in one of the clean new-papered rooms, had a sooty, cobwebby look that filled me with forebodings of

trouble. However, it was too late to withdraw.
There was no going back to that abandoned place
down in the valley. There was nothing to do but
hope for the best.

Hope seemed justified for a week or two, while
Bettesworth's new garden, heretofore a wilderness,
assumed a new order. He had sowed early peas—
probably other things too—having actually paid a
neighbour to help him get the ground dug ; and he
was extremely happy, until a day came when he
said, cautiously and bitterly, " I thinks I got a
enemy." He went on to explain that some one, he
suspected, wanted his cottage, and was trying to get
him out of it. I have forgotten what raised his sus-
picions. He did not even then realize that himself,
or rather his wife, was the only enemy he had to
fear.

That was the miserable truth, however. Down
in that other place, secluded from the neighbours,
the old woman had grown utterly squalid, though
Bettesworth had not seen it. And now the owner
of the new cottage, perhaps from the grounds of the
large residence destined for his friends, had caught
sight of old Lucy Bettesworth, and had been, as
anyone else would have been, horrified at her filthy
appearance. But he did not act on that single impression : it was not until kindly means had been
taken to ascertain the truth of it that he first expostulated, and then told Bettesworth that he could
not be permitted to stay. Nay, I was allowed to

try first if persuasion of mine could remedy the evil.

Unfortunately, remedies were not in Bettesworth's power, or he would by now have employed them, being alarmed as well as indignant. He listened to my hints that his wife was intolerably dirty, but (I write from memory) " What can I do, sir ?" he said. " I knows she en't like other women, with her bad hand and all." (She had broken her wrist some years before, and never regained its strength.) " But I can't afford to dress her like a lady. I told 'n so to his head : ' I can't keep a dressed-up doll,' I says." Neither could he, being so nearly blind, see that his wife was going about unwashed, grimy, like a dreadful apparition of poverty from the Middle Ages. To her it would have been useless to speak. Her epilepsy had impaired her intellect,. and any suggestion of reform, even from her own husband, seemed to her a piece of persecution to be obstinately resented.

So there was nothing to be done. The prospective tenants of the big house near by could not be expected to endure such a neighbour ; the cottage itself, which had cost £20 for repairs, the owner told me, was no place for such a tenant. The Bettesworths therefore must go. They received formal notice to quit ; then, as nothing appeared to be happening, a more peremptory notice was sent limiting their time to three weeks, yet promising a sovereign as compensation for the work done and

the crops planted in the garden. In the meantime
they had probably done more than a sovereign's
worth of damage to the cottage interior, with its
new paper and paint.

But though nothing appeared to be happening,
the two old people were secretly in a state near to
distraction. The reader will remember the peculiar
topography of this parish, with the tenements dotted
about for a mile or more on the northern slope of
the valley. All up and down this district, and then
on the other side, where he was less at home, Bettesworth hunted in vain for an available cottage
within possible reach of his work : there was not one
to be found. And now he realized his physical
feebleness. Years ago, miles would not have mat-
tered ; he could have shifted to another village and
defied the demands of our new-come town civilization ; but now a walk of a mile would be a consideration. His legs were too old and stiff for a long walk
as well as a day's work.

For several days—and days are money, especially
to a working-man—he searched up and down, his
despair increasing, his dismay deepening, at every
fresh disappointment. I began to fear he would
break down. He could not sleep, nor yet could his
wife. She had been crying half the night—so he told
me after the misery had endured the best part of the
week. " She kep' on, ' Whatever will become of us,
Fred ? Wherever *shall* we go ?' " and he, trying to
reassure her that they would " find somewhere to

creep into," seemed to be face to face with the workhouse as his only prospect. So they spent their
night, and rose to a hopeless morning.

It was time, evidently, for me to take the matter
up. Besides, the old people's trouble was getting
on my nerves. Across the valley there was an
empty cottage—one of a pair—which the owner had
refused to let on the strange plea that the tenants
who had just left had been so troublesome and destructive that he was resolved against taking any
others. Such a dry, whimsical old man was this
landlord that the story was not incredible. A
retired bricklayer, and a widower, he lived by himself on next to nothing, not from miserliness but from
choice, and his chief object in life seemed to be to
avoid trouble. He had, however, worked with
Bettesworth in years gone by, and was, in fact, a
sort of chum of his, so that it seemed worth while to
try what persuasion would do to shake his resolution
of keeping an empty cottage. And where Bettesworth had failed, I might succeed.

So, one fine morning—it was near the middle of
March by now—I hunted up this old man—a man
as genial and kindly as I wish to see—and made
him a proposal. He showed some reluctance to
entertain it. Why ? The truth came out at last :
he did not want the Bettesworths for tenants ; he
knew the indescribable state of the old woman ;
it was to her that he objected ; and it was to
spare his old chum's feelings that he had invented

that story about being unwilling to let the cottage at all.

But the case was desperate. How I pleaded it I no longer remember, nor is it of any importance. I think there were two interviews. In the end the cottage was let, not direct to Bettesworth, but to me with permission to sublet it to him ; and two, or at most three days afterwards, Bettesworth was in possession, and the other cottage once more stood empty.

So the squalid episode was over. After such a narrow escape from the workhouse, it was as it were with a gasp of relief that the old couple settled down in their new abode, safe at last. The place, though, was not one which Bettesworth would have chosen, had there been a choice. Down there by the meadow where he had come from, though the cottage might be crazy, the outlook had been fair. He had been peacefully alone there ; in summer evenings he had heard the men mowing ; on winter nights there was the wind in the withies and the sound of the stream. But from this time onwards we have to think of him as living in one of a mean group of tenements which exhibit their stuccoed ugliness nakedly on a bleak slope above the meadow. As to the neighbours—some of them resented his coming, for of course the scandal of his wife's condition was public property by now. With a certain defiant shame, therefore, he crept in amongst them. Fortunately, the people in the next-door cottage—an unmarried labourer and his mother—knew Bettesworth's record, and regarded him as a veteran to be cared for ; and not many weeks passed before the old man felt himself established in their good-will, and was trying to persuade himself that all was for the best.

Of course, he was only partially successful in that endeavour. Occasional bitter remarks showed that he still harboured a resentment against the owner of the cottage from which he had been turned out, and, in fact, there were circumstances which would have made it difficult for him quite to forget the affair. Perched on one of the steepest of the bluffs, high above the stream, the cottage in which he was not good enough to live stood beside the path he now had to travel to and from his work every day. Often, as his legs grew weary and his breath short with ascending the footpath, he must have felt tempted to curse the place. Often it must have seemed to taunt him with his unfitness. Even when he was at work, there it was full in sight. In bad weather, and as he grew feebler, it stood there on its uplifted brow, not sheltering the wife to whom he wanted to go at dinner-time, but like an obstacle in his way. Instead of being his home, it cut him off from his home ; and he took to bringing his dinner with him, wrapped in a handkerchief ; poor cold food which he frequently left untasted, preferring a pipe.

Yet it was not his nature to be embittered. When the peas he had sown came up, though for another man's benefit, he looked across at them from this garden and admired them.   They were a fine crop and remarkably early.   If, however, they made him a little envious, he was generous enough to be pleased too.   Perhaps the sight comforted him, proving that he would have done well there, at least with the garden, if they had let him stay.   And certainly he was flattered when the new tenant, wholly grateful, asked him what sort of peas these were.   " Earliest of All," he replied, giving the name by which he had really bought them.   And by-and-by a joke arose out of the answer, because the other man would not believe that the peas were really so called, but thought Bettesworth was " kiddin' of 'n " with a name invented by himself.   The old man had many a chuckle over this piece of incredulity.   " I tells 'n right enough," he laughed ; " but he won't have it."

XX

As may be imagined, the troubles through which
Bettesworth had thus come did nothing to re-
juvenate him. On the contrary, they openly con-
victed him of old age, and made it patent that he
was no longer very well able to take care of himself.
In fact, the man's instinctive pride in himself had
been shaken, and though I do not think he consciously slackened his efforts to do well, his unconscious, spontaneous activity was certainly impaired.
It was as though the inner stimulus to his muscles
was gone. He forgot to move as fast as he was
able. Sometimes he would, as it were, wake up, and
spur himself back into something like good labouring
form ; but after a little time he would relapse, and
go dreamily humming about his work like a very old
man. In these days, my own interest in him reached
its lowest ebb. I found myself burdened with a
dependent I could not in honour shake off ; but
there was little pleasure to be had in thinking of
Bettesworth. Only now and again, when he
dropped into reminiscence, did he seem worth attention ; only now and again, in my note-books of the

period, does he re-emerge, telling chiefly of things the present generations have forgotten.

To the earliest notice of him for the year an irony attaches, since it begins by recording with extreme satisfaction the first of those summer rains which were to make 1903 so memorable and disastrous. How little did we guess, on that June 10, what was in store for us ! My note describes, almost gloatingly, " one of those gloomy summer evenings that we get with thundery rain. There is scarcely any wind ; grey cloud, well-nigh motionless, hangs over all the sky ; the distant hills are a stronger grey ; the garden is all wet greenness—deep beyond deep of sombre green, turning black under the denser branches of the trees. Now and again rain shatters down into the rich leafage—a solemn noise ; and thrushes are vocal ; but these sounds do not disturb the impressive quietness."

So the entry proceeds, noting how stiff and strong the grass was already looking after a threat of drought ; how the hedgerows were odorous with the pungent scent of nettles ; how the lustrous opaque white of horse-daisies starred certain grassy banks ; and at last, how all my neighbours who have gardens were as well pleased as myself with the weather.

And so the note comes round to Bettesworth. He too, with his head full of recollections of past summer rains, and of hopes of rich crops to result from this present one, was glorying in the gloom of the day.

As the old wise toads crept out from hole and wall-cranny and waddled solemn and moist-skinned across the lawn about their affairs, so Bettesworth about his, not much regarding a wet coat. He had theories as to hilling potatoes, or rather as to not hilling them until the ground could be drawn round the haulm wet. And here was his chance. In the afternoon he took it, joyfully, and the earth turned up rich and dark under his beck.*

The tool set him talking. For hilling potatoes he reckoned, a beck is much better than a hoe : " leaves such a nice crumb on the ground." He was resolved to have his " five-grained spud " or garden fork turned into a beck—the next time he went to the town, perhaps, " 'cause it wouldn't take 'em long, jest to turn the neck, and then draw the rivets an' take the tree out an' put in a handle. 'T'd make a good tool then—so sharp !

" This old beck I'm usin'," he went on happily, " I warrant he's a hunderd year old. He belonged to my wife's gran'father afore I had 'n ; and *I*'ve had 'n this thirty year or more. . . . He's a reg'lar hand-made one—and a good tool still. That's who he belonged to—my old gal's gran'father.

" He " (the grandfather) " had this place over here o' Warner's—'twas him as built that, you know." The property mentioned is a large cottage and

* A tool of which the iron part resembles that of a garden fork, the handle, however, being socketed into it at right angles, as in a rake.

garden, adjoining that from which Bettesworth and his wife had so lately been turned out. " And he was the one as fust planted Brook's Field. He had Nott's, down here, and Mavin's, and Brook's Field—and a *purty* bit that was, too ! He was the fust one as planted it. Dessay he had a hunderd acres. Used to keep a little team, and a waggon shed—up the lane here, an' come down this lane an' right in there. . . ."

But we need not follow Bettesworth into these topographical details. Returning, in a moment, to the prosperity of his wife's grandfather, he hinted at the basis of it. The man was a peasant-farmer, producing for his own needs first, and enjoying certain valuable rights of common.

" He used to keep two or three cows," said Bettesworth. " Well, moost people used to keep a cow then, what *was* anybody at all. Ye see, the commons was all open, and the boys what looked after the cows used to git so much for every one ; so the more (cows) they could git the better their week's wages was for lookin' after 'em.

" They *was* some boys too, some of 'em—when there got two or three of 'em up there in the Forest together, 'long o' the cows !" The old man chuckled grimly. " I rec'lect one time me an' Sonny Mander and his brother went after one o' the forest ponies. There was hunders o' ponies then. Deer, too. And as soon as we caught 'n, I was up on his back. I didn't care after I got *upon* 'n. I clung on to his

mane—his mane was down to the ground—and off
he went with me, all down towards Rocknest and "—
well, and more topography. "He tore through everything, an' scratched my face, and I was afraid to
get off for fear he should gallop over me. . . . And
they hollerin' after 'n only made 'n worse. He run
till he was beat, afore I got off.

"*Purty* tannin' I got, when I got 'ome ! 'Cause
me clothes was tore, and me cap was gone. . . .
Oh, *I* had beltinker ! They had the news afore I
got 'ome, 'cause so many cowboys see me."

Smiling, Bettesworth resumed work with his
ancient beck, by dexterous twist now right and now
left turning the dark wet earth in to the potato
haulm.

It was about this time that, our talk working
round somehow to the subject of donkeys, Bettesworth remarked, as if it were a part of the natural
history of those interesting animals, and indeed one
of their specific habits, "Moost donkeys goes after
dirty clothes o' Monday mornin's." I suppose that
is true of the donkeys kept by the numerous cottage
laundresses in this parish.

From this he launched off into a long rambling
narrative, which I did not understand in all its
details, of his "old mother-in-law's donkey," named
Jane, whom he once drove down into Sussex for the
harvesting. "She drinked seven pints o' beer
'tween this an' Chichester. Some policemen give

her one pint when we drove down into Singleton. There was three or four policemen outside the public there," Goodwood races being on at the time ; and these policemen treated Jane, while Bettesworth went within to refresh himself. " That an' some bread was all she wanted. I'd took a peck o' corn for her, but she didn't sim to care about it ; and I give a feller thruppence what 'd got some clover-grass on a cart, but she only had about a mouthful o' that." In short, Jane preferred bread and beer. " Jest break a loaf o' bread in half an' put it in a bowl an' pour about a pint o' beer over 't. . . . But she'd put her lips into a glass or a cup and soop it out. Reg'lar coster's donkey, she was, and they'd learnt her. Not much bigger 'n a good-sized dog— but *trot !*"

How she trotted, and won a wager, against another donkey on the same road, was told so confusedly that I could not follow the tale.

In Sussex, Jane was the delight of the farmer's children. " ' May I have a ride on your donkey ?' they'd say, twenty times a day. ' Yes,' I'd say, ' if you can catch her.' And she'd let 'em go up to her, but as soon as ever they got on her back they was off again. ' You give her a bit o' bread,' I'd say ; ' p'raps she'll let ye ride then.' And they used to give her bread," but she would never suffer them to ride her.

People on the road admired the donkey—nay, the whole equipage. " Comin' home, down Fernhurst Hill, I got up—'cause I rode down 'ills—I walked all the rest—and says, ' Now, Jane, there's a pint o' beer for ye at the bottom of the hill.' So we come down " to the inn there, named by Bettesworth but forgotten by me, " and three or four farmers there says, ' Here comes the man wi' the little donkey !' And I called out for a pint, and she thought she was goin' to have it ; but I says, ' No, this is for me. You wait till you got your wind back.' "

We spoke afterwards of other donkeys, and particularly of one—a lady's of the neighbourhood— which, as Bettesworth had been told, was " groomed and put into the stable with a cloth over him, jest like the other horses. . . . Law ! if donkeys was looked after, they'd *kill* all the ponies (by outworking them), but they don't get no chance."

The harvesting expeditions into Sussex, and the keeping of cows on the common, were parts of an antique peasant economy now quite obsolete. In August of this year a further glimpse of it was obtained, in a conversation which, I grieve to say, I neglected to set down in Bettesworth's own words.

August 21, 1903.—There was a time shortly after his marriage, and, as I guess, between forty and fifty years ago, when he rented a cottage and garden quite close to this house. The price of wheat being then two shillings the gallon, he used to grow wheat in his garden ; and his average crop was at the rate of fourteen or fifteen sacks to the acre, or nearly twice as much as local farmers now succeed in growing.

In making this use of his garden he was by no means singular. Many of his neighbours at that date grew their own corn ; and it was Mrs. Bettesworth's brother (a man still living, and now working a threshing engine) who dibbed it for them. The dibber (" dessay he got it now ") was described by Bettesworth—a double implement, made for dibbing two rows at a time. It had two " trees," like spade handles, set side by side, each of which was socketed into an iron bent forwards like a letter L. On the under-side of each iron, four excrescences made four shallow holes in the ground, " about like a egg "; and a rod connecting the two irons kept the double tool rigid. Walking backwards, the man using this implement could press into the ground two rows of egg-shaped holes at a time, as fast as the women could follow with the seed. For it seems that two women followed the dibber, carrying their seed-corn in basins and dropping one or two grains into each hole. The ground was afterwards rolled with a home-made wooden roller ; and as soon as the corn came up the hoe was kept going, the rows being about eight inches asunder, until the crop was knee high.

Is it wrong to give so much space to these haphazard recollections ? They interrupt the narrative of Bettesworth's slow and weary decline—that must be admitted. Yet, following as they do so close upon his wretched experiences in contact with more modern life, they help to explain why he and modernity were so much at odds. He had been a labourer, a soldier, all sorts of things ; but he had been first and last by taste a peasant, with ideas and interests proper to another England than that in which we are living now.

In course of time, but not yet, a good deal more was to be gleaned from him about this former kind of country existence. I shall take it as it comes, and, while Bettesworth is losing grip of life, let the contrast between him dying and the modern world eagerly living make its own effect. As now this detail, and now that, is added to the mass, perhaps a little of the atmosphere may be restored in which his mind still had its being, and through which he saw our time, yet not as we see it.

Meanwhile, there is one reminiscence which stands by itself and throws light on little or nothing, but is too queer to be omitted. Having no place of its own, it is given here because it comes next in my note-book.

October 24, 1903.—It was the weather that started our talk. Bettesworth could not remember anything like this year 1903 for rain. But there! he supposed we should get some fine weather again " somewhen ?"

Now, I had just been reading some history, and

was able to answer with some confidence, " Oh yes. There have been wet years before this." And I mentioned the year after the Battle of Waterloo.

Then Bettesworth, " Let's see. Battle of Waterloo ? That was in '47, wa'n't it ?"

I chanced to be able to give him the correct date, which he accepted easily, as if he had known all the time. " Oh ah," he said. " But there was something in eighteen hunderd and forty-seven—some great affair or other ? . . . I dunno what 'twas, though, now. . . . Forty-seven ? H'm !"

What could it have been ? No, not the Mutiny. " That come after the Crimea. 'Twa'n't that. But there was something, I know."

I could not imagine what it could have been ; but Bettesworth still pondered, and at last an idea struck him. " June, '47. . . . H'm ! . . . Oh, I knows. Old Waterloo Day, that's what 'twas ! There used to be a lot of 'em " (he was hurrying on, and I could only surmise that he meant Waterloo veterans) " at Chatham. I see one of 'em there myself, what had cut one of his hamstrings out o' cowardice, so's he shouldn't have to go into the battle. So then they cut the other, too, an' kep' 'n there " (at Chatham) " for a peep-show. He wa'n't never to be buried, but put in a glass case when he died.

" He laid up there in his bed, and anybody as mind could go up an' see 'n. They used to flog 'n every Waterloo Day—in the last years 'twas a bunch o' black ribbons he was flogged with. He had a wooden ball tied to a bit o' string ; and you go up, and ast 'n about the 71st (?), and see what you'd git ! 'Cause one of the soldiers o' the 71st went up there once, an' called 'n all manner o' things. O' course, when he'd throwed this ball he could always draw 'n back again, 'cause o' the string. . . . And every mornin' he was ast what he'd have to drink. They said he was worth a lot, and 't'd all go to a sergeant-major's daughter when he died, what looked after 'n.

" He was worth a lot o' money. Lots used to go up to see 'n—I did, and so did a many more, 'cause he was kep' there for show, and everybody as went up he'd ast 'm for something. He'd git half a crown, or ten shillin's, or a sovereign sometimes. But lots o' soldiers used to go an' let 'n have it.

" Ye see, he couldn't git up. He cut his own hamstring for cowardice, so's he shouldn't go into battle, and then they cut the other. 'Twas the Dook o' Wellington, they says, ordered it to be done, for a punishment. And, o' course, he never was able to walk again. That done him. There he laid on the bed, with waddin' wrapped all round to prevent sores. And in one part o' the room was the glass case ready for when he died, for 'n to be embarmed an' kep'—'cause he was never to be buried. Fifty year he laid there ! I shouldn't much like his bit, should you ?"

XXI

November 4, 1903.—One morning—it was the 4th of November—Bettesworth said, " I got a invitation out to a grand dinner to-night, down in the town. Veterans of the Crimea. But I shan't go. I'd sooner be at home and have a bit o' supper an' get to bed early. . . . No ; it don't cost ye nothin' —an' plenty *of* everything ; spirits, good food, a very good *dinner*. Still, you can't go to these sort o' things without spendin' a shillin'. And then be about half the night. I don't care about it. If I was to go, 't'd upset me to-morrer."

All this bewildered me. For one thing, it was plain that the fact of Bettesworth's having been a soldier was no secret after all. As he now went on to tell me, he had actually attended two previous dinners. Who were they, then, who knew his record, and got him his invitation ? Who, indeed, was giving the dinner ? Rumours of some such annual celebration, it is true, had reached me ; but it was no public function. Even by name the promoters were unknown to me ; and yet somehow they had known for several years before I did that my man had been a soldier in the Crimea.

At the moment, however, it was Bettesworth's refusal of the invitation that most surprised me, although his alleged reasons were very good. He so loved good cheer, and he had so few opportunities of enjoying it—the Oddfellows' dinner was the only other chance he ever had in any year— that I immediately suspected him of having been swayed in this instance by something else besides prudence. He sounded over-virtuous. And presently it struck me that there might have been something offensive to him in the way the invitation was given.

It had been received on the previous evening. He had just got round to the public-house, " 'long of old White," when " a feller come in," inquiring for him. Bettesworth did not know the man ; it was "somebody in a grey suit." " Stood me a glass of hot whisky-and-water, he did, and old White too." And, referring to Bettesworth's military service, " ' What was ye ?' he says. ' A man,' I says. He laughed and says, ' What are ye drinkin' ?' ' Only a glass o' cold fo'penny,' I says." And Bettesworth seems to have said it in a very meek voice, subtly insinuating that " the feller " might stand something better.

I inferred, further, that Bettesworth's conscience was now pricking him for some incivility he had shown in declining the invitation. At any rate, he made a lame attempt, not otherwise called for, to prove that a self-respecting man would not humble himself to anyone upon whom he was not dependent. He had evidently been the reverse of humble ; and possibly the invitation was patronizing, and raised his ire.

"Or else," he concluded, "I be purty near the only veteran left about here. There used to be Tom Willett and "—another whose name I have forgotten—" in the town, but they be gone, and I dunno who else there is. And I knows there's ne'er another in this parish. Dessay they'll get a few kiddies from Aldershot. 'Cause there's any amount o' drink. . . ."

Well, Bettesworth did not go to the dinner, and I never quite understood why. Possibly he really felt too old for dissipation, even of a decorous kind : still more likely, he dreaded being at once under-valued and patronized, among the " kiddies " from Aldershot. He certainly did well to avoid their company. Long afterwards, when for other reasons I was making inquiries about this dinner, I learnt that the behaviour of some of the guests had been scandalous. Some had been carried away, drunk. Others had taken with them, hidden in their pockets, the means of getting drunk at home. So I was told ; but not by the promoters, who had shortly after-wards left the neighbourhood.

On this same date (4th November, 1903) Bettes-worth informed me of another circumstance which affected him seriously. It was that he had lately been superannuated from his club, which he had joined in July, 1866. At that distant time, when he was still a young man, and a strong one, how should he look forward to the year 1903 ? By what then seemed a profitable arrangement, he paid his subscription on a lower scale, on the understanding that he would receive no financial help in time of sickness after he was sixty-five years old. He had now passed that age. Henceforth, for a payment of threepence a month, he was to have medical attendance free, and on his death the club would pay for his funeral.

He was mighty philosophical over this. For my part, it was impossible to look forward without apprehension to the position he would be in during the approaching winter. A year previously he had shown symptoms of bronchitis. But what was to become of him now, if he should be ill, and have no " sick-pay " upon which to fall back ?

XXII

I think it must have been during the winter we
have reached that the village policeman stopped
me in the road one night to talk about old Mrs.
Bettesworth. He told me, what I vaguely knew,
that she was increasingly ill. Once, if not oftener
(I write from memory), he had helped get her home
out of the road, where she had fallen in a fit ; and
a fear was upon him that she would come to some
tragical end. Then there would be an inquest ;
Bettesworth might be blamed for omitting necessary precautions ; at any rate, trouble and scandal
must ensue. The policeman proposed that it would
be well if a doctor could see the old woman occasionally, and suggested that through my influence
with Bettesworth it might be arranged.

Although I promised to see what could be done
to carry out so thoughtful a suggestion, and meant
to keep my promise, as a matter of fact no steps
towards its performance were ever taken ; and the
thing is mentioned here only as a piece of evidence
as to the conditions in which Bettesworth passed
the winter. In the background of his mind, there
stood always the circumstances which had inspired

apprehension in the policeman. I never noted down his dread, because it was too constant a thing; and for a like reason, he seldom spoke of it; but there it always was, immovable. The policeman's talk merely shows that the reasons for it were gathering in force.

Save for one or two other equally vague memories, that winter is lost, so far as Bettesworth is concerned. We had some cold though not really severe weather—nothing so terrible as an odd calculation of his would have made it out to be. "For," said he, "we *be* gettin' it! The Vicar's gardener says there was six degrees o' frost this mornin'. . . . And five yesterday; an' seven the mornin' before. That makes eighteen degrees!" So he added up the thermometer readings; and, associated with his words, there comes back to me a winter afternoon in which the air had grown tense and still. Under an apple-tree, where the ground, covered with thin snow, was too hard frozen for a tool to penetrate, the emptyings of an ash-bin from the kitchen lay in a little heap; and a dozen or so of starlings were quarrelling over this refuse, flying up to spar at one another, and uttering sharp querulous cries. A white fog hung in the trees. It was real winter, and I laughed to myself, to think what a record Bettesworth might make of it by the following morning.

Seeing that every winter now he was troubled with a cough, I may as well give here some undated sentences I have preserved, in which he described how he caught cold on one occasion. "If I'd ha' put on my wrop as soon 's I left off work," he said, " I should ha' bin aw-right. 'Stead o' that, I went scrawneckin' off 'ome jest's I was, an' that's how I copt it." The word scrawnecking, whatever he meant by it, conjures up a picture of him boring blindly ahead with skinny throat uncovered. He took little care of himself ; and considering how ill-fed he went now that his wife was so helpless, it was small wonder that he suffered from colds. They did not improve his appetite. They spoilt many a night's rest for him, too. At such times, the account he used to give of his coughing was imita-tive. " Cough cough cough, all night long." A strong accent on the first and fourth syllables, and a " dying fall " for the others, gives the cadence.

Beyond these memories nothing else is left of Bettesworth's experiences during those three months —December, 1903, and January and February, 1904. Coming to March, I might repeat some interesting remarks of his upon an affair then agitating the village ; but after all they do not much concern his history, and there are strong reasons for with-holding them. And suppressing these, I find no further account of him until the middle of May.

The interval, however, between the 3rd of March and the 16th of May, was sadly eventful for Bettes-worth. I cannot say much about it. As once before when his circumstances grew too tragical, so on this occasion a vague sense of decency forbade me to sit down and record in cold blood his sufferings, perhaps for future publication.

What happened was briefly this : that some time in March one of the colds which had distressed him all the winter settled upon his chest and rapidly turned to bronchitis. If his wife's condition is taken into account, the seriousness of the situation will be appreciated. At his time of life bronchitis would have been bad enough, even with good nursing ; but poor old Lucy Bettesworth was far past devoting to her husband any attention of that sort. Even in her best state she was past it, and she was by no means at her best just now. She needed care herself ; had a heavy cold ; was at times beyond question slightly crazy ; and, to aggravate the trouble, she was insulting even to the two or three neighbours who might have conquered their reluctance to enter the filthy cottage and help the old man. For perhaps a week, therefore, he lay uncared for, and none realized how ill he was. Only the next-door neighbour spoke of hearing him coughing all night long.

The old woman received me downstairs when I went to make inquiries. She sat with her hand at her chest, dishevelled and unspeakably dirty. And she coughed ; tried to attract my sympathy to herself ; assured me " I be as bad as he is "; looked indeed ill, and half-witted. " You can go up and see 'n," she said. I stumbled up the stairs and found Bettesworth in bed, with burning cheeks and eyes feverishly bright. The bedding was disgusting ; so were the remains of a bloater left on the table beside him, so much as to give me a feeling of nausea. As for nursing, he had had none. He had got out of bed the previous night and found a packet of mustard, of which he had shaken some into his hand, and rubbed that into his chest, dry ; and that was the only remedy that had been used for his bronchitis, unless—yes, I think there was a bottle of medicine on the mantelpiece ; for he was still entitled to the services of the club doctor, who had been sent for. But in such a case, what could a doctor do ?

The next day the old man was worse, at times wandering in his mind. And, as there was no one else to take the initiative, and as he looked like dying and involving us all in disgrace, I interviewed the doctor and—but the story grows wearisome.

To finish, then : the workhouse infirmary was decided upon, as the only place where Bettesworth could get the nursing without which he would probably die. Fortunately, he received the proposal reasonably ; he was ready to go anywhere to get well, as he felt that he never would at home. He merely stipulated that his wife must not be left. A walk to find the relieving officer and get the necessary orders from him was to me the only pleasant part of the episode. It took me, on a brilliant spring evening, some three miles farther into the country, where I saw the first primroses I had seen outside my garden that year. It also enabled me to see how parish relief looks from the side of the poor who have to ask for it, but that was not so pleasant. However, the officer was civil enough ; he gave me the necessary orders ; we made all the arrangements, and on the following day the two old Bettesworths were driven off miserably in a cab to the workhouse.

How fervently everybody hoped, then, that Bettesworth would leave his wife behind, if he ever came out of the institution himself alive ! And yet, though it's true he was dependent on me for the wherewithal to keep his home together, how much nobler was his own behaviour than that we would have commended ! Once in the infirmary, he recovered quickly ; and in ten days, to my amazement (and annoyance at the time), word came that the old couple were out again. They had toddled feebly home—a two-mile journey ; they two together, not to be separated ; each of them the sole person in the world left to the other. The old woman, people told me, was amazingly clean. Her hair, which had been cut, proved white beyond expectation ; her face was almost comely now that it was washed. Had I not seen her ? What a pity it was, wasn't it, the old man wouldn't leave her up there to be took care of, and after all the trouble it had been, too, to get 'em there !

I believe it was on the day before Good Friday

(1904) that they returned home. When Bettesworth got to work again is more than my memory
tells me. I suppose, though, that I must have paid
him a visit first—probably during the following
week ; for I remember hoping to see the old woman's
white hair and clean face, and being disappointed
to find her as grimy as ever—her visage almost as
black as her hands, and her hair an ashy grey.

XXIII

May 16, 1904.—" It is long," says a note of the 16th
of May, "since I wrote down any of Bettesworth's
talk ; but it flows on constantly—less vivacious than
of old, perhaps, for he is visibly breaking since his
illness in the spring, and is a stiff, shiftless, rather
weary, rather sad old man ; but his garrulity has
not lost its flavour of the country-side ; and many
of his sayings sound to me like the traditional quips
and phrases of earlier generations."

This was apropos of a remark he had let fall
about a certain Mr. Sparrow in an adjacent village,
for whom Bettesworth's next-door neighbour Kiddy
Norris had been labouring, until Kiddy could no
longer endure the man's grasping ways. Stooping
over his wooden grass-rake, Bettesworth murmured,
as if to the grass, " Old Jones used to say Sparrows
pecks." Then he told how Sparrow, deprived of
the services not only of Kiddy, but of Kiddy's mate
Alf, was at a loss for men to replace them ; and,
" Ah," Bettesworth commented, " he can't have
'em on a peg, to take down jest when he mind to."
The saying had a suggestive old-world sound : I
could imagine it handed about, on the Surrey hill-

sides, and in cottage gardens, and at public-houses, over and over again through many years.

Presently Bettesworth said casually, " I hear they're goin' to open that new church over here in Moorway's Bottom to-morrer. Some of 'em was terrifyin' little Alf Cook about it last night " (Sunday night ; probably at the public-house), " tellin' him he was goin' to be made clerk, and he wouldn't be tall enough to reach to ring the bell."

" Little Alf," I asked, " who used to work for So-and-so ?"

" Worked for 'n for years. The boys do terrify 'n. Tells 'n he won't be able to reach to ring the bell. They keeps on. Why, he en't tall enough to pick strawberries, they says."

" He's got a family, hasn't he ?"

" Yes — but they be all doin' for theirselves. Two or three of 'em be married. *He* might ha' bin doin' very well. His old father left 'n the house he lives in, and a smart bit o' ground : but I dunno —some of 'em reckons 'tis purty near all gone."

" Down his neck ?"

" Ah. They was talkin' about 'n last night, and they seemed to reckon there wa'n't much left. But he's a handy little feller. Bin over there at Cashford this six weeks, so he told me, pointin' hoppoles for they Fowlers. He said he'd had purty near enough of it. But he poled, I thinks he said, nine acres o' hop-ground for 'em last year. He bin pointin' this year. He says he might do better if 'twas nearer home—he can't git rid o' the chips over there ; people won't have 'em. If he'd got 'em here, they'd be worth sixpence a sack—that always was the price. He gits so much a hunderd for pointin' ; and he told me it was as much as he could do to earn two-and-nine or three shillin's " (a day). "Then o' course there's the chips, only he can't sell 'em. Cert'nly they'd serve he for firin' ; but that en't what he wants."

May 20.—"There's a dandy. You lay there." Bettesworth chose out and put on one side a dandelion from the grass he was chopping off a green path. "I'll take he home for my rabbits," he said.

A sow-thistle in the near bank caught my eye. "Your rabbits will eat sow-thistles too, won't they ?" I asked.

"Yes, they likes 'em very well. They'll eat 'em —an' then presently I shall eat they."

I pulled up the thistle, and another dandelion, while Bettesworth discoursed of the economics of rabbit-keeping. "'Ten't no good keepin' 'em for the pleasure. . . . But give me a wild rabbit to eat afore a tame one, any day. My neighbour Kid kills one purty near every week. He had one last Sunday must ha' wanted some boilin', or bakin', or somethin'."

"What, an old one ?"

"Old buck. I ast 'n, 'What, have ye had yer

teeth ground, then ?' I says.   He's purty much of
a one for rabbits."

I was not so wonderfully fond of them, I said.

"No ?   I en't had e'er a one—I dunno *when*.
Well—a rabbit, you come to put one down afore a
hungry man, what is it ?   He's mother have gone
an' bought one for 'n at a shop, when he en't happened to have one hisself—give as much as a shillin'
or fifteenpence.   'Ten't worth it.   Or else I've
many a time bought 'em for sixpence—sixpence, or
sixpence-ha'penny, or sevenpence.   And they en't
worth no more."

During all this he was sweeping up his grass
cuttings.   The children came out of school for afternoon recess, and their shoutings sounded across the
valley.   " There's the rebels let loose again," said
Bettesworth.   From where we stood, high on one
of the upper terraces of the garden, we could see far.
The sky was grey and melancholy.   A wind blew
up gustily out of the south-east, and I foreboded
rain.   " We don't want it from that quarter,"
Bettesworth replied.   " That's such a *cold* rain.
And I've knowed it keep on forty-eight hours,
out o' the east. . . .   I felt a lot better " (of the
recent bronchitis) " when she " (the wind) " shifted
out o' there before."

Meanwhile I had pulled up one or two more dande-
lions, to add to Bettesworth's heap ; and now I
espied a small seedling of bryony, which also I was
careful to pull out.   The root, already as big as a

man's thumb, came up easily, and I passed it to Bettesworth, asking, " Isn't that what they give to horses sometimes ? "

He handled it. " I never *heared* of anybody," he answered, perhaps not recognizing it at this small stage of growth. " Now, ground *ivy !* That's a rare thing. If you bakes the roots o' that in the oven, an' then grinds it up to a powder, you no need to *call* yer horses to ye, after you've give 'em that. They'll foller ye for it. Dandelion roots the same. Make 'em as fat ! And their coats come up mottled, jest as if you'd knocked 'em all over with a 'ammer. They'll foller ye about anywhere for that. *I*'ve give it to 'em, many's a time ; bin out, after my day's work, all round the hedges, purpose to get things for my 'osses. There's lots o' things in the hedgerow as is good for 'em. So there is for we too, if we only knowed which they was. We shouldn't want much *doctor* if we knowed about herbs.

" Old Waterson, he used to eat dandelion leaves same as you would a lettuce, and he said it done 'n good, too. Old Steve Blackman was another. He used to know all about the herbs. If you went into his kitchen, you'd see it hung all round with little bundles of 'em, to dry. *He* was the only one as could cure old Rokey Wells o' the yeller janders. Gunner had tried 'n—all the doctors had tried 'n, and give 'n up. He'd bin up there at the infirmary eighteen months or more, till old Steve see 'n one day and took to 'n. And he made a hale hearty man of 'n again.

"That 'ere Holt—Tom Holt, *you* know, what used to be keeper at Culverley—*he* got the yeller janders now. He's pensioned off—twelve shillin's a week, and his cot and firin'. Lives in Cashford Bridge house—you knows that old farmhouse as you goes over Cashford Bridge. He lives there now. If old Steve's son got his father's book now, he'll be able to cure 'n. He used to keep a book where he put all the receipts, so 't is to be hoped his son have kep' it. They says Holt 've got the yeller janders wonderful strong, but if . . ."

May 24.—In Bettesworth's opinion, an important part of the training of a labourer relates to getting about and finding work. The old man was at the Whit Monday fête with a man named Vickery, of whom he talked, imitating Vickery's gruff voice with appreciation. Vickery—sixty or seventy years old—came (I learn) from a village out Guildford way—"that was his native," says Bettesworth—but was adopted by an aunt in this parish, who left him her two cottages at her death. All this, if not interesting to us, was deeply so to Bettesworth. And Vickery, it appears, has worked all his life in one situation, at Culverley Park. He began as a boy minding sheep. As a man, he managed the gas-house belonging to the mansion ; and when the electric light was installed, he took over the management of that, making up his time with chopping fire-wood, and so forth. And, says Bettesworth, " They'd ha' to set fire to Culverley to get rid of 'n. He never worked nowhere else. That's how they be down there. Old Smith's another of 'em. He bin there forty year. He turned seventy, here a week ago. Never had but two places, and bin at Culverley forty year. Why, if they was turned out they wouldn't know how to go about. Same when Mr. John Payne died : there was a lot o' young fellers turned off. They hadn't looked out for theirselves ; their fathers had always got the work for 'em, and law! they didn' know where to go no more than a cuckoo ! But I reckon that's a very silly thing."

XXIV*

June 1, 1904.—A cool thundery rain this first of June drove Bettesworth to shelter. As usual at such times, he busied himself at sawing and splitting wood for kindling fires.

At the moment of my joining him he was breaking up an old wooden bucket which had lately been condemned as useless. " Th' old bucket's done for," he said contemplatively. " I dessay he seen a good deal o' brewin' ; but there en't much of it done now. A good many men used to make purty near a livin' goin' round brewin' for people. Brown's in Church Street used to be a rare place for 'em. Dessay you knows there's a big yard there ; an' then they had some good tackle, and plenty o' room for firin'. Pearsons, Coopers "—he named several who were wont to make use of Brown's yard and tackle. I asked, Did the cottage people brew ? But Bettesworth shook his head. " I never knowed none much —only this sugar beer."

" But they grew hops ?" I asked.

" Oh yes," Bettesworth assented, " every garden

* The earlier portions of this chapter have already appeared in *Country Life*.

172

had a few hills o' hops. But 't wa'n't very often they brewed any malted beer. Now 'n again one 'd get a peck o' malt, but gen'ly 'twas this here sugar beer. Or else I've brewed over here at my old mother-in-law's, 'cause they had the tackle, ye see ; and so I have gone over there when I've killed a pig, to salt 'n."

A suggestion that he would hardly know how to brew now caused him to smile. " No, I don't s'pose I should," he admitted.

I urged next that nearly all people, I supposed, used at one time to brew their own beer. To which Bettesworth :

" And so they did bake their own bread. They'd buy some flour. . . ."

I interrupted, remembering how he had himself grown corn, to ask if that was not rather the custom.

" Sometimes. Yes, I *have* growed corn as high as my own head, up there at the back of this cot. . . . But my old gal and me, when hoppin' was over, we'd buy some flour, enough to last us through the winter, and then with some taters, and a pig salted down, I'd say, ' There, we no call to *starve*, let the winter be *what* it will.' Well, taters, ye see, didn't cost nothin' ; and then we always had a pig. You couldn't pass a cottage at that time that hadn't a pigsty. . . . And there was milk, and butter, and bread. . . ."

" But not many comforts ?" I queried.

" No ; 'twas rough. But I dunno—they used to

look as strong an' jolly as they do now. But 'twas poor money. The first farm-house I went to I never had but thirty shillin's and my grub."

"Thirty shillings in how long?"

"Twal'month. And I had to pay my washin' an' buy my own clothes out o' that."

The point was interesting. Did he buy his clothes at a shop, ready made?

"Yes. That was always same as 'tis now. Well, there was these round frocks—you'd get *they*"— home-made, he meant. And he told how his sister-in-law, Mrs. Loveland, and her mother "used to earn half a living" at making these "round" or smock frocks to order, for neighbours. The stuff was bought: the price for making it up was eighteen-pence, "or if you had much work on 'em, two shillin's."

Much fancy-work, did he mean?

"The gaugin', you know, about here." Bettes-worth spread his hands over his chest, and continued, "Most men got 'em made; their wives 'd make 'em. Some women, o' course, if they wasn't handy wi' the needle, 'd git somebody else to do 'em. They was warmer 'n anybody 'd think. And if you bought brown stuff, 'tis surprisin' what a lot o' rain they'd keep out. One o' them, and a woollen jacket under it, and them yello' leather gaiters right up your thighs—you could go out in the rain. . . . But 'twas a white round frock for Sundays."

At this point I let the talk wander; and presently

Bettesworth was relating perhaps the least credit-
able story he ever told me about himself. In judg-
ing him, however, if anyone desires to judge him
after so many years, the circumstances should be
borne in mind. The farm-lad on thirty shillings a
year, the young soldier from the Crimea where he
had been rationed on rum, marrying at last and
settling down in this village where the rough
eighteenth-century habits still lingered, might almost
be expected to shock his twentieth-century critics.
Be it admitted that his behaviour on the death of
his father-in-law was disgraceful; but let it be allowed also that that father-in-law, the old road-fore-
man, was a drunken tyrant—at times a dangerous
madman—at whose death it was natural to rejoice.
However, I will let Bettesworth get on with his story.

The " white round frock on Sundays " reminded
him of his father-in-law's costume—frock as described, tall hat, and knee-breeches; and this recalled (here on this rainy June day where we talked
in the shed) how tall a man he was; and how, lying
on the floor in the stupor of death, just across the
lane there, he looked " like a great balk o' timber."
Confusedly the narrative hurried on after this. A
cottage was mentioned, which used to stand where
now that resident lives who could not endure the
Bettesworths for his tenants. This was the maiden
home of Bettesworth's mother-in-law; and to this
the mother-in-law would flee for refuge, in terror of
being murdered by her husband in his drunken

frenzies. Then would the husband follow, and
" break in all the windows "; for which he was
" kept out " of the owner's will, and lost much
property that would have been his. Particulars of
his suicide followed : the man cut his throat and
lay speechless for eight days before he died. But
at the first news Bettesworth, being one son-in-law,
was dispatched to a village some five miles distant,
to fetch home another. He borrowed a pony and
cart ; found his brother-in-law, " and," he said, " we
both got as boozy as billyo on the way home. . . .
' 'Arry,' I says, ' the old foreman bin an' done for
hisself.' " At every public-house they came to
they had beer, treating the pony also ; and finally
they came racing through the town at full speed.
" We should ha' bin locked up for it now. No
mistake we *come*, when we did get away. And
when we got 'ome, 'Arry stooped over to speak to
'n, an' fell over on his face. I didn't wait for *my*
lecture : I had to get the pony home. It was
runnin' off 'n, when I got 'n down to his stable,
with the pace we'd made, an' the beer he'd had.
We should ha' got into trouble for it if 't had been
now. The old woman come out, an' begun goin'
on about it ; but the old man says, ' You might be
sure they'd travel, for such a job. And he won't
be none the worse for it.' We put 'n in the stable,
an' give 'n another pint o' beer, and rubbed 'n
down an' throwed two or three hop-sacks over 'n ;
an' next mornin' he was as right as ever."

"How long ago ?" I asked.

" I 'most forgets how long ago 'twas. A smartish many years. His wife—she bin dead this—let's see—three-an'-twenty year ; and she lived a good many years after he."

She had property—her husband's, no doubt—which her son Will (Bettesworth's wife's brother, remember) inherited, yet only by the skin of his teeth. For if some infant or other had breathed after birth, that infant's relatives would have been the heirs. On this sort of subject people like Bettesworth are always most tedious and obscure. As to the household stuff, it was to be divided ; " and when it come to our turn to choose," Bettesworth said, " my old gal and me said Will could have ourn. We'd got old clutter enough layin' about, and Will hadn't got none, ye see, always livin' with his mother. So he had the stuff an' the cot. They " (the rival party) "had two or three tries for it ; but 'twas proved that the child never breathed. My wife's sister Jane thought *she* was goin' to get it. But I says, ' No, Jane ; you wears the wrong clothes. That belongs to William.' "

Bettesworth ceased. In the ten or fifteen minutes while he had been talking we had got far from the subject of peasant industries ; and yet somehow the thought of them was still present to both of us, and when he grew silent I nodded my head contempla- tively, murmuring something about " queer old times." " Yes," he returned, " a good many wouldn't be able to tell ye how they *did* bring up a family o' childern, if you was to ast 'em." And so, with the rain pattering down upon the shed roof, I left the old man to his wood-chopping.

June 11, 1904.—The twentieth century is driving out the old-fashioned people and their savagery from the village, but here and there it lets in savagery of its own. Into that hovel down by the stream, which Bettesworth had vacated, there had come fresh tenants, as I knew ; but that was all I knew until one morning Bettesworth told me something, which I lost no time in hurrying down on to paper, while his sentences were hot in my mind, as follows :

" Ha' ye heared about our neighbours down 'ere runnin' away ?"

" No ! Where ?"

" Down here where I used to live. Gone off an' left their little childern to the wide world."

" Well, but . . . who . . . ?"

" Worcester they *calls* 'n. But I dunno what his name is."

" Where did he come from ? I don't seem to know him."

" No, nor me. I dunno nothin' about 'n. He bin a sojer an' got a pension. He bin at work down at this Bordon. But his wife bin carryin' on purty much. Had another bloke about there this fort-night. An' then went off, an' give one of her little childern a black eye for a partin' gift. He come 'ome o' Sunday, and didn't find nobody about there; and took all there was and his pension papers and was off. And there's them two poor little dears left there alone wi' nobody to look after 'em or get 'em a bit o' vittles."

Of course I exclaimed, while Bettesworth went on,

"Ah . . . I reckon they ought to be hung up by the heels, leavin' their childern like that. I always *was* fond o' childern, but if 't 'd bin older ones able to look after theirselves I shouldn't ha' took so much notice. But these be two little 'ns ben't 'ardly able to dress theirselves : two little gals about five or six. Poor little dears, there was one of 'em went cryin' 'cause her mother was goin' away, and her mother up with her hand and give her one. Law! somebody ought to ha' bin there with a stick and hit her across the head and killed her dead !

"There they was all day and all night. Mrs. Mardon went to the policeman about it. He said she better take care of 'em. 'But I can't afford to keep 'em,' she says. 'No,' he says, ' cert'nly not. 'Ten't to be expected you should. But you look after 'em for a week, an' we'll see if their parents comes back. And if they don't, we'll see the relievin' officer, an' pay you for your trouble ; and the children 'll be took to the workhouse, and then we shall very soon *have* 'em ' " (the parents). "And

so they will, too.   They says he's gone to Salisbury.
But they'll have 'n.   Old soldier, and a pensioner,
and all : they'll find 'n."

" What's his name, do you say ?"

" They *calls* 'n Worcester : we dunno whether 'tis
his right name, or only a nickname.   He ought to
ha' Worcester !   He's like 'nough to cop it, too !"

XXV

June 20.—On the afternoon of June 20th, once more
Bettesworth was at work among the potatoes, yet
not in the circumstances of last year, when we were
rejoicing in the rain. According to my book, this
was "a real summer afternoon—Hindhead showing
the desired dazzling blue; soft high clouds floating
from the westwards; a soft wind occasionally
stirring the trees." Blackbirds, it seems, were
flitting about the garden to watch their young,
warning them, too, with an incessant "twit-twit,
twit-twit"; and no doubt, besides this June sound,
there was that of garden tools struck into the soil.

And yet, for me, rather than the far-reaching daylight or the vibrating afternoon air, another of the
great characteristics of English summer clings to
this and the following few fragments about Bettesworth. I might look away to Hindhead and rejoice
in the sense of vast warm distance; I might admire
the landscape, and practise my æsthetics; but he
was becking in amongst the potatoes, and it is his
point of view, not mine, that has survived and given
its tinge to these talks.

Forgetful, both of us, that the same subject in

almost the same place had occupied us a year ago, we spoke of his work ; and first he admired the potatoes, and then he praised his beck. " Nice tool," he said. I took hold of it : " Hand-made, of course ?" " Yes ; belonged to my old gal's gran'mother. There's no tellin' how old he is."

He went on to explain that it was a " polling beck," pointing out peculiarities hardly to be described here. They interested me ; yet not so much as other things about the tool, which it was good to handle. From the old beck a feeling came to me of summer as the country labourers feel it. This thing was probably a hundred years old. Through a hundred seasons men's faces had bent over it and felt the heat of the sun reflecting up from off the potatoes, as the tines of the beck brightened in the hot soil. And what sweat and sunburn, yet what delight in the crops, had gone to the polishing of the handle ! A stout ash shaft, cut in some coppice years ago, and but rudely trimmed, it shone now with the wear of men's hands ; and to balance it as I did, warm and moist from Bettesworth's grasp, was to get the thrill of a new meaning from the afternoon. For those who use such tools do not stop to admire the summer, but they co-operate with it.

The old man took his beck again, and I saw the sunlight beating down upon his back and brown arms as he once more bent his face to the work. Then our talk changed. Soon I fetched a tool for myself, so as to be working near him and hear his chatter.

He touched on scythes for a moment, and then glanced off to name a distant village (a place which lies on a valley side, facing the midday heat), and to tell of a family of blacksmiths who once lived there. " They used to make purty well all sorts o' edge-tools. And they earned a name for 't, too, didn't they ? I've see as many as four of 'em over there at a axe. Three with sledge-'ammers, and one with a little 'ammer, tinkin' on the anvil." " And he is the master man of them all," I laughed. Bettesworth laughed too—we were so happy there in the broiling sunshine — " Yes, but I've often noticed it, the others does all the work." To which I rejoined, " But he keeps time to the sledges ; and it's he who knows to a blow when they have done enough." " There was one part of making a axe," said Bettesworth, " as they'd never let anybody see 'em at." What could that have been ? We agreed that it had to do with some secret process of hardening the steel.

Another shifting of the talk brought us round to his brother-in-law — that accomplished farm-labourer, who was then, however, driving a traction engine, with one truck which carried three thousand bricks. " That must do away with a lot of hoss hire," said Bettesworth. " And yet," I urged, " there seem more horses about than ever." " And they be dear to buy, so Will Crawte says," added Bettesworth.

" How many load," I asked ignorantly, " do you reckon three thousand bricks ? More than a four-horse load, isn't it ?"

Bettesworth made no effort to reckon, but said easily, " Yes. They reckons three hunderd an' fifty is a load, of these here wire-cut bricks ; four hunderd, of the old red bricks ; and stock bricks is five hunderd. And slates, ' Countess ' slates—they be twenty inches by ten—six hunderd o' they goes to a load."

Wondering at his knowledge, I commented on the endless variety of technical details never dreamt of by people like myself ; and Bettesworth assented, without interest, however, in me or other people or anything but his subject. " That's one o' the things you wants to learn, if you be goin' with hosses—when you got a load. Law ! half o' these carters on the road dunno whether they got a load or whether they en't. I've almost forgot now ; but I learnt it once."

" How do you mean ' learnt ' it ? Picked it up ?'

" No. 'Tis in a book. You can learn to reckon things. . . . If you be goin' for a tree, or a block o' stone, or bricks, you wants to know what's a load for a hoss, or a two or a three hoss load. A mason told me once, when I was goin' for a block o' stone. He put his tape round it, an' told me near the matter what it weighed. He said you always ought to carry a two-foot rule in your

pocket ; and then put it across the stone—or p'r'aps
'tis two or three bits you got to take. . . ."

As there is nothing in the talk itself to give the
impression, it must have been my working in the
sunshine when I heard of these details, that now
makes them—the glaring stone-mason's yard, the
village smithy, the engine hauling bricks along the
high road—seem all sun-baked and dusty, in the
heat which men like Bettesworth have to face, while
I am admiring the summer landscape.

Twice in the early days of July the old man's
homely rustic living is touched upon. By now, in
the cottage gardens, the broad-beans are at their
best ; and he desires, it is said in one place, no
better food than beans, served for choice with a bit
of bacon. But there are peas too ; and one day he
tells me simply that he " had peas three times
yesterday. There's always some left from dinner,
and then I has 'em in a saucer for my supper."

July 29.—As July ran to its close, the weather,
though still warm, turned gloomy, and showers
came streaking down in front of the grey dismal
distance. "They gives a *poor* account of the
harvest," says Bettesworth. "What ? have they
started ?" I ask ; and he, "Yes, I've heared of a
smartish few."

I supposed he meant in Sussex ; but it appeared
not. "No," he said, "I dunno as they've begun

in Sussex, but about here. Lent corn, oats, an'
barley, an' so on. There's So-and-so "—he named
three or four farmers reported to have begun cutting,
and went on, " But 'tis all machine work, so there
won't be much " (extra work). " But the straw en't
no higher 'n your knees in some parts, so they says.
. . . 'Twas the cold spring—an' then the dryth.
But it don't much matter about the barley. I've
heared old people say they've knowed barley sowed
and up and harvested without a drop o' rain on it
fust to last. Where you gets straw " (with other
crops, I suppose, is the meaning) " there en't no fear
about the barley : 'tis a thing as 'll stand dryth as
well as purty near anything."

He had " heard old people say "—things like
these that he was now saying. And Bettesworth's
phrase will bear thinking of, for its indication of
the topics which the progress of the summer months
had always been wont to renew in his brain year by
year.

Unhappily, about this period something less pleasing was beginning to force itself upon his attention.

XXVI

INTO the peacefulness of Bettesworth's last working summer a disquieting circumstance had been slowly intruding; and now, with August, it developed into a subject of grave fears. I do not know when I first noticed a small sore on the old man's lower lip, but I think it must have been in May or early June. On being asked, he said it had been there since his illness in the spring, and " didn't seem to get no worse." Certainly he was not troubling about it.

Weeks passed, perhaps six weeks, in which, though the ugly, angry look of the thing sometimes took my attention, I forbore to speak of it again, being unwilling to arouse alarm. Then it occurred to me that if I was too fanciful, Bettesworth was not fanciful enough. In his robust out-door life he had never learnt to be nervous and anticipate horrors ; and he might not be sufficiently alive to the dreadful possibilities which were presenting themselves to my own imagination. I urged him accordingly to see his club doctor.

He did so, not immediately, though after how long an interval I am unable to say, since none of this affair got into my note-book. The doctor no

sooner saw the sore than he said it must be cut out.
" Do you smoke ?" was one of his first questions ;
and " Where is your pipe ?" was the next. Bettesworth produced his pipe—an old blackened briar—
and was comforted to learn that it was considered
harmless. But he must have the sore removed, and
his two or three remaining teeth near it would have
to come out. When could he have it done ? the
doctor asked. Bettesworth said that he must consult me on that point, and came away promising to
do so.

Considering how sure he must have been that I
should put no obstacle in his way, I incline to think
that by now he must himself have begun to feel
alarm. He waited, however, about a week, and
then one morning off he went again to see the
doctor, half expecting, I believe, to have the operation done then and there, before he came home.

An hour afterwards I met him returning, looking
worried. The doctor was just setting off for his
holiday, and could not now undertake the operation, but advised him to go to Guildford Hospital.
Perhaps Bettesworth would have liked me to pooh-
pooh the suggestion—he little relished the idea of
leaving his wife and his work, and taking a railway
journey to so dismal an end ; but even as he talked,
I was watching on his lip that which might mean
death. So I sent him off straightway to the Vicarage,
where he could obtain a necessary letter of introduction to the hospital.

Of what immediately followed my memory is quite blank. I only recall that the old chap started at last all alone on his journey to Guildford, not knowing how long he would be away, or what was likely to happen to him. A niece of his had provided him with a stamped addressed envelope and a clean sheet of note-paper, in case he should need to get anyone at the hospital to send a message home.

August 6, 1904.—So he disappeared for a time. Three or four days, we supposed, would be the extent of his absence ; but the days went by and no word came from him. For all we knew he might never have reached the hospital ; and it began to be a serious question what would become of his wife, and whether she would not have to be sent to the workhouse for want of a protector. At last, I wrote for information to the matron of the hospital. Her answer, which lies before me now, and is the only piece of evidence I have preserved of the whole business, is dated August 6th. On that day, it stated, Bettesworth was to be operated upon, and, if all went well, he would most likely be able to leave the hospital in ten days or a fortnight.

Unless I mistake, the ten days or a fortnight dragged out to nearly three weeks, in which I had the old wife on my mind. A visit to her one Sunday morning reassured me. Poor old Lucy Bettesworth ! I did not anticipate, then, that I should never again see her alive. Dirty and dishevelled as ever, alone in the squalid cottage, she received me with a meek simplicity that in my eyes made amends for many faults. She was more sane than I had dared to hope I should find her, eager for "Fred" to come home, but contented, it seemed, to wait, if it was doing him good. She did not want for anything; she ate no meat, and it cost her nothing to live. Would I like a vegetable marrow? There was a nice one in the garden that "wanted cuttin'."

Perceiving that she desired me to have the vegetable marrow, I allowed her to take me out into the garden to get it. "Could I cut it?" Of course I could, and did. Then a qualm struck her: perhaps I shouldn't like carrying it! But she might be able to wrap it up in a piece of newspaper. . . .

To that, however, I demurred. There was no harm in being seen with a vegetable marrow on Sunday morning; and I took it, undraped by paper, aware that the despised old woman had done me the greatest courtesy in her power. And that was, as it proved, the last time I ever saw her.

Bettesworth, meanwhile, in the hospital, was not quite forgotten. His niece has been mentioned who gave him the stamped envelope which he had not used. We shall hear a good deal of her, later on— a helpful but delicate woman, who was Bettesworth's niece only by marriage with a nephew of his, of whom also we shall hear. These two on that Sunday morning—it being a quiet, half-hazy, half-sunny August day—walked over to Guildford, and brought back néws that the old man was doing as well as could be hoped. They proposed to repeat the visit the following week. It made a pleasant Sunday outing.

But before that week was ended Bettesworth was suddenly home again, unannounced. An odd look about him puzzled me, until I realized that he had grown a beard—a white, scrubby, short-trimmed beard, which gave him a foxy expression that I did not like. His lip was in strapping, a little blood-stained, but he reported that all was going on well. The surgeons had carved down into his jaw, and believed the operation to have been quite successful. Satisfied as to this, I could endure his changed appearance.

Something about his manner was less satisfactory. Looking back, I think I know what was the matter; but at the time a sort of levity in him struck a false note. Besides, he seemed not to realize that his wife might have suffered by his absence, or that others had put themselves about on his behalf. He struck me as selfish and self-satisfied. I forgot what a lonely expedition his had been, and how he had had to start off and face this miserable experience without a friend at hand to care whether he came through it alive or not.

Left to himself (it is obvious enough now) and determined to go through the business in manly fashion, he had rather overdone it—had overplayed his part. In refusing to admit fear, he had erred a little on the other side, and he still erred so in telling his experiences, perhaps because he was still not quite free of fear. By his account, his stay in the hospital had been an interesting holiday. Everything about it was a little too good to be believed. He had jested with the doctors and the nurses. They called him " Dad," and " a joking old man," and he felt flattered : they had had a " fire-drill," and from his bed, or his seat under the veranda among the convalescents, he had entered into the spirit of the thing. Grimmer details, too, did not escape him : the arrival of new patients in the night—" accident cases " brought in for immediate treatment ; the sufferings he witnessed ; the hopeless condition of a railway porter, and so forth. All this was told in his own manner, with swift realistic touch, convincingly true ; with a genuine sense of the humour of the thing, he mentioned the operating-room by the patients' name for it—" the slaughter-house "; but none the less his narrative had an offensive emptiness, an unreality, a flippancy, unworthy, I thought, of Bettesworth.

A little more sense would have shown me the clue to it, in his behaviour just before the operation. He was dressed in " a sort of a white night-gown," waiting for his turn ; and, he said, " I made 'em laugh. I got up and danced about on the floor. ' Now I be Father Peter,' I says." Then the nurse

came to conduct him to "the slaughter-house."
"'Old Freddy's goin' to 'ave something now,' they"
(the nearer patients) "says. I took hold o' the nurse's
arm. 'Now I be goin' out for a walk with my young
lady,' I says. 'We be goin' out courtin'.'" And
in such fashion, over-excited, he maintained his
fortitude, with a travesty of the courage he was all
but losing. He never confessed to having felt fear.
The nearest approach to it was when he was actually
lying on the operating-table. Left quite alone there
(for half an hour, he alleged and believed), " I looked
all round," he said, " and up at the skylight, and I
says to myself, 'So this is where it is, is it?'"

With these tales he came home, repeating them
until I was weary. By and by, however, he settled
down to work, although one or two visits had to
be paid to the hospital, for dressing the lip ; and
as he settled down, his normal manner returned.
For some weeks—nay, for longer—his friends were
not free of anxiety about him. There were pains
in his jaw, and in his lip too, enough to draw dire
forebodings from those of pessimistic humour. But
Bettesworth owned to no fears. So it went on for
a month or so, when that occurred which effectually
banished from his mind all remembrance of this
trouble.

XXVII

September 19, 1904.—Because they can so little
afford to be ill, it is habitual among the very poor
to neglect an illness long after other people would
be seriously alarmed at it ; and the habit had been
confirmed in Bettesworth with regard to his wife's
maladies, by her having so many times recovered
from them without help. It was almost a matter
of course to him, when about the middle of September, and less than a month after his return from
the hospital, she became once more exceedingly
unwell. So she had often done : it was not worth
mentioning, and was not mentioned, to me. I knew
of no trouble. If I had been asked about his welfare
at that time, I should have said that the old man
was rather unusually happy. I should have said
so especially one Monday morning (it was the 19th
of September) ; because on that day we were picking apples, and his conversation was so delightfully
in harmony with the sunshine glinting among the
apple-boughs. He told of cider and cider-making ;
and then of shepherds he had known on the Sussex
Downs, and of their dogs, and their solitary pas-
times upon the hills. Hearing him, no one, I am

sure, could have supposed that at home his wife had been dangerously ill for nearly a week, and that consequently his own comfort there had for the time ceased to exist.

Later on that Monday his wife's condition (not his own) was somehow made known to me. I suppose Bettesworth consulted me on the step he was contemplating, of going to the relieving officer tomorrow to get an order for medical attendance for old Lucy. At any rate, by Monday night that is what he had resolved to do, and I knew it and approved, remembering what the policeman had said to me. It seemed a wise precaution to take, but evidently it could not be urgent. Bettesworth was choosing Tuesday, because on Tuesday mornings the relieving officer is in attendance in the parish, and the order could therefore be got without a five-mile walk for it.

From various circumstances it may be inferred that the early part of Tuesday was an unhappy time for Bettesworth : a time of fretful watching for the dawn, perhaps after a wakeful night ; of impatience to come and begin his day's work, and then of impatience for eleven o'clock to arrive, and of brooding obstinate thoughts, until at eleven he might go and get the miserable interview over. For it made him miserable to have to sue in the form of a pauper, and he was prepared, as poor folk generally are, to find in the relieving officer a bully if not a brute. I may say at once that he was agreeably deceived, and said as much afterwards—he was treated humanely and with appreciation ; but the relieving officer's account of the interview sufficiently proves that the old man went to it in but a surly temper. I imagine him standing up as straight as his crooked old limbs would let him, rolling his head back defiantly, with tightened lips and suspicious eyes, and answering as uncivilly as he dared. A compliment was offered him, on his haste to get away from the infirmary in the spring. " *I* en't no workhouse man !" he answered brusquely. And he did his best to persuade the relieving officer that he would never want relief for himself, asserting that he belonged to a club, and concealing the fact that he was a superannuated member of it, no longer entitled to benefit from the club funds.

And then, the interview over, and the order obtained, his cheerfulness for the rest of the day is suggestive of an ordeal successfully passed. True, I have lost record of how he pottered through the afternoon—it was, of course, useless to go to the parish doctor at that time of day—but he seemed to have suddenly lost the weakness still lingering from the operation in the hospital ; and being short of money, he proposed an extra job for the evening. He wanted to clear out a cesspit in my garden. I urged that he had better rest, and take care of himself as well as of his wife. " *I* be gettin' bonny !" he said happily.

He carried his point, too. As if he had no wife ill at home, at about eight o'clock, which was usually his bed-time, he came back and began his self-imposed task, with a young labourer to help. And he must have been in merry spirits, for he kept his mate amused, so that from the house I could hear the man laughing, in frequent bleating outbursts of hilarity, at some facetious saying or other. One of these sayings I heard, on going out to see how the work was progressing. " He must be a greedy feller as wants more 'n one or two whiffs o' this," Bettesworth remarked ; and his companion let out another good-tempered laugh. From the old man's manner I argued that his wife must be doing well ; but probably it indicated only a reaction from the moody temper of the morning. The job was finished at about half-past nine, and conscious of a good day's work done, Bettesworth once more crept over the hill and across the valley, home.

But not to go to bed, or to sleep. While he was at work in the moonlight and making his friend laugh, I did not know, but he did, what was in store for him. Having no spare bed, be began his night downstairs and dozed for a while in an easy-chair ; then roused and went out into the moon-light to smoke a pipe ; and so he got through the night. Tobacco was his solace. He smoked, he told me, a full ounce in the ensuing twenty-four hours. At seven in the morning—his usual hour—

he was here beginning work : at nine he left off, to go into the town and present his order at the doctor's.

That journey on the Wednesday morning proved the beginning of a period of intenser wretchedness for the old man. He set out in apparent equanimity ; but the fatigue of the night was upon him, the glow of yesterday's contentment had died out, and his nerves must have been all on edge to take as he did a remark of the doctor's—" What do you want of an order ?   You're in constant work, aren't you ?" It seemed to him that he was being insulted for coming as a pauper, and it was all he could do to refrain from a rejoinder that would have resulted in his being summarily ejected from the doctor's presence.   And was he as submissive as he fancied ? It is more likely that the ungraciousness of his manner was to blame for what he regarded as pure heartlessness in the other. That he must be at home to meet the doctor was self-evident ; but it was important to him not to lose a whole day from his work, and he desired to know whether the visit would be made before his dinner-time or after it ?   I hazard a guess that he stated the case in tones of defiant bargaining ; at any rate, he could get no answer but that the doctor would call during the day.   With that he returned here—a quivering mass of resentment ; and in that temper, to which nothing is so repugnant as waiting, by my persuasion rather than by his goodwill he left his work and went home to wait.

With what increasing bitterness he wore through the day, with what fretfulness and final despair as of a man despised and forgotten, must be left to conjecture. For the doctor did not come, after all. Conjecture, too, must picture if it can the night that followed—the attempts to sleep in the chair, the restless wanderings into the garden to smoke, the repetition, in fact, of the preceding night's misery, but with a great addition of weariness and distress. Bettesworth, when he came round the next morning to tell me how he was situated, did not so much as mention all this ; he only let fall one pitiful detail. Some time in the night he had given his wife a little brandy ; and about daybreak he went out to draw fresh water into the kettle " so's not to have it no-ways stale," for making her a cup of tea. But, partaking of a cup himself at the same time, he " hadn't had it above five minutes afore he was out in the garden " to let the tea come back again. After that, he appears to have abandoned the attempt to get sustenance elsewhere than from tobacco. It was a dismal story to hear : but there was nothing to be done ; and having heard it, I sent him home again to go on waiting. This was Thursday, two days after he obtained the relieving officer's order for medical assistance, and by now the state of his wife was causing him grave fears.

But why had the doctor not been near ? To Bettesworth's wounded feelings the explanation needed no seeking : he was being made to wait for

richer people, because he was poor and unimportant.
Meanwhile, happening to meet with the relieving
officer, I laid the case before him, and heard that a
call to a distance had obliged the doctor to leave
his work for a day or two in the hands of a *locum
tenens*, who must have blundered. And this proved
to be the fact. On Thursday afternoon a doctor
who was a stranger at last found his way to Bettesworth's cottage, and the unhappy old man's long
suspense was so far over. At once all his bitterness
died out. The doctor " was as nice a gentleman
as ever I talked to," he affirmed. "He said she
was very bad. She wasn't to have nothing but only
milk an' beef-tea an' brandy, an' she wasn't to be
left alone." Bettesworth therefore did not leave
home again that day. He got his niece, whose
young family prevented her from giving much help,
to go to the town and bring home the medicine,
and so he settled down for another night like those
that had gone before.

It was on the next morning (Friday) that he told
me these few particulars, and how his wife seemed
a trifle—only a trifle—better ; how, too, he had
" washed her as well as he could," and, being asked,
how he had not been to bed himself. And now he
was on his way to the town to buy a few necessaries.
Who was with his wife meanwhile ? That was a
question I dared not ask, because I knew that the
distressful old woman was a by-word for sluttishness
among the neighbours, so much that they would

hardly go near her ; and I knew that Bettesworth,
though silent on the subject, was sore about it.
Without doubt the old woman was quite alone,
whenever circumstances compelled him to leave
her.

The "necessaries" he was going to buy included
beef-tea "and some cakes," he said. At the
mention of cakes I exclaimed, but he protested
reproachfully, "Well, but she en't had *nothin'* to
eat !" Clearly he did not regard milk as food, or
indeed anything else that was not solid. In the
matter of beef-tea, "I can't make it myself," he
said, "but you can buy it, can't ye, in jars ?"
He was perhaps thinking of Bovril, or something of
the kind. Fortunately there were those at hand
who knew how to make beef-tea, and undertook at
once to relieve the old man of this burden.

Taking him apart then, I asked if he needed a
shilling or two. He almost groaned in deprecation,
" I owes you such a lot now, and keeps on gettin'
into debt. I'd sooner rub along with jest as little
as ever I possibly can." It was of his rent he was
thinking, which of course was payable for those
weeks of his own illnesses, as well as for his absence
from work now, when he was not earning any wages
from which the rent could be deducted. Perhaps
he was unaware that I had no account of the debt ;
in any case, it seemed to be preying upon his mind.
I did not press the point, therefore, and he started
off for the town without aid from me.

In another way, too, the old man's reluctance
to be a burden manifested itself. What he had
told me so far was told because I wished to hear it,
and he wished me to understand. He made no
long tale : he was brief, unaffected, and as for
seeking compassion, it was far from his intention.
Of one thing only did he complain : a near relative's
indifference. " He was over by our place twice
o' Sunday," Bettesworth said scornfully, " and
couldn't look in to see how the poor old gal was.
He was ready enough to send to me when he had
his mishap " (falling from a rick, and finding himself
in agony at night), " and I run off an' went all down
to the town for 'n, late at night. But now *I* wants
help—no : he won't come anear. That's the sort
o' feller *he* is." So Bettesworth, uttering his sole
complaint. But he did not demand from others
the sympathy he looked for from a relation, or seek
to inflict them with the tale of troubles which, after
all, he would have to bear by himself.

At this point, if the actual course of this over-
crowded Friday were to be followed strictly, the
narrative would suffer a strange interruption. For,
having business of my own in the town, I set off
at the same time with Bettesworth, expecting little
cheerfulness from him on the way. But I had
failed to appreciate the man's stoicism, or the strong
grip he had over his feelings. For several nights
he had not rested on a bed ; he had taken during

the same period next to no food ; he had been
harassed by suspense, worn by indignation, baffled
constantly by the obstacles which his poverty set
in his way ; and it would have been pardonable if
he had proved himself but a gloomy companion for
a walk. Yet from the moment of our setting out
he put aside all his difficulties, and not only did he
not distress me, but for the half-hour before we
separated he kept me interested in his sensible
conversation on local topics, or charmed by the
pleasant rustic flavour of some of his reminiscences.
Here, therefore, would be the natural place for
inserting some fragments of this talk, which I wrote
down in the evening. It happened, however, that
in writing I gave precedence to an important
change which by then had come over the situation
at Bettesworth's home ; and as I propose to take
the account of this development and the issue of
it straight from my note-book, the bits of gossip
too had better come in just as they stand there.

It appears, then, to have been at about six o'clock
in the afternoon that I was writing, as follows :

Bettesworth has just been over (from his home)
to consult me, and perhaps to have a chat and relieve
his overburdened soul. When he got back from the
town this morning, he found the doctor paying
another visit, who was " wonderful nice," and
offered to give him a certificate for admitting the
old woman to the infirmary, if he would care to
have it and would call for it at the surgery. Bettes-

worth only wanted my encouragement. He is going down this evening for the certificate, and hopes to get his wife removed to-morrow.

It will be none too soon. The watching is wearing him out. Last night he had left her and gone downstairs, and sat dozing in the chair, when she tried to get out of bed, and fell heavily on the floor. He ran up—and forgot to take the candle back with him, thereby adding to his difficulties—and somehow managed to get her back into bed again and covered up, without aid. But now, says he, " I said to Dave Harding as I come up the road, ' What I should like to do 'd be to crawl up into the fir-woods where nobody couldn't see me, and lay down an' get three or four hours' sleep.' ' You couldn't do it,' he says ; ' 't'd be on your mind all the time. You might get off for ten minutes, p'raps, an' then you'd be up an' off again.' But that's what I sims as if I should like, more 'n anything : jest to crawl away somewhere, where nobody wouldn't come, for a good sleep. Then wake up and 'ave a floush—'t'd freshen me up."

Certainly he is overdone. Upon my renewing offers of a little help, he became tearful, almost sobbing : " You be the only friend I got. . . . I bin all over the country," and have faced all sorts of things, " but I *be* hammer-hacked about, now, no mistake." His grief consists in being able to do so little for his wife. He has given her since his dinner-time her medicine, then a sip of brandy "to take the taste out of her mouth . . . And then I said, ' Now here's a cake I bought for ye in the town ; have a bit o' that.' So she nibbled a bit, and I says, ' Eat 'n up.' No, she didn't want no more. ' But you got to 'ave it,' I says. I a'most forced it down her throat. I do's the best I can for her ; but I en't got nobody to tell me what to do."

And he is galled by turns, by turns amused, at her behaviour towards himself. "I can't do nothink right for her. She's more stubborn to me than to anybody else : keeps on findin' fault. Last night, in the night, she roused up an' accused me o' goin' away. ' You bin away somewheres,' she says. ' Oh yes, you 'ave ; I heared ye come creepin' back up the road.' And I'd bin sittin' there all the time."

This and much more he told. I tried to get away (we were in the garden), for I was busy ; but he followed me, to talk still, and wandered off into recollections of his experiences at Guildford Hospital.

7.30 *p.m.* Bettesworth has called once more, coming from the town, to show me the doctor's certificate (gastritis, it says), and to let me know that to-morrow morning he will not be here at his usual time. He proposes going to the relieving officer to obtain his order for a conveyance to move the old woman. "I shall be over there by seven o'clock," he says. The cumbersomeness of all these formalities is sickening. Having got the order, he will probably need to go right back to the town to arrange about the conveyance.

He was very tired, and rather wet, the night having set in with showers coming up on the east wind. So I got him a chair in the scullery, for the wet was making his old corduroys smell badly, and gave him a small glass of brandy-and-water. He refused a biscuit; "I couldn't swaller it," he said. "I can't eat, for thinkin' o' she."

He is not without a kind of pitiful consolation. "Seven or eight," he says, have professed their willingness to receive him into their homes, if need should be. One, even now, on the road from the town, has said, "Don't you trouble about *yerself*, Freddy; you can have a home with me, if you should want one." But the idea associated with this, of parting from his wife, breaks him down. The doctor who granted the certificate—the right doctor, this time—was sympathetic. "He come out to me because he see I was touched, and says, ' You no call to be *oneasy*, old gentleman ; she'll be looked *after* up there. Everything 'll be done for her as can be done.' "

But these nights, in which he does not go to bed ! His ankles and calves get the cramp, for he seems not to have thought, so little practice has he had in making himself comfortable, of resting his feet on another chair, while he is lying back in the easy-chair downstairs. . . . He has gone home now, to make up a fire and get what rest he may. " But then," he says, " she'll holler out, an' I got to run." He told me again how she " fell out o' bed flump " last night, and he stormed upstairs and found her on the floor, for " she didn't know how to get in again, not no more'n a cuckoo."

The group of cottages where he lives stands high above the road, which is reached by steps roughly cut into the steep bank. On one of these recent nights, having gone down the steps meaning to buy his wife sixpennyworth of brandy, Bettesworth felt in his trousers pocket for the shilling he had put there, and—it was gone. " Oh, I was in a way! I went back, an' crawled all up they steps, feelin' for it," the hour being eight o'clock, and moonlight. " As I went past old Kiddy's, I called out to 'n, ' Kid!', 'cause I wanted to tell 'n what trouble I was in, and I knowed he'd ha' come and helped me to find 'n, if he'd bin about. But he was gone to bed, 'cause he starts off so early in the mornin'." Thus the old man got back home, disconsolate, without the necessary brandy for his wife ; and, calling upstairs to her, " Lou, I've lost that shillin'," he began to prepare for his night in the easy-chair. But, first feeling in his pocket once more, he discovered there (fruits of his wife's incapacity) " a hole," he said, " I could put my finger through."

He pulled up his trouser legs to the knee, " because

I always ties my garters up above the knee," and, with his foot on " the little stool I always puts 'n on to lace up my boots—I've had 'n ever since my boy was born—I thought I felt somethin' in the heel o' my shoe, and as soon as I pulled 'n off it rattled on the floor. *Wa'n't* that a miracle ? My hair stood bolt upright ! I gropsed an' picked 'n up, and hollered up the stairs, ' I've found 'n !' ' Oh, have ye ?' she says. ' I thought you'd bin an' spent 'n.' " Quickly he was off again to the public-house—Tom Durrant's—and " I says, ' I lost that shillin' once. I'll take good care I don't lose 'n again !' And I chucked 'n up on the counter. Durrant says, ' Oh, did ye lose 'n ?' So then I come back 'ome with my sixpenn'oth o' brandy. But wa'n't it a miracle ? My hair stood reg'lar bolt upright, and I was that *contented !*"

There was much, very much, that I am missing ; but I must not quite pass over the old man's talk on the way to the town this morning. He did not once mention his trouble. All the way it was his ordinary chatter—the chatter of a most vigorous mind, which had never learnt to think of things in groups, but was intensely interested in details.

It began at once, with reference to a cottage—a sort of " week-end " cottage—we were passing, into which, Bettesworth said, new tenants were coming. " How they keep changing !" said I ; and he, " Well enough they may, at the price." " What is it, then ?" " Four pound a month. Furnished, o'

course ; but there en't much there. And," he added,
" I can't see payin' a pound a week for a place to
lay down in."

Next—but what came next had better be omitted
now. It related to the family affairs of a certain
coal-carter, and so led up to discourse of other
carter men who lived in the village. From them,
the transition to the employer of two of them was
easy. He " got the two best carters in the neighbourhood now," said Bettesworth ; but as for horses,
" he en't got a hoss fit to put in a cart, 'cause he
en't never had anybody before as understood anything about 'em. Somebody ought to put the
cruelty inspector on to him, to go to his place and
see. He *did* go, once ; but he " (the horse-owner)
" got wind of it and," as far as could be gathered
from Bettesworth's talk, is suspected of having
" squared " the inspector. But " there's a lot
talkin' about the condition of the hosses down
there," and, indeed, things " down there " seem to
be generally mismanaged. The premises are " a
reg'lar destructive old place " : the carts, " he won't
never have 'em only botched up, an' they be all to
pieces ; " and the harness is treated no better.
" The saddles, they says, the flock 's all in lumps :
sure a hoss's back an' shoulders 'd get sore. That's
where they do's all the work, poor things. When I
had hosses to look after, as soon as I got 'em in I
always looked to their back an' shoulders first.
I'd get a sponge, or a cloth. . . ."

One of the two good carters above mentioned "can trace up a hoss's tail, you know, with straw. There en't one in ten knows how to do that. I've earnt many a shillin' at it." But Bettesworth had known one man who used to earn as much as thirty shillings in a day at this work, at horse-fairs. Him Bettesworth has occasionally helped, I understand; and also, "Old Bill Baldwin—I've sometimes bin down an' done it for him."

Now, I had thought Bill Baldwin knew all that was worth knowing about horses and horse manage-ment; so I asked, surprisedly, "What, can't he do it?"

"He can do the tracin', in a straight run; but he can't tie up. I could do it all: the tails, and the manes too—you've see it. I'd get a bit o' live" (lithe?) "straw . . . 't was when I was a boy-chap, a little bigger 'n that 'n " (whom at the moment we were meeting) "down at Penstead at Farmer Barnes's. I used to be such a one for the hosses; and I could do it, because my fingers was so lissom." (Poor old stubbed, stiff, bent fingers! to think of it!) "And then, I took such a delight in it. And Mrs. Barnes—she was a Burton—she was as proud o' them hosses! Used to get up at four o'clock in the mornin', purpose to see 'em start off. And the harness was all as clean—the brass used to shine as bright as ever any gold is, and she *was* proud. Twenty thousand pound, was the last legacy she had. She was just such another woman to look at as old Miss Keen, what used to live down in the town ; and a better woman never was.

"That's where I got all my scholarship. . . . Well, I could read—a little—but not to understand it. But she—she give me shirts, an' trousers —'cause we wore smock-frocks then—but she give me shirts an' trousers to go to night-school in. Course, I couldn't have had proper clothes without. 'Cause 'twas only thirty shillin's a year besides grub an' lodgin'. . . . And 't wan't no use to talk about runnin' away. I hadn't got no home. Besides, we was hired from Michaelmas to Michaelmas."

We spoke again of various neighbours, and thus drifting on (I am omitting vast quantities) Bettesworth presently told of a recent attempt at starting a village football club, or rather, of the subsequent discussion of the affair at the public-house. An enthusiast there wished to get " as many members as ever they could." " But how be ye goin' to pick 'em for play ?" asked another. " Oh, pick the best." Bettesworth tells me this, adding, " I don't call that fair do's at all. I can't see no justice in that, that one should pay to be a member of a club, purpose for somebody else to have all the play. That's the way they breaks up a club. Break up any club, that would."

September 24.—Word was brought this afternoon (Saturday) that Bettesworth was at the kitchen door, wishing to see me. Of course he has not been to work to-day. I found him standing outside, patient and quiet, until, being asked how things were going, he began to cry, and shook his head, so that I feared something had miscarried and asked, " Why, haven't you got your wife away ?"

" Yes, we got her away, but she was purty near dead when we got her there. The matron shook her head, and said, ' You'll never see her home again alive.' "

There were repetitions and variations of this ; but I, reiterating my assurances that " she had got a lot of strength," and that in fine the old wife would yet live to come home again, quite forgot to observe exactly what Bettesworth said. His distress was too afflicting.

It would take long, too, to tell of his morning in his own words, beginning with the early walk to Moorways for the relieving officer's order, and telling how old chums starting off to work were astonished to see him thus unwontedly on the road, and what they said as he passed them by as if with a renewal of vigour, and how one was " puffed, tryin' to keep up." The long waiting at the office door (the officer had been out in his garden getting up potatoes), and Bettesworth's meditations, " I wish he'd come," and the instructions furnished him as to how to go on—they were all narrated simply, because they happened ; but the touch of grey morning mist which somehow pervaded the talk while I was hearing it could not be reproduced with its words.

The old man was back here soon after eight o'clock, on his way to the town to order the fly which should take his wife to the infirmary. He had had no breakfast. I gave him tea and bread and butter ; but he left the bread and butter—couldn't swallow it, he said. He had had a glass of beer at the Moorways Inn.

He went into the town, and I met him on the road, returning. The fly proprietor had recognized him and behaved kindly. " Got a bit o' trouble then, old gentleman ?" Yes, the fly should be there to the minute.

At noon, to the minute, it arrived, the driver of it being a son of an old neighbour of Bettesworth's. Meanwhile, Bettesworth's niece, " Liz," and a neighbour's wife—a Mrs. Eggar—whom he spoke of as " Kate," were there trying to dress the old woman—and failing. They got her stockings on, but no boots ; a petticoat or so, but no bodice with sleeves ; and for that much they had to struggle, even calling on Bettesworth to come upstairs and help them. Then the fly came, " and all she kep' sayin' was, ' Leave me to die at home. I wants to die at home ';" and she fought and would not be moved.

To get her downstairs the help of two men besides the driver was enlisted, Kate's husband being one of them. By a kindly policy, Bettesworth himself was sent to hold the horse (" 'cause he wanted to start off "), in order that the sight of her husband might not increase the poor old woman's reluctance; and so they carried her downstairs, "bodily," he said, meaning, I suppose, that she did not support herself at all.

The doctor had advised, and the neighbours too, that Bettesworth himself should not accompany his wife. But now the niece Liz, being unwell, was afraid to be alone with what looked a dying woman, and at the last moment Bettesworth jumped into the cab. As it started, the old woman's head fell back, her mouth dropped open. A pause was made at the public-house, to get brandy for her, which, however, she could not, or would not, take. Gin was tried, and she just touched it. Liz took the brandy; Bettesworth and the driver shared a pint of beer; then they drove off again. Once, on the way, Liz said, "Uncle, she's gone! Hadn't ye better stop the fly?" But he put his head down against her cheek, and found that she was still living; and so they came to the outer entrance of the infirmary. Further than that Bettesworth was dissuaded from going: it was not well that his wife should be agitated by the sight of him at the very gates; and accordingly he came away.

So he is alone in his cottage, and may rest if he can. He is to have meals at his niece's, but will sleep at home. The kindness is touching to him, not alone of the nephew and niece, but of his neighbours generally. "Kate said she'd ha' went down in the fly, if I'd ha' let her know in time. An' she'd wash for me—if I'd take anything I wanted along to her Monday or Tuesday, she'd wash it. I says to her, ' You be the first friend I got, Kate.' Well, Liz had told me she *couldn't* undertake it. She was forced to get somebody to do her own, and the doctor come to see her one day expectin' to find her in bed, and she was gettin' the dinner. There's Jack " (her husband) " and four boys. . . . So Kate's goin' to do the washin' for me, and she and her daughter's goin' one day to give the place a scrub out. More'n that she *can't* do—with eight little 'uns, and then look at the washin' !" For Mrs. Eggar takes in washing, to eke out her husband's fifteen or sixteen shillings a week.

Besides these friends, there are those who are willing to find the old man a home, " if anything should happen to the old gal." " 'Tis a sort o' comfortin'," he says, " to think what good neigh-bours I got ;" but he hopes not to break up his home yet. In an unconscious symbolism of his affection for all the home things he bought this afternoon a pennyworth of milk for the cat, who came running to meet him on his return to the lonely cottage, and then ran upstairs " to see if the old gal was there."

He will keep his home together if he may, with warm feelings towards his neighbours. " But as for these up here," and he points contemptuously in the direction of the old woman's relatives, " I dunno if they knows she's gone, and I shan't trouble to tell 'em."

[So I wrote on the Saturday evening. Four clear days pass, without any note about Bettesworth; then on the following Thursday the narrative is reopened. It is given here, unaltered.]

September 29.—Bettesworth's wife died at the workhouse infirmary, about midnight of the 27th.

She had been unconscious since her admission, and spoke only twice. Once she said, " Bring my little box upstairs off the dresser, Fred ;" the other time it was, " Fred, have ye wound up the clock ?" These things were reported to him by the nurse, when he reached the infirmary on Tuesday afternoon—the usual afternoon for the admission of visitors.

He had gone down then, with his niece Liz, to see the old lady. And of course I heard the details of the expedition when he came back. Stopping at a greengrocer's in the town, he bought two ripe pears, at three halfpence each. " Did ye ever hear tell o' such a price for a pear ? What 'd that be for a bushel ? Why, 't'd come to a pound ! But I said, 'I'll ha' the best.' Then I bought her some sponge-cakes at the confectioner's ;" and with these delicacies he went to her.

She could not touch them. She lay with her eyes open, but unconscious even of the flies, which he, sitting beside, kept fanning from her face. There was no recognition of him ; so he asked which was " her locker," proposing to leave the pears and sponge-cakes there for her, on the chance of her being able to enjoy them later. " Poor old lady, she'll never want 'em," the nurse said ; and he replied, " Now I've brought 'em here I shan't take 'em back. Give 'em to some other poor soul that can fancy 'em."

They gave him permission to stay as long as he liked ; but, said he, " I bid there an hour an' a quarter, an' then I couldn't bide no longer. What was the use, sir ? She didn't know me." So at last he came away, provided with a free pass, " to go in at any hour o' the day or night he mind to."

Yesterday (Wednesday) morning he was about his work here when a letter was brought to him. It contained only a formal notice that " Lucy Bettesworth was lying dangerously ill, and desired to see him." Probably the notice was mercifully designed to prepare him for the worse news it might have told, but of course he did not know it, even if that was the case. He left here at once, to go and see his wife.

Between two and three hours afterwards he was back again. " How is it ?" I asked, guessing how it was. " She's gone, sir "—and then he broke down, sobbing, but only for a minute. He had already ordered the coffin—" a nice box," he called it. The remainder of the day was spent in getting the death certificate and observing other formalities. He had the knell rung, too. Nothing would he neglect that would testify to his respect

for the partner he had lost ; and I think in all this
he was partly animated by a savage resentment
towards her relatives, who had ignored her, and by
a resolved opposition to those who had contemned
his wife while she lived. " Everybody always bin
very good, to *me*," he has said, with significant
emphasis on the last word.

In the evening he had the corpse brought away
to his nephew Jack's. He also slept at Jack's, and
in numerous ways Jack is behaving well to him.
To spare the old man's weariness he spent the evening
in going to see about the insurance money ; and
to-day it is Jack who is getting six other men to
carry the coffin at the funeral on Saturday.

This morning Bettesworth went to the Vicar to
arrange about the funeral. " He spoke very nice
to me," he said. Thence he was sent to the sexton,
near at hand ; and soon he came to me to borrow a
two-foot rule, because the sexton wanted to know
the exact measurements of the coffin before digging
the grave ; " and *don't* let's have any mistakes !"
he had said, for there had been a mistake not so
long ago, a grave having been dug too small for
the coffin.

Knowing Bettesworth's fumbling blindness, and
seeing him nervous, " Can you manage it ?" I asked,
" or would you like me to go over and measure it
for you ?" There was no hesitation : " It *would*
be a kindness, if you don't mind, sir. . . ." I have
but just now returned.

I think I will not record particulars of that visit. If I had not previously known it, I should have known then that Bettesworth is—but there are no fit epithets. Nothing sensational happened, nothing extravagantly emotional. But all that he did and said, so simple and unaffected and necessary, was done as if it were an act of worship. No woman could have been tenderer or more delicate than he, when he drew the sheet back from the dead face, to show me. . . . The coffin itself (because he is so poor and so lonely)—a decent elm coffin—is a kind of symbol, and so a comfort to him, enabling him to testify to his unspoken feelings towards his dead wife.

October 1.—I went to the funeral of Bettesworth's wife this Saturday afternoon. In his decent black clothes and with his grey hair the old man looked very dignified, showing a quiet, unaffected patience.

There were but few people present : four or five relatives besides the bearers and the undertaker and sexton ; while a young woman (Mrs. Porter) with her little boy Tim stood in the background, she carrying a wreath she had made. She is a near neighbour to us, and a very impoverished one, to whom the old man has shown what kindness has been in his power ; while she on many mornings has called him into her cottage at breakfast time, to give him a cup of hot tea.

XXVIII

Shutting his mouth doggedly, Bettesworth went back to his cottage, to live alone there with his cat. There had been some talk of his going into lodgings ; but after all, this was still his home. Should he once give it up, he reasoned, and dispose of his furniture, it would be impossible ever again to form a home of his own, however much he might desire to do so. To live with neighbours might be very well ; yet how if he and they should disagree ? He would have burnt his boats ; he would be unable to resume his independence. Better were it, then, to keep while he still had it a place where he was his own master, and take the risk of being lonely.

For some seven weeks after the wife's funeral there is next to nothing to be told of him. I find that I am unable to remember anything about him for that period, unless it was then—and it could not have been much later—that he renewed some of his household goods, and amongst them his mattress, being visited apparently by a wish to regain the character for cleanliness which had been lost in his wife's time. It must have been then also that he first talked of buying muslin for blinds to his windows. It is further certain that he chatted a great deal about his next-door neighbours—the Norrises, mother and son, upon whose society he was now chiefly dependent ; but of all this not a syllable remains, nor is there any dimmest picture in my memory of what the old man did, or even how he looked, in those seven weeks.

November 22, 1904.—At the end of them, on a raw morning in November, amid our struggles to heave out of the ground a huge shrub we were transplanting, it was remarkable how strong Bettesworth seemed, because of the cunning use he made of every ounce of force in his experienced old muscles. How to lift, and how to support a weight, were things he knew as excellently as some know how to drive a golf-ball. Nor was my theory quite so good as his experience, for showing where our skids and levers should be placed. It was Bettesworth who got them into the serviceable positions.

Something about those skids set us talking of other skidding work, and especially of the extremely tricky business of loading timber on a trolly. " I see a carter once," said Bettesworth, " get three big elm-trees up on to a timber-carriage, with only hisself and the hosses. He put the runnin' chains on and all hisself."

" And *that* takes some doing," I said.

" Yes, a man got to understand the way 'tis done. . . . I never had much hand in timber-cartin' myself ; but this man. . . . 'Twas over there on the Hog's Back, not far from Tongham Station. We all went out for to see 'n do it—'cause 'twas in the dinner-time he come, and we never believed he'd do it single-handed. The farmer says to 'n, ' You'll never get they up by yourself.' ' I dessay I shall,' he says ; and so he did, too. Three great elm-trees upon that one carriage. . . . Well, he had a four-hoss team, so that'll tell ye what 'twas. They *was* some hosses, too. Ordinary farm hosses wouldn't ha' done it. But he only jest had to speak, and you'd see they watchin' him. . . . When he went forward, after he'd got the trees up, to see what sort of a road he'd got for gettin' out, they stood there with their heads stretched out and their ears for'ard. ' Come on,' he says, and *away* they went, *tearin'* away. Left great ruts in the road where the wheels went in—that'll show ye they got something to pull."

We got our shrub a little further, Bettesworth grunting to a heavy lift ; then, in answer to a question :

" No, none o' we helped 'n. We was only gone out to see 'n do it. He never wanted no help. He didn't say much ; only ' Git back,' or ' Git up,' to the hosses. When it come to gettin' the last tree up, on top o' t'other two, I never thought he could ha' done it. But he got 'n up. And he was a oldish man, too : sixty, I dessay he was. But he jest spoke to the hosses. Never used no whip,

'xcept jest to guide 'em. Didn't the old farmer
go on at his own men, too! 'You dam fellers call
yerselves carters,' he says; 'a man like that's
worth a dozen o' you.' Well, they couldn't ha'
done it. A dozen of 'em 'd ha' scrambled about,
an' *then* not done it! Besides, their *hosses* wouldn't.
But this feller—the old farmer says to 'n, 'I never
believed you'd ha' done it.' 'I thought mos' likely
I should,' he says. But he never had much to say."

Sleet showers were falling, and a north wind was
roaring through the fir wood on top of the next hill
while we worked. Dropping into the vernacular,
"I don't want to see no snow," said I. "No,"
responded Bettesworth, "it's too white for me."
"January," I went on, "is plenty soon enough for
snow to think about comin'." "April," he urged.
"Ah well, April," I laughed; and he, "Let it wait till
there's a warm sun to get rid of it 's fast as it comes."

Then he continued, "That rain las' night come
as a reg'lar su'prise to me. I was sittin' indoors by
my fire smokin'—I 'ave got rid o' some baccer
lately—and old Kid went up the garden. He see
my light, and hollered out, 'It don't half rain!' '*Let*
it rain,' I says. I was in there as comfortable . . ."

In the next night but one a little snow fell, enough
to justify our forecast and no more; and then we
had frost, and garden work could hardly go on. I
was meaning to lay turf over a plot of ground where
the shrubs had stood; but the work had to wait:
the frozen turfs could not be unrolled.

Bettesworth did not like the weather. I have told of those steps connecting his cottage with the road. They were slippery now, and the handrail to them was icy when he clutched it, coming down in the dark of the mornings. At the bottom of the steps, before the road is reached, there is a steep path, commonly known as " Granny Fry's." Boys were sliding there after breakfast, and they called out to Bettesworth, " Be you roughed, Master Bettesworth ?" According to his tale, he spoke angrily : " 'Tis *you* ought to be roughed,' I says ; ' you ought to be roughed over the bank. You be old enough to know better.' And so they be, too. They be biggish boys ; and anybody goin' there might easy fall down and break their back—'specially after dark."

When he came back from his dinner, he said, " Somebody 've bin an' qualified old Granny Fry's." How ? " Oh, somebody 've chucked some dirt over where they boys had made it so slippery."

He was obliged to admit, though, that in his own boyhood he had been as careless as any of these. And a few minutes later he was confessing to another boyish fault. In a cottage hard by, little Timothy Porter—a chubby little chap about five years old—was on very friendly terms with old Bettesworth. He had but lately started his schooling, and almost immediately was taken unwell and had to stay at home a week or two. I happened now to ask Bettesworth how little Tim was getting on.

" Oh, he's gettin' all right : goin' to school again

Monday. He've kicked up a rare shine, 'cause they wouldn't let 'n go. I likes 'n for that. I likes to hear of a boy eager for learnin'—not to see 'm make a shine and their mothers have to take 'em three parts o' the way. Not but what I wanted makin' when I was a nipper. Many's a time I've clucked up to a tree jest this side o' Cowley Bridge, and that old 'oman " (I don't know what old woman) " come out an' drive me. There wa'n't no school then nearer 'n Lyons's—where Smith the wheelwright lives now. He used to travel with tea, and I dessay half a dozen of us 'd come to his school from Cowley Bridge. We'd start off an' say we wouldn't go to school ; but we *'ad* to."

The frost, had it continued, would very soon have been calamitous to the working people. As it was, I saw bricklayers—good men known to me, and neighbours, too—standing idle in the town, at the street corners. And Bettesworth said,

" Some o' the shop-keepers down in the town begun to cry out about it. They missed the Poor Man. And I heared the landlord down 'ere at the Swan say he was several pounds out o' pocket by it."

December 2, 1904.—Fortunately it was not to last. The men got to work again ; our gardening tasks could go forward. My notebook has this entry for the 2nd of December :

" Laying turf this afternoon, in wonderful mild dry weather."

XXIX

THE thought came to me one of those afternoons,
Was it I, or was it Bettesworth, who was growing
dull ? It might well have been myself ; for at the
unaccustomed labour of turf-laying, in weather
that had turned mild and relaxing, mind no less
than body was aware of fatigue, and perhaps on
that account the old man's talk seemed less vivid
than usual, less deserving of remembrance. At
the same time I could not help speculating whether
the livelier interests of his conversation might not
be almost over. Had he much more to tell ? Or
had I heard it practically all ?

At this turf-laying the parts were reversed now.
Time had been when, at similar employments, I
was the helper or onlooker ; but now Bettesworth's
sight was so bad that I could no longer leave him
to unroll two turfs side by side and make their
edges fit. I had to be down on the ground with
him, or instead of him.

And yet he would not accept criticism. Did I
say, " Shove that end up a little tighter," he would
rejoin, " That's jest what I was a-goin' to do."
Or, to my comment, " That isn't a first-rate fit just

there," "No, sir," he would admit, "I was only jest layin' it so ontil," etc., etc. "You'll see that'll go down all right. That'll go down all right. . . . Yes, that'll go down all right." And he would fumble unserviceably, while the sentence trailed away into inaudible reiterations. Still, it was a rich, creamy, very quiet and pleasing old voice that spoke.

The habit of repeating his own words was growing upon the old man fast since his wife's death ; and it irritated me at times, filling up the gaps and interrupting my share of the conversation. Instead of listening to me, he mumbled on, dreamily. Now and again, however, he appeared to become aware of the habit. More than once, after relating something he had said at home, he added in explanation, "I was talkin' to *myself*, you know. I en't got nobody else to talk *to*." This was almost the only indication he allowed me to see of that loneliness which others assured me he was feeling. Did he, I wonder, fear that if I knew of it I should be urging him to give up his cottage ? For whatever reason, he made no confidant of me on that point. Once, indeed, there was mention of sitting indoors one evening by his fire, "till he couldn't sit no longer," but got up and walked up and down his garden, driven by crowding thoughts. Another time, "All sorts o' things keeps comin' into my mind now," he said. And these were the utmost complainings to which he condescended, in my hearing.

It was very fortunate that he had excellent neighbours in old Mrs. Norris (old Nanny, he called her) and her son, known as Kid, Kiddy, or Kidder. While stooping over our turfs I heard many tiny details of Bettesworth's kindly relations with these good people; and, as pleasantly as oddly, between them and myself a sort of friendship grew up, through the old man's mediation. We seldom met; we knew little of one another save what he told us; but he must have gone home and talked to them of me, just as he came here and told me about them; and thus, while I was learning to like them cordially, I think they were learning to like me, and it seemed to stamp with the seal of genuineness my intercourse with Bettesworth himself. But it was truly queer. Old Nanny Norris—the skinny old woman with the strange Mongolian or Tartar face and eyes—took to stopping for a chat, if we met on the road. In the town once, where I stood talking with some one else, she, coming up from behind me, could not pass on without looking round, nodding joyfully and grimacing her countenance—the countenance of an eastern image—into a jolly smile. She wore a Paisley shawl, and a little bonnet gay with russet and pink.

Bettesworth was distressed only by Nanny's deafness. "*En't* that a denial to anybody!" he exclaimed feelingly. "There, I can't talk to her. I always did hate talkin' to anybody deaf. Everybody can hear what you got to say, and if 't en't

nothing, still you don't want everybody to hear it. . . .
Old Kid *breaks* out at her sometimes : ' Gaw' dangy !
I'll *make* ye hear !' Every now an' then I laughs
to myself to hear 'n, sittin' in there by myself.''

He handed me another turf, and continued :
" 'Tis a good thing for she that old Kidder en't
never got married. But she slaves about for 'n ;
nobody *could*n't do no more for 'n than she do.
When I got home to dinner she come runnin' round.
She'd jest bin to pay all his clubs for 'n. He belongs
to three clubs : two slate clubs an' the Foresters.''

" He doesn't mean to be in any trouble if he's
ill," I grumbled up from the turf.

" Not he. Thirty-two shillin's a week he'll get,
if he's laid up. There's Alf '' (one of his half-brothers)
" and him—rare schemin' fellers they be, no mistake.'' Particulars followed about this family of
strong brothers ; but, in fine, " Kidder 've always
bin the darlin'. He's the youngest.''

Fearless, black-bearded strong man that he is,
though very quiet, even silky and soft in his ordinary
demeanour, it was laughable to think of Kid Norris
as a " darling.'' Along with Alf he was at work
all through the summer on the new railway near
Bordon Camp, they two being experts and earning
a halfpenny an hour more than the common navvy.
Their way was to leave home at four in the morning and walk the eight miles to their work. In the
evening the 7 p.m. up-train brought them within a
mile and a half of this village. Once or twice they

overtook me, making their way homewards, long-striding; and sometimes they would work an hour or two after that in their gardens, in the summer twilight.

When the weather worsened and the days short-ened, Kid threw up his railway-work, and took a job at digging sea-kale for a large grower. The fields were scattered about the district; some of them within two miles, and the remotest not more than three, from his home. He was the leading man of a gang of labourers; and at my paltry turf-laying I heard of his work, which, it appears, was new to him. " They had to save," he said (and the fact was interesting to old Bettesworth), " jest the parts he should ha' throwed away. . . . It did take some heavin': they stamms was gone down like tree-roots," especially down there in such-and-such a field. " Up here above Barlow's Mill 'twan't half the trouble." The master said to Kid, " You no call to slack. I got plenty o' trenchin' you can go on at, when the kale's up." Then said Kid to his gang, " Some o' you chaps 'll have to move about a bit quicker, if you're goin' trenchin' 'long o' me." He sent one of them packing—a neigh-bour from this village, too. " Not a bad chap to work, so far as that goes, but too stiff, somehow," Bettesworth said, evidently knowing the man's style.

Towards the end of one afternoon, " It looks comin' up rainy," Bettesworth observed, " but old

Kid wants it frosty. Where he is now—trenchin'
up there at Waterman's—he says this rain makes
it so heavy ; it comes up on they spuds jest as much
as ever a man can lift."

"And that's not a little," said I ; " Kid's a strong
man."

"Well—he's jest the age ; jest on forty. I says
to 'n, ' Some of 'em 'd go for you, if they knowed
you was wantin' frost.' He laughed. "We all
speaks for ourselves, don't we ?' he says."

Then Bettesworth added, " There, I never could
have a better neighbour 'n he is. Always jest the
same. He looks out for me, too."

I grieve that I have forgotten the particular instance of looking out : it was a case of Kid's mother
telling him that she was short of some commodity
or other—hot water, perhaps, for tea ; upon which
Kid said, " Well, see there's some left for old
Freddy." On another occasion, " I had," Bettesworth remarked, " my favourite dish for supper last
night—pig's chiddlins," and he owed the treat to
his neighbours. " They'd killed their pig, and old
Nanny brought me in a nice hot plateful. I *did*
enjoy 'em : they was so soft an' nice. There's
nothin' I be more fond of, if I knows who cleaned
'em. But I en't tasted any since I give up keepin'
pigs myself."

I could not spare many hours a day for it, so that
our turfing work dragged out wearisomely ; but

throughout it Bettesworth's conversation maintained the same homely inconspicuous character. Once it was about the celery in the garden : " 'Tis the nicest celery I ever had—so crisp, an' so well-bleached. I've had two sticks." (He had been told to help himself.) " Last night I put some in a saucepan an' boiled it up; an' then a little pepper an' salt and a nice bit o' butter." He has no teeth now for eating it uncooked ; " or else at one time I could," he assured me.

One after another his simple domestic arrangements were talked over. He made no fire at home in the morning ; Nanny gave him a cup of tea ; and so he saved coal, which he had been buying from one of the village shops, half a hundredweight at a time. But the price was exorbitant, and Bettesworth had found a way of buying for fourpence the hundredweight cheaper. And " fo'pence—that's a lot. Well, there's the price of a loaf *soon* saved." " And a loaf," I put in, " lasts you . . . ?" " Lasts me a long time, and *then* I gives the crusts and odd bits to Kid for his pig. . . . One way and another I makes it all up to 'em."

Of a well-to-do neighbour, " He don't shake off that lumbago in his back yet, so he says. . . . Ah, he have bin a strong man. So he ought to be, the way he eats. His sister was sayin' only t'other day how every mornin' he'll eat as big a plateful o' fat bacon as she puts before 'n."

A difficulty with a turf which was cut too thick at

one corner made a queer diversion. The old man
was wearing new boots, and already I knew how
he had bargained for them at Wilby's shop, getting
a pair of cork socks, besides laces and dubbin,
thrown in for his money. And now, this little
corner of grass obstinately sticking up, " Let's see
what Mr. Wilby 'll do for 'n," said Bettesworth,
and he stamped his new boot down hard and the
thickened sod yielded. " Do they hurt you at all ?"
I asked then. " No," he said, " not no more'n
you may expect. New boots always draws your
feet a bit. That one wrung my foot a little yest'-
day. When I got home, 'fore ever I lit my candle,
I'd unlaced 'n and fetched 'n off. I flung 'n down.
But I be very well pleased with 'em. 'Tis jest across
here by the seam where they hurts. . . . No, I
en't *laced* 'em tight. I don't hold with that, for
new boots. Of course they en't leather ; can't be
for the money. When you've paid for the makin'
what is there left for leather, out of five-and-six-
pence ? No, they *can't* be leather. . . .

" Little Tim " (Bettesworth's five-year-old chum)
"jest got some new uns, with nails in 'em. Nex'
pair he has, he says, he's goin' to have 'em big, with
big nails, jest like his father's. ' You ben't man
enough yet, Tim,' I says. But he got some little
gaiters too. ' Now I be ready,' he says, ' if it snows
or anything.' "

As a rule we endured in silence the minor discomforts incidental to work like ours, in a raw

winter air. But there were exceptions, as when we agreed in hating to handle the tools with our hands so caked over with the black earth. To me, indeed, the spade felt as if covered with sand-paper, so that sometimes it was less painful to use fingers, although of course they did but get the more thickly encrusted with soil by that device. This state of our hands was the cause of another small distress : one could not touch a pocket-hand-kerchief. And of this also we spoke, once, when I all but laughed aloud at what Bettesworth said.

It began with his testily remarking, " My nose is more plag' than enough !" There was, indeed, and had been for a long time, a glistening drop at the end of it.

My own was in like case, no pocket-handkerchief being available. So I said, " Mine would be all right in a second, if I could only get to wipe it."

Then said Bettesworth, innocently (for he had no suspicion how funny his reply was), " Ah, but that's what you can't do, without makin' your face all dirty."

With our noses distilling dew-drops, and our hands gloved-over with mud and aching with cold, we may be pardoned, I hope, for complaining some-times of the weather. I believe that really we liked it ; for down there so close to the grass and the soil we were entering into intimacies like theirs, with the cool winter air ; but our enjoyment was sub-conscious, whereas consciously we criticized and were not too well pleased. After one interval of grumbling, I tried to cheer up, with the suggestion, "We must be thankful it isn't so cold as yesterday." Bettesworth, however, was not to be so easily appeased, but replied, "We don't feel it down here, where 'tis so sheltered, but depend upon it, 'tis purty cold down the road, when you gets into the wind. I met old Steve when I was comin' back from dinner. 'How d'ye get on up there?' I says." (*Up there* is on the ridge of the hill, where Steve works in a garden.) " ' 'Tis purty peaky up there,' he says. I'll lay it is, too. I shouldn't think there's anybody got a much colder job than he have. 'Pend upon it, he *do* feel it."

"I was afraid on Sunday we were in for more snow."

"Ah, so was I. I found my old hard broom. Stacked in he was, behind a lot o' peasticks an' clutter. I'd missed 'n for a long time—ever since our young Dave" (his nephew's son) "come to clear up the garden for me. He'd pulled up the peasticks an' put 'em in the old shed—well, I'd told 'n to. And I *fancied* that's where the broom must be. So Sunday I fetched 'em all out of it and got 'n out and took 'n indoors with the shovel, in case any snow *should* come.

"Little Dave's gone on 'long o' George Bryant, up at Powell's. Handy little chap, he is. . . ."

In this way, so long as the turf-laying lasted,

Bettesworth's talk went drivelling on. Was he really getting dull ? I had begun by fancying so ; and yet as I listened to him, perhaps myself benumbed a little by the cold open air, something rather new to me—a quality in the old man's conversation more intrinsically pleasing than I had previously known—began to make its subtle appeal. Half unawares it came home to me, like the contact of the garden mould, and the smell of the earth, and the silent saturation of the cold air. You could hardly call it thought—the quality in this simple prattling. Our hands touching the turfs had no thought either ; but they were alive for all that ; and of such a nature was the life in Bettesworth's brain, in its simple touch upon the circumstances of his existence. The fretful echoes men call opinions did not sound in it ; clamour of the daily press did not disturb its quiet ; it was no bubble puffed out by learning, nor indeed had it any of the gracefulness which some mental life takes from poetry and art ; but it was still a genuine and strong elemental life of the human brain that during those days was my companion. It seemed as if something very real, as if the true sound of the life of the village, had at last reached my dull senses.

The themes might be trivial, yet the talk was not ignoble. The rippling comments upon their affairs, which swing in perpetual ebb and flow amidst the labouring people, lead them perhaps no farther ; and yet, should they not be said ? Could they be dispensed with ? Are they not an integral part of life ? Let me quote another fragment :

" After that rain yesterday, old Kid says, up in that clay at Waterman's when you takes your spud out o' the ground you can't see whether 'tis a spud or a board. And it's enough to break your shoulders all to pieces. He *was* tired last night, he says."

Well—to me the observation justifies itself, and I like it for its own sake. It touched me with an elusive vitality of its own, for which after our turf-laying I began generally to listen in Bettesworth's talk, and which nowadays I hear in that of his neighbours, as when old Nanny Norris meets me on the road and stops for a gossip.

XXX

CHRISTMAS was approaching near—was "buckin'
up," as Bettesworth quaintly phrased it ; and that
it contributed to the melancholy of his existence
will easily be understood. It is nowhere mentioned
in my book, but a remorse was beginning to haunt
him, for having let his wife be taken away to the
infirmary, to die there. "I done it for the best,
poor old dear," I remember his saying several
times ; "but it hurts me to think I let her go." In
the long evenings before Christmas, alone in his
cottage and unable to pass time by reading, he had
too much time for brooding over his loss.

The nights as well as the evenings were probably
too long for him, and I make no question that his
happiest hours were those he spent at work, when he
could forget himself and still talk cheerfully. Thus
there is quite a gleam of cheerfulness in the following instructive fragment, of the 17th of December.

December 17, 1904.—" When the wind blowed up
in the night I thought 'twas rain. I got out an'
went to the winder—law! 'twas dark! But the
winder an' all seemed as dry !"

" What time was that ?"

" I *dunno*, sir."

" The moon must have been down ?"

" Yes, the moon was down."

" Then it must have been getting on for morning."

" I dunno. . . . But I'd smoked two pipes o' baccer before Kid called me. I *have* smoked some baccer since I bin livin' there alone. The last half-pound I had is purty well all gone ; and 'tent the day for another lot afore Monday." (This was Saturday.) " But I shall ha' to get me some more to-night. Why, that's quarter of a pound a week !

" Old Kid says, ' Don't it make ye *dry ?*' this smoking. °No,' I says, ' that " (namely, to drink) "en't no good.' Kid don't smoke. Reg'lar old-fashioned card, he is. 'Ten't many *young* men you'll see like 'n. But he's as reg'lar in his habits as a old married man. Ay, and he's as good, too. 'T least, he's as good to me. So they both be."

" Isn't he to his mother ?"

" Ah ! an' she to him. No woman couldn't look after a baby better. Every night as soon as he's home and ready to sit down, there's his supper on the table. ' Supper's ready, Kid,' she says. ' So's yourn too, Freddy,' she says to me. ' Ah,' I says, ' Wait a bit, Nanny, till my kettle's boilin'.' Because I always has tea along o' my supper. Kid, he don't have his till after ; but I likes mine with my supper. So I tells her to put it in the oven till I'm ready. Cert'nly, my little kettle don't take long to boil.

But I shall ha' to get me quarter of a ton o' coal, soon as Chris'mas is over."

A faint memory, for which I have had to grope, restores a mention by Bettesworth of three glasses of grog to which he treated Kid Norris and himself and old Nanny. Perhaps this was at Christmas time ; at any rate I am not aware that the season was brightened for him by any other celebration. It passed, and the New Year came in, and still he was living the same broken life, yet telling rather of the few pleasures it contained than of its desolation. I am sure he did not mean to let me know that he was being constantly reminded of his wife, yet the next conversation gives reason to suppose that such was the case.

January 10, 1905.—He had spent two vigorous days in cutting down and sawing into logs an old plum-tree, and grubbing out its roots. That was a job which he might still be left to do without supervision ; but I had to assist, when it came to planting a young tree in the vacant space. A pear-tree, this new one was; and he asked, " Was it a ' William ' pear ?" It was a *Doyenne du Comice,* I said. His shrug showed that he did not get hold of the name at all, and I fancied him a little contemptuous of such outlandishness ; so I added that I had seen some of the pears in a fruiterer's window, and wished to grow the like for myself.

" Ah "—the suggestion was enough. He wondered if that was the sort he had bought for his
" poor old gal " ; and then he told again how he
had given three halfpence apiece for pears to take
to her at the infirmary, and would have given
sixpence rather than go without them. " And
then the poor old gal never tasted 'em. . . . She
wa'n't up there long. . . . That Blackman what
drove the fly that took her ast me about her t'other
day. He didn't know " (that she was dead), " or he
said he didn't. ' She was only up there three days,'
I said. Since then, he've took old Mrs. Cook—
Jerry's mother. . . . Jerry kep' her as long as he
could, but 't last she 'ad to go. Yes, he stuck to
'er as long as he could, Jerry did. None o' the
others didn't, ye see. . . . But he had money : there
was two hunderd pound, so they said, when his
wife's mother died, and nobody couldn't make out
what become of it exactly. But Jerry had some,
an' purty soon got rid of it. Purty near killed 'n.
'Fore he'd done with it he couldn't stoop to tie up
his shoelaces, he was got that bloaty. . . . I reckon
he bides down there by hisself, now."

In that he resembled Bettesworth, then. I
asked if Jerry had no wife.

" She died about two year ago. Poor thing—
she'd bin through *every*thing ; bin to hospitals and
all." It was one hop-picking, about nine years
ago, and just after she was married, that " they
was larkin' about—jest havin' a bit o' fun, ye know :

there wasn't no spite in it—and one of 'em swished her right across the eye with a hop-bine. . . . I s'pose 'twas something frightful, afore she died : 't had eat right into her head."

The old man pondered over the horror, then continued, " There must be something poisonous about hop-bine. Same as with a ear o' corn. How many you sees have lost an eye by an ear o' corn swishin' into it ! En't you ever heard of it ? *I*'ve knowed it, many's a time. There was " (I forget whom he named)—" it jest flicked 'n across the sight, and he went purty near mad wi' the pain of it. Oats is the worst. Well, as you knows, oats is so thin, 't'll stick to the eyeball purty near like paper. . . . But I'd sooner cut oats than any other ; it cuts so sweet. That was always my favourite corn to cut. Cert'nly I en't never had no accident with it. Barley cuts sweet, but 't en't like oats."

The next day's chatter gives one more touch to the picture of Bettesworth's pleasant intercourse with his neighbours at this period. Apropos of nothing at all the old man began his story.

January 11, 1905.—" When I went home last night I see my door was open ; but I never went in, because you knows I had to go on further to take that note for you. But after I'd done that I come back same way, and then I see a light in the winder. ' Hullo !' I says to myself. ' What's up now, then ?'

So I pushed on ; and when I got indoors there was old Nanny—she'd made up my fire an' biled my kettle, an' was gettin' my dinner ready. Ah, an' she'd bin upstairs, too : she'd scrubbed it out—all the rooms ; and she says, ' I've made yer bed too, Fred. . . .' But I give her a shillin', so she can't go about sayin' she done all this for me for nothin'. *She* en't got nothin' to complain of. Besides, 't wants a scrub out now an' again. Not as 'twas anyways *dirty*, 'cause *t'en't*. She said so herself. ' If it's a fine day to-morrer, Fred, I'll come an' scrub your floors out for ye : 't'll do 'em good. Not as they be *dirty*,' she says ; ' I see 'em myself, so I knows. . . .' Well, so she did. She come in last week, and hung my new curtains. . . . I've had new curtains " (little muslin blinds) " to the winders, upstairs an' down—I bought 'em week afore last—and ol' Nan 've made 'em an' put 'em up for me. No mistake she is a one to work ! Works as hard as any young gal—and she between seventy an' eighty."

I said, " Yes, she's one of the right sort, is Nanny."

" One o' the right sort for me. 'Tis to be hoped nothin' 'll ever happen to *she* !"

Such were the makeshift, yet not altogether unhappy domestic, conditions by which Bettesworth was enabled for a little while to maintain his independence, and carry on the obstinate and now hopeless struggle to earn a living for himself. He was a man with work to do, and with the will to do it, as yet. On this same eleventh of January we may picture him forming one of a curious group of the working men of the parish, who gathered in a rainy dawn on a high piece of the road, and looked apprehensively at the weather. " I thought," Bettesworth told me afterwards, " we was in for a reg'lar wild day ; and so did a good many more. The men didn't like startin'. . . . I come out to the cross-roads 'long of old Kid, and he said he didn't hardly know what to think about it. And while we stood there, Ben Fowler come along. ' I don't hardly know what to make of it,' he says. And then some more come. There was a reg'lar gang of 'em ; didn't like to go away. Well, a man don't *like* to set off for a day's work an' get wet through afore he begins."

January 17.—Not many more days of work, however, were to be added to the tale of Bettesworth's laborious years. On the 17th of January it appears that he was still going on, for old Nanny seen at an unaccustomed hour on the road, spoke of him as getting about with difficulty. This is what she said, in her gruff, quick, scolding voice : " I couldn't git to the town fust thing, 'twas so slippery. Bettesworth said he couldn't git down our steps this mornin', so I bin chuckin' sand over 'em. Don't want ol' Freddy to break his leg. . . . All up there by Granny Fry's the childern gets slidin,' an' makes it ten times wuss than what 'twas afore, an' the more you says to 'm the wuss they be."

With this last glimpse of him fumbling painfully on the slippery pathway, we finish our acquaintance with Bettesworth's working life.

XXXI

January 22, 1905.—The 22nd of January was the
date, as nearly as I can make out now, of Bettesworth's being seized by another of his bronchial
colds, from which he had hitherto been tolerably
free this winter. An influenza attacking myself
about the same time prevented me from going out
to see how he fared, and for about ten days I know
only that he did not come to work. Then, on the
3rd of February, leaning heavily on his stick and
looking white and feeble, he managed to get this
far to report himself. It would take over long to
tell how he sat by the kitchen fire that day and
discussed sundry affairs of the village. For himself, he was rapidly getting well, and hoped to be
back at work in a few days. I surmise that he had
been lonely. Kid Norris had not come near him,
but had been audible through the partition wall,
asking his deaf mother " How old Freddy was ?"
Old Nanny herself had an extremely bad cold.

February 8.—A few more days pass ; and then on
February the 8th there is the following brief entry
in my note-book :

" Bettesworth started work again yesterday. He planted some shallots, and even while I watched him smoothing the earth over them, he raked out two which, failing to see, he trod upon and left on the ground."

And that was Bettesworth's last day's work. He never again after that day put hand to tool, and probably some suspicion that the end had at length come to the usefulness of his life prompted me the next morning to make that entry in my book.

On that day he had professed to be fairly well, and so he seemed. He mentioned, however, when I asked if Kid Norris had yet been to see him, that the kindness of the Norrises had " fell away very much. Very much, it have. I en't *told* nobody, but. . . ." He talked of giving up his cottage and accepting an offer to lodge with George Bryant. This young labourer, who has been spoken of before, was now and to the end a stanch friend and admirer of Bettesworth. With him Bettesworth fancied he would be comfortable, and I thought so too, and encouraged him in the project, for the old man's illness had shown that it was not right for him to live alone.

But the proposal came too late. On the following morning (the 8th : a Tuesday) no Bettesworth appeared ; but about nine o'clock a messenger, who was on the way to fetch a doctor, called to say that Bettesworth was very ill ; and then I remembered that on the previous afternoon he had spoken of having been shivering all through his dinner-hour.

It was a wet day : the influenza had barely left me, and I dared not go out to visit Bettesworth. Towards evening, as there had been no news of him, a member of my family started out across the valley to make inquiries, and had not long been gone, when one of his neighbours arrived here. It was Mrs. Eggar—" Kate," as he called her : the same good helpful woman who had volunteered to do his washing when his wife was ill, and had despatched the messenger for a doctor this morning. On this evening she had stepped into the gap again. Her errand was to urge that Bettesworth should be sent off at once to the infirmary, and to persuade me to write to the relieving officer asking him to take the necessary action. Her daughter, she said, would carry my letter to him in the morning, and would bring back any message or instructions he might send.

From her account of him it was evident that Bettesworth was in a critical state. He ought not to be left alone for the approaching night ; but the question was, who would sit up with him ? As it was out of my own power to do that, and as the old man's life might depend on its being done, my duty was clear enough : I could make it worth somebody's while to undertake the watching ; and accordingly I made the offer. The woman hesitated, thinking of her family and her laundry work, and of her husband's toilsome days too ; and then, seeing that with all their toil they were very poor (she told me much about her circumstances afterwards), she finally decided that she and her husband would see Bettesworth through the night. Her husband had work three or four miles away, and was leaving home at four in the morning : she herself had a young baby at the time ; but, says my note-book, " they did it."

And on the following morning, as we had arranged, their daughter went that weary journey to the relieving officer, and brought back to me by ten o'clock his order for the medical officer's attendance. It seemed that the old pitiful routine we had been through several times before was to be entered upon once more ; but to expedite matters I enclosed the order for attendance in a note of my own to the doctor ; and the girl started off with it to the town, to add another three miles to the five or six she had already walked that morning.

That, one would have supposed, should have almost ended the trouble ; but though a man be dying it is not easy, under the existing Poor Law, to get him that help which the ratepayers provide, for the machinery is cumbersome, and the people who should profit by it do not appreciate its intricacies, or know how to make it work smoothly. In the present instance much trouble would have been saved, if Bettesworth's neighbours had known enough to correct an oversight of the doctor's.

There was no delay on his side ; but unfortunately it was the *locum tenens* again who called ; and he contented himself with giving his verbal assent to Bettesworth's going to the infirmary. That, of course, was useless ; but the women attending Bettesworth did not know it. On the contrary, they supposed that the formal certificate could be dispensed with, and that a note from myself would satisfy the relieving officer. A message from them reached me, begging me to write such a note, which, they said, Bettesworth's nephew would take over to Moorway's in the evening.

Of course the suggestion was utterly futile. The relieving officer could not recognize a request from me as an order, and an attempt to make him do so, if it effected nothing worse, would certainly delay Bettesworth's removal for yet another day, although, as it was, the unhappy old man must be left a second night in the care of his ignorant if well-meaning neighbours. But worse might easily follow the sending of Bettesworth's nephew for a long walk on such a fool's errand. Strong passionate man that he was, it was more than likely that he would quarrel with the officer ; and to applicants for relief a relieving officer is an autocrat with whom it is not well to quarrel. These considerations, duly weighed, persuaded me not to do what I was asked ; but I sent the messenger back with the request that Bettesworth's nephew should call upon me.

He came in the evening : a black-haired powerful builder's-labourer, tired with his day's work, but prepared to be sent on a five-mile walk. As we discussed Bettesworth's condition, and the desirability of getting him to the infirmary, the man's tone jarred a little. He said, " It's the best place for him. But it strikes me he'll never come home again." A feeling passed over me that a wish was father to this thought : that Jack Bettesworth was not eager for the responsibility which would rest upon him, if his uncle should come home. After events seem to prove that I wronged the man : on this occasion I was chiefly eager to secure his help. Almost apologetically I said, " It makes a lot of running about." " Well, can't 'elp it," was the laconic answer. We did help it to some extent, however, by sending him, not to the relieving officer, which would have cost another five miles, but to the doctor, at the expense of no more than three. The nephew was to get the doctor's certificate, and post it in the town to the relieving officer ; and for this purpose he was furnished with a stamped and addressed envelope, in which was enclosed a letter to the relieving officer, begging him to attend to the case on his way through the village in the morning. It was the best we could do. Should all go well, not more than ten or twelve miles of walking (I omit the carrying of messages to and from me) and not more than two days of waiting would have sufficed for getting Bettesworth the help of which he was officially certified to be in need.

February 9, 1905.—And all did go well. On Thursday morning, the 9th of February, I went to Bettesworth's cottage, and found preparations in progress for his going away. There was more than preparation. With all their kindliness, it must be said of the labouring people that they want tact. Bettesworth's poor home had become a sort of show, in its small squalid fashion. The door stood wide open ; there were half a dozen people in the living-room, where the old man had of late shut himself in with his loneliness and his independence ; and upstairs in his bed he must have been aware of the nakedness of the place now displayed. The unswept hearth and the extinct fire were pitiful to see ; yet there stood women and children, seeing them. Mrs. Eggar (" Kate ") had a good right to be there. She had sat up a second night, and, albeit sleepy-eyed and untidy, there was helpfulness in her large buxom presence. Perhaps there were reasons too for her daughter's being there with the baby. Another woman, tall, grave, and sympathetic of aspect, had brought two more children ; and she told me that upstairs Jack Bettesworth's wife Liz was washing the old man. Liz, by the way, was prepared to go with him on his journey.

I went up into the little square-windowed dirty bedroom and saw him. He was inclined to cry at the prospect of shutting up his home ; but a little talk about my garden — perhaps dearer to him now than even his home was — brightened him up. It pleased him to learn that some early peas had been sown. In what part ? he wanted to know. And being told, " Ah," he said, " and there's another place where peas 'd do well : up there under George Bryant's hedge." When I left, it was with a promise to go and see him in the infirmary on the next visiting day. Going out I saw old Nanny Norris at her door, observant of all that went on, but unserviceably deaf. She was wearing her bonnet and black shawl, looked ill, and complained of cough and of pains across her shoulders. I think there were two or three other women standing near. They were probably waiting to see Bettesworth removed, as he duly was, at mid-day.

XXXII

February 10.—The day after his departure a rather annoying circumstance came to light. The monthly contribution to the club was found to be a whole year in arrear. As the sum was but threepence a month, so that even now only three shillings were due, it seemed a little too bad of Bettesworth to have neglected the payments which at least secured him a doctor's attendance and at his death would produce four pounds for funeral expenses. Perhaps, however, he was not so much to blame as appeared ; at any rate, the manner by which we learnt of his carelessness offers to the imagination the material for an affecting picture of the old man on his sick-bed. It was Mrs. Eggar who, in some trouble for him, brought his club-membership card to me, and told how he had asked her to find it. On the eve of his departure he had taken her into his confidence, spoken of the possibility that he might be going away only to die, and desired, in that event, to be brought home from the infirmary and buried decently, " same as his wife," with this sum which the club would pay. Of course the money for the arrears had to be found, and Mrs.

Eggar undertook to pay it to the club secretary on
the next day, when she went to the town to do
her Saturday's shopping. Bettesworth had further
asked her, she said, to find his discharge papers from
the army, and see what reason for his discharge was
stated, since he had forgotten. I have never understood why he should have been curious on that
point, at such a time. Defective sight seems to
have been the unexciting reason alleged.

And now, its occupant gone and Mrs. Eggar's
rummagings done, the squalid tenement next door
to the Norris's stood shut up, with the door locked
on the few poor belongings it contained. To the
neighbours there seemed to be all the circumstances
of a death, except the death itself. People began
to remember, what I had failed to observe yet
could well believe, how greatly Bettesworth had
changed of late ; others recalled complaints he had
uttered of being unbearably lonely. It was the
general opinion that, even if he lived, he would never
work again, and never again come back to the place
he had left. Three or four men approached me in
the hope of getting work in my garden ; while as
for the cottage, had I cared to give it up, there
were already (the owner told me) four or five
applicants eager to take it. What I should do, and
what Bettesworth, formed the subject of a good deal
of speculation. Old Nanny, meeting me in the road,
plunged excitedly into the middle of the discussion.
In her harsh snapping voice she assured me that the

cottage was " as dirty as *ever !* " and that, as regarded
Bettesworth, the infirmary was " the best place *for*
him !" " Have ye give up the cot ?" she asked.
" No." " Oh ! . . . Beagley " (the owner) " told
young Cook as you had ?" " I haven't." " Well,
he *said* you had." For some reason that was never
divulged, Nanny had conceived a violent animosity
towards Bettesworth, which I then supposed to be
peculiar to herself ; but in other respects her un-
mannerly questionings only betrayed the attitude
of almost all the other neighbours. Bettesworth
was done for : he had better stay at the infirmary
and let others have his work and his cottage. Such
was the prevailing opinion. The people were not
intentionally unkind ; but in the merciless working-
class struggle for life one may admire how long
Bettesworth had held his own.

On the other hand, the opposite side, Bettesworth's side, was championed probably by not a
few labouring men, who had learnt to appreciate his
quality. Among these was George Bryant. Bryant
had been doing a few necessary jobs for me during
Bettesworth's illness, and it was to his interest, if
anybody's, that the old man should not come home
again. When I repeated to him, however, what
people had been saying—namely, that Bettesworth
ought now to stay in the infirmary, he said " H'm !"
and clearly did not agree. Finally, " Well, of
course, we knows 'tis a place where old people *ought*
to be looked after, but—well, Bettesworth likes

his liberty. And so should I, if I was in his place!"

With a cordial feeling which warmed me at the time and may give a little colour now to the grey narrative, he spoke of the change he had lately observed in Bettesworth, who had confessed to him that life had grown so lonely "he didn't know how ever to put up with it." On the very last Sunday evening Bryant had been over at the old man's cottage, "and 'tis a *lot* cleaner 'n what it used to be in the old lady's time." But the difficulty was that Bettesworth could not see. I assented, mentioning his last labours at planting shallots. Bryant smiled; from his adjoining garden he had noticed the same thing a year ago, with some peas. But, in general, he admired Bettesworth. "He's a man that don't talk much till he's started, and then. . . . He was tellin' me Sunday about the things he see in the war. I reckon that got a lot to do with the way he is now: the cold winds, when the tents blowed over, and he'd have to lay out all in the mud. He might think 't didn't hurt 'n," but in all likelihood Bettesworth was now feeling the effects of these sufferings of so long ago. The Crimean wind, as described by Bettesworth, seemed to have impressed Bryant. "'He did tell me what regiment it belonged to, but I forgets which 'twas; but one o' the regiments had the big drum lifted right up into the air an' carried out to sea by the wind."

XXXIII

THE remainder of Bettesworth's story may for the most part be told in the notes made at the time, without much comment. I was unable to go to the infirmary on the first visiting day after his admission, as I had promised that I would ; but I managed to get to him a week later, namely on Tuesday, the 21st of February, when he had been there twelve days ; and on the next day the following account of the visit was jotted down.

February 22, 1905.—At the infirmary yesterday I found Bettesworth still in bed, in a large ward on the ground floor. Out of doors, though it was a day of fair sunshine generally, the north-east wind was bitter, and a storm of sleet and sparse hail which I had been watching as it drove across the eastern sky, and which had reached me as I neared the gate, made it agreeable to get inside the fine well-warmed building. From Bettesworth's bedside I could see, through the tall windows of the ward, distant fields and the grey storm drifting slowly over them. Trees on the horizon stood out sombre against the sombre sky.

Within, was plentiful light—plentiful air and warmth too, and cleanly order. The place looked almost cheerful, although some twenty men lay there, suffering or unhappy. One only was sitting up, who coughed exhaustedly, not violently ; he seemed able to do no more than sit up, shaking with debility. In the beds the patients mostly lay quite still. The man next beyond Bettesworth drew the counterpane up over his ears, and I saw a glowing feverish eye watching me. There were but few other visitors—only four, I think, besides myself. Somewhere an electric bell sounded. A little nursing attendant with sleeves stripped up came stumping cheerily all down the ward. She had been washing dishes or something in a kind of scullery just outside when I came in. As she passed through she said, as though to interest the sick men, " This is how I do my work—see ? Walkin' about like this !"

My first impression of the place was favourable ; all looked so well-appointed, so sumptuous even. And there lay Bettesworth under his white counterpane, himself wonderfully clean and trim, and wearing a floppy white nightcap. I had hoped to find him sitting up ; but still. . . .

" How are you ?" I shook his hand—unrecognizably thin and clean and soft—and he flushed and sat up, pleased enough. But, " I'm as well as ever I shall be," he murmured ; or was it (I don't quite remember) " I shan't never be no better."

Shocked, and not sure of having heard aright, I asked again, and the answer came, " I shan't never be no better, so long as I bides here."

What was the matter, then ? Everything. The interview turned forthwith into one protracted, unreasoning grumble from the old man. He had not food enough. Bread and butter—just a little piece at one time, and a little piece more at some other time. And beef-tea—" they calls it beef-tea, but 'tis only that stuff out o' the bottle—*I* forgets the name of it. Bovril ? Ah, that's it. One cup we has at home 'd make twenty o' these."

I tried to reason with him, but it was useless. Evidently he was very weak. He coughed at times, but said he had no pain now. What he wanted was to get up, and be about, where he could obtain for himself such things as he might fancy. If a man, he argued, feeling as he did, was allowed to get up and put on his clothes for an hour or two, and have a sluice down, wouldn't it brighten that man up ? But last night—he didn't know what time it was, and he got out of bed. One of the nurses came in just then. " ' What are you doin' out there ?' she said; 'you ought to be in bed.' ' And so did you ought to be,' I says." To judge from his tone in narrating, he said it in no amiable voice. He added petulantly, " There ! give me Guildford Hospital before this, twenty times over !"

Thus he grumbled continuously. " There's old Hall in that bed over there. *He's* wantin' to go 'ome, too." Bettesworth spoke with a sneer, not at our poor old neighbour Hall, but at Hall's pitiful prospect of getting release from this imprisonment. He told me of the other's bad cough, and of his age, and so forth, and for a minute or two forgot his own grievances, but only for a minute or two. I asked some question about the doctor. The doctor ? They never set eyes on him, for two or three days at a time. And he didn't give him any medicine much, either. That bottle he " (Bettesworth) "had from the club doctor before leaving home—he only had two doses out of it, but that was a *lot* nicer than this stuff. And the bed was hard—" nothin' soft to lay on," and his back was getting sore. " Let's see—'twas a fortnight last Thursday I come here, wasn't it ?" " No, a week." " Oh, only a week ? I thought 'twas a fortnight. The time seems so *long*."

A woman and a girl were at old Hall's bedside, farther down the ward. I could see him sitting up, panting, white, the picture of despair. Then the woman turned and came towards us ; it was Bettesworth's niece Liz. She was smiling a little bewilderedly. " He wants me to send for the nurse," she said, alluding to Hall ; " he wants to go home."

She joined me in talking to Bettesworth. One or two things I told him about the garden awakened but a faint interest in him ; and meanwhile I could see Hall sitting up, his under-lip drooping, his eyes abnormally bright. Yet I think he could not see

much. Usually he wears spectacles, being eighty
years old. And still we talked to Bettesworth.
His niece was as unsuccessful as myself in trying
to reason with him. To some remark of hers,
suggesting that if he were at home he would be
without anyone to nurse him, he replied fiercely
(and I have no notion of his meaning), "No! and
there won't *be* none, neither, once I gets home and
got my key. I shall lock my door! . . ." Liz
argued then that this place was so comfortable and
so clean. " 'Tis the patients has to do that," said
Bettesworth.

At last a nurse came to old Hall, and we listened
while he proffered his request to go home. "To-
morrow," he said. "Oh, you can't go till you've
seen the doctor!" The nurse spoke pleasantly,
though of course with decision, and bustled away.
But Bettesworth, with his sneer, commented, "Ah!
I *thought* she'd snap his head off!"

Weary of him, I went over to speak to Hall,
who was now looking utterly baffled. Until I was
quite close he did not recognize me, but then he
shook hands joyfully. To him, as to Bettesworth, I
counselled patience. Ah, but he felt he shouldn't
get on, so long as he bid there. He couldn't get
on with the food. The bread in the broth did not
get soft, and as for the dry bread—" I've no teeth
at all in the top row," he said, and therefore he
could not masticate it. Another reason for his
wishing to leave was that his wife was ill with

bronchitis at home, and he longed to return to her.

Well, I had no comfort for him, any more than for Bettesworth. And when I left, they were still dissatisfied, and I was equally sure that their grievances were unreal. What, then, was the matter with them ? The root of it all, I think, was in this : that they were homesick. The good order, the cleanliness, the sense of air and space, the routine of the institution, had overwhelmed them. They were no longer their own masters in their own homes. They were pining for their little poky rooms, nice and stuffy, with the windows shut and the curtains half drawn ; they missed their own furniture, pictures, and worthless rubbish endeared to them by old associations. They did not care, at their age, to begin practising hygiene and learn how to live to grow old. They were old already, and wanted to be at home.

February 28.—I have no record of my second visit to the infirmary a week later; but, as I remember, Bettesworth was then sitting up in a day-room, so that he was evidently better, although still extremely feeble.

XXXIV

March 7, 1905.—Bettesworth left the infirmary on
Saturday morning, March the 4th. I met him half
a mile away from it, in the town, and he was
trembling with weakness where he stood. But he
protested that he should get home well enough;
he had just had a nice rest, a friend of mine having
taken him into his house to sit down by the fire.
My friend told me afterwards how the old man,
invited in because of his pitiable condition, had
seemed to crawl in a state of collapse to the chair
set for him.

His tale to my friend was curiously different
from the account he gave me of his leaving the
infirmary. To the former he explained that on the
Thursday he had desired to be allowed to go home.
The wish was communicated on the next day to
the doctor, who asked, "Do you want to go then?"
and was answered ungraciously, "I shan't get no
better here." On Saturday, therefore, his clothes
were brought to him, and out he came.

But this was not quite the same story that he
told me. Perhaps I should premise that I felt
annoyed with him for coming out, since it was

plain who would have to provide for him ; and he may have seen that I was displeased when I said, " You have no business out ! You're not fit for work, and you ought to have stayed another week or two." Somehow so I greeted him, none too kindly. He replied that there were seven or eight " turned out " that morning, their room being wanted for others. Nor did he forget to complain. His clothes, he said, having been tied in a bundle with a ticket on them, and tossed into a shed, had been returned to him so damp that he felt "shivery" getting into them ; and there was no fire by which to dress.

What did he propose to do ? was my next question. He was going home, to make up a fire in his bedroom and air his bed. Already he had arranged with Liz and Jack to come and help him do that. Such of his things as were worth anyone's buying he should sell—Mrs. Eggar, for instance, would take the Windsor chairs ; and then he was going to live, probably, at Jack's. But his first care was to go and air his bed. Firing—coal, at least—he possessed ; wood could be provided by knocking up two old tables which were grown rickety. To my protest against such destruction, he replied that already before his illness he had touched one of the tables with his little axe.

He trembled, but his mouth shut resolutely, so that I got the impression, and that not for the first time of late, of something desperate about him, something hard, fierce, suspicious.

The discrepancy between his stories to my friend and to myself strengthens the impression, and as I write this a hypothesis shapes itself : that he fears to lose his employment with me ; fears that I am weary of him and anxious to get him permanently settled in the workhouse. For this reason, perhaps, he reviles that hated place, hurries from it, will not own to weakness though I see him shaking, will be independent as to coal and the rest. I asked him how he was off for money. He could do with a shilling or so ; but he did not want to get into debt.

That was three days ago. I was from home to-day when he came to see me, announcing himself vastly better. He has gone to live with Jack, in whose house he has a room to himself and " a nice soft bed," and is well looked after, he says. Liz has even been giving him a cup of tea in bed—or desiring to do so.

I understand him to have said that the old cot used to cost him as much as six shillings a week to keep going. And that, he added, would be nearly enough for him to live upon, in his new quarters.

March 8.—I have promised Bettesworth (we walked down the garden this morning to talk it over out of earshot) that when he finds himself past work I will make him an allowance, to keep him from the workhouse. He is to tell me, when the time comes ; at present, he still hopes to do a little more.

I was wrong, it seems, in surmising that dread of losing his employment made him so anxious to quit the infirmary. " Was it so ?" was a question put to him this morning, point blank. He denied it. " No," he said ; " I was afraid I should die. That's what made me so eager to get away. I felt I should die if I bid there another week." So many died, he said, while he was there—several in one day, I understood, one being the man in the bed next to Bettesworth's. This man " made up his mind " and was gone, in twenty minutes—one Freeland, from Moorways. There also died there a certain old Taff Skinner, an old neighbour whom Bettesworth, in his own convalescence, tried to get upstairs to see. A nurse turned him back, he protesting that he " didn't know as he was doin' wrong," and she explaining that he might only visit another room or ward on visiting day. " Or else," he told me, " Old Taff's wife an' daughter was there, and ast me if I wouldn't go an' see 'n to cheer 'n up."

Having got home and shifted a few things to Jack's, Bettesworth's great joy was in his " nice soft bed." He has been used to feathers, and found the mattress hard at the infirmary. He said with gusto, " That was a treat to me, to get into that bed and roll myself over. And my poor old back seemed almost well the next morning." Across the loins and down the back of his thighs he is tender, and his elbows were beginning to get sore from hoisting himself up on the mattress. To ease the loins Jack has been rubbing in " some o' that strong liniment." On the whole Jack seems to be treating the old man very well.

That he will continue to do so is devoutly to be hoped. For there are not many refuges open to Bettesworth now, nor can the infirmary any more be looked to as one of them. According to his last version of it, when the doctor asked him if it was really his wish to leave, he answered, " Once I gets away I'll never come here no more, not if there's a ditch at home I can die in."

March 12.—I find there is a steady set of public opinion—that is to say, the opinion of his own class—against Bettesworth, which has grown very marked since he came out of the infirmary, although probably it is not quite a new thing.

One of the first indications of it, besides old Nanny's animosity already mentioned, appeared while he was still away, when Bill Crawte spoke to me in the town, alleging that the old man had been misbehaving of late in his evenings. I received an impression of drinking bouts and disorder, which was conveyed in innuendo rather than directly. " He spends too much money at the public-house ; and he can't take much without its going to his head "—such was Crawte's expression, intended, it seemed, to warn me that I was deceived in my protégé.

A few days ago I met old Mrs. Skinner. I remember that I crossed the street to speak to her

" because she was such a stranger," and she looked flattered, but complained of " such a bad face-ache, sir," and grimaced, holding her black shawl over her mouth. Then she hurried into the subject of Bettesworth's home-coming, and did not hesitate to assure me that he was " a *bad* old man." Once again I felt that I was being warned that the old man was unworthy of my help. I had heard Mrs. Skinner before, however—months before—on the same subject. In her way she is a good woman whom I like and respect, but she has a taste for commenting on other people's faults. Moreover, there was never much love lost between her and Bettesworth : his old tongue, I suspect, has been too shrewd for her at times.

Yesterday I met old Nanny, with a bundle on her back, and I stopped to speak, partly sheltered from a driving rain by the umbrella she held behind her. She, too, has not scrupled before to complain of Bettesworth's behaviour, and always with the air of saying to me " he's not the good old man you take him for." But yesterday her tongue knew no reticence ; she felt wronged herself, and she lashed Bettesworth's character mercilessly, in the hope of hurting him in my esteem. Swift and snappish, out came the long screed, while the old woman's eyes were fiery and her cheeks flushed. Oh, but she felt righteous, I am sure. She was exposing a black-guard, a scamp ! And if she could injure him, she would.

I do not recall many of her words. His ingratitude to her was Bettesworth's chief offence—after all she had done for him! So she told what she had done : how she had cooked his supper night after night, and got it all ready while he sat down there at the public-house waiting to be fetched. She wouldn't have done it, but Kid said, " Poor old feller, help 'n all you can. He en't got nobody to do anything for him." And she had washed his clothes, and scrubbed out his house ; and he was such a dirty old man that it almost made her sick. And when he was ill, Mrs. Cook watching (downstairs, I gathered) was obliged to sit all night with the window open, because the place so stank. I heard how many pails of water it took to scrub the floor ; how the boards upstairs—new boards " as white as drippen snow " when the Bettesworths took possession—would in all likelihood never come white again ; and how the landlord had said that he should demand a week's rent (from me, of course) to pay for cleaning, when Bettesworth moved. And now Bettesworth was gone away, " taking his money " (his wages or his allowance), and " I don't like it, Mr. Bourne !" said old Nanny, vehemently. Not, apparently, that the money was an object to her, but that all her good offices had gone unthanked, nay, minimized. Had not Bettesworth complained that he had no one to do anything for him ? And all the time Mrs. Norris was slaving for him. Had he not told me during his illness that he had taken nothing, when, in fact, Mrs. Cook not long before had taken him up a cup of tea and two slices of bread and butter, which he had eaten ? " I don't *like* it, Mr. Bourne." No, I could see that she did not ; I could hear as much in the emphasis of the words, rapped out like swift hammer-strokes ; and the old woman looked almost handsome in the flush of her indignation.

I left her and passed on, wondering what the original offence could have been to produce such bitterness. Probably it was some harsh speech of Bettesworth's, some antique savagery drawn from him in the despair of his lonely situation, with his powers failing, the workhouse looming. Suspicious, hard, obstinate, wrapped-up now wholly in himself, he may easily . . . but it is useless to surmise.

Useless is it, too, to pretend that the repeated insinuations have had no effect upon me. As a rule backbiters succeed only in making me see their own unreason, while mentally I take sides with their victims ; but in this case fancies of my own were corroborated by the slanders of the neighbours. I have believed, and think it likely, that Bettesworth is ready to deceive me to his own advantage, just as I have long known that he has not really been worth half his wages. He is in desperate plight, dependent on my caprice, and he cannot afford to be over scrupulous on a point of honour. As for old Nanny and the others, I suppose their sense of justice is outraged by Bettesworth's good fortune in having my protection. They are jealous ; they resent the imposition which they suppose is being put upon me, and imagine me a blind fool who ought to be enlightened.

To-day I fell in with old Mrs. Hall, whose husband is still at the infirmary. She had nothing hopeful to tell me about that old man's condition. He had been more contented, however, since his master had written to him, though he did talk, bedridden as he is, of digging a hole somewhere under the infirmary wall, so that he might escape to the cab that would bring him back home. But Mrs. Hall didn't think—if she said what she really thought—that he would ever come home again. At his great age (why, he is eighty to-morrow !) how could she hope that he would recover ? Poor little dumpy old woman, with the plump face, and dainty chin, and round eyes—her lips trembled, talking of her husband and of her own difficulties. " For while he lays up there," she said, " I got nothin' to live on," except a little help from the Vicar. Her daughter, married and away in Devonshire, will pay the quarter's rent, but . . .

" And Mr. Bettesworth's out, it seems," the old woman continued. " It seems to me he's an ungrateful old man. For 'tis all nice and comfortable up there. It do seem ungrateful."

Such was Mrs. Hall's unasked for, unexpected comment, on Bettesworth's behaviour. Poor old woman, to me too it seemed unjust that she should be so unaided, and he, perhaps, so over-aided. He is no old woman, though ; allowance must be made for that. He could not away with the sort of comfort so praised by Mrs. Hall.

Is, then, the last word about Bettesworth to be that he is dirty, dishonest, degraded ? He may be all three (he certainly is the first) and yet have a claim to be helped now and remembered with honour.

For, as another recent incident has served to remind me, our point of view is in danger of growing too narrow. One of the kindest of cultured women, going about her work of visiting the sick, asked me how Bettesworth was doing. Then, in her amiable way, she talked of him and of his wife, and soon was speaking of the extreme dirtiness in which they had lived. As a district visitor she had once or twice come upon them at meal-times, when their food on the table caused her a physical loathing—just as once I had been nauseated myself by the sight of a kippered herring by the old man's bedside. The district visitor—being invited and finding no courteous excuse for refusal—had sat down in Bettesworth's easy-chair, not without dread of what she might bring away. Most cottages she could visit without such terrors ; most people, she supposed, " managed to get a tub once a week " ; but the Bettesworths. . . . The lady spoke laughingly. In her comely life, an experience like this is afterwards an adventure.

I smiled, and said, " They are survivals."

" Of the fittest ?"

We both laughed ; but when I added, " Yes, for some qualities," we knew (or I at least knew) that indeed that squalor of an earlier century is associated with a hardness of fibre most intimately connected with the survival of the English people.

Suppose that now in stress of circumstances, the toughness warps, turns to ill-living, suspicion, selfishness and dishonesty, in the grim determination not to " go under ": is it then no longer venerable, because it has ceased to be amiable ? The onlooker should give an eye to his own point of view.

XXXV

March 13, 1905.—This (Monday) morning Bettesworth came, slowly hobbling with his stick. Last
week he had promised himself to be at work again
to-day ; but no—he is less well, and fancies he has
taken fresh cold.

He looked white, weak, pathetically docile and
kind, as he led the way from the kitchen door to
the wood-shed, evidently desirous of a private talk.

He said he was " purty near beat, comin' over
Saddler's Hill "; he had never before had such a
job, having been forced to stop to get breath. It
" felt like a lot o' mud in his chest ; it was all slushin'
and sloppin' about inside him, jest like a lot o'
thick mud." But he had been worrying so : he
wanted to pay me his rent. And then about his
club pay—that worried him, too. He need not
have worried ? Ah, but he had done so, none the
less ; and Liz had said to him, " You better go up
an' see about it, and you'll feel better when you
got it off your mind "; or else he was hardly fit to
be out in this cold wind. He had stayed indoors
from Saturday afternoon until this morning. At
tea-time, " about four o'clock yesterday," Liz had

brought him a cup of tea with an egg beaten up in it, which had seemed to do him good. And she had got him half a quarte'n of whisky to hearten him up as he came away this morning. But he could not eat. " Law! they boys o' Jack's 'll eat three times what I do. I likes to see 'em. Jack says, ' What d'ye think o' that for a table ?' " and indicates to Bettesworth the plentiful supply.

A hint brought the wandering talk back readily to the subject which the old man had on his mind. " *I* never owed that money to the club, what you says Mrs. Eggar drawed from you. . . . She've done me out o' that, ye see." Just as he had supposed, so it proved, he affirmed : he had paid up to last August ; and the inference was that Mrs. Eggar had drawn the money from me for her own uses, and now Bettesworth must repay it.

He produced two membership cards in support of his statements. The first was the same which Mrs. Eggar had brought me, at that time bearing no receipt later than February, 1904, but now certifying a further payment of 1s. 6d. up to August. The other was a new card, giving receipt in full to February of this year. To judge by the ink, these two receipts had been given at the same time ; in other words, they had been obtained by Mrs. Eggar in return for the money duly paid in by her. But it took me long to satisfy Bettesworth (if he was satisfied) that she had not " done " me out of three shillings on his behalf.

And then there was his rent, which had been running on all the time that he was at the infirmary. He had brought the money for that now, to get out of my debt.

Of course it was refused. In consideration of this rent, I said, I had not helped otherwise during his sickness, and I did not wish him to repay it. What he said to that I regret that I do not exactly remember, but it went somehow in this way :— " You done a *lot* for me, sir ; more 'n you any call to. And I thinks of you. . . .' He was unable to go on and express his meaning, but his tone rang very sincere. I did not find any ingratitude in him ; nor was there any dishonesty in the purpose for which he had come to me.

He, however, found dishonesty in the neighbours, who have bought his household goods and now hang back with the purchase money. So cheap, too, he had sold his things ! " That landlord at the Swan said 'twas givin' of 'em away. . . . But what could I do ?" Bettesworth urged. His brother-in-law had advised him " not to stand out for sixpence ; 't wa'n't as if they was new things," and had warned him against giving trust. But what could he do ? Even as it was, the trouble of attending to the business had been too much for him in his weak state. So, one had had a table, and another two saucepans, and so on ; and now he could not get the money. Instead of twenty-two shillings which should have been received on Saturday, he found himself with no more than five ; and this morning only another five shillings had come in.

Yes, the people had " had " him ; he was sure of that. There was " that Tom Beagley's wife. . . . She come to me Saturday sayin' Tom was on the booze and hadn't given her no money, so she couldn't pay me. . . . ' That's a lie,' our Tom says ; ' he en't bin on the booze. He bin at work all the week, over here at Moorways.' So I told her I should have the things back, if she didn't pay me this mornin'." Other instances were generalized ; Bettesworth thought himself cheated all round.

By this time we had left the shed, and were standing in its shadow, where the wind blew up cold and draughty. " Let's get into the sunshine," I proposed.

As we moved, " Wasn't it a day yesterday ?" I remarked ; and Bettesworth assented, " No mistake !" It had in fact been a Sunday of March gales, of furious rain and hail-storms, and then gay bursts of sunshine hurrying down the valley. With none to sweep it, the path where we stood was still bestrewn with a litter of dead twigs, which the east winds had left, but this fierce westerly wind had finally torn out from the lilac bushes. " It's a sort of pruning," I said, and was answered, " Yes, that must do a lot o' good. Done it better 'n you could ha' done, too." We found a sunny place, although still a draughty wind searched us out, and fast-changing clouds sometimes drew across the sun-

shine and left us shivering. " More showers," we
predicted, " before the day is out."

There, in the sunshine, Bettesworth coughed—a
little painful cough without variety. It seemed as if
it need not have begun, yet, having begun, need never
cease. " You must get rid of that cough," said I.
" I en't got strength to cough," he replied. Then
he put his hands against the pit of his stomach.
" That's where it hurts me. Sims to tear me all
to pieces." I advised care in feeding, and avoidance of solids. " Bread an' butter's the only solid
food I takes," he said. " Liz wanted me to have a
kipper. ' Naw,' I says, ' I en't much of a fish man.'
But I don't want it. I en't got no appetite." It
was suggested that the warm weather presently
would restore him; but he returned, very quietly;
" I dunno. I sims to think I shan't last much
longer. I got that idear. I can feel it, somehow."

" How long have you felt like that ?"

" This six weeks I've had that sort o' feelin'." He
went on to repeat what he had said to Jack in consequence. When he had got his bed and other
things into Jack's house, " ' It's all yours now,' I
says. ' You take everything there is. All you got
to do is to see me put away.' "

His weakness was distressing to see, and he had
to get back home somehow. Would a little more
whisky help him ? We adjourned to the kitchen,
sat down there near the fire, and while the old man
had his stimulant he talked of many things.

At first, handing me the key of his cottage, he told of his cat, how plump she looked, and how she had welcomed him home in such fashion as to make Liz say with a laugh, " No call to ask whose cat she is ! " Sometimes he thought of " gettin' old Kid to put a charge o' shot into her "; sometimes, of " puttin' her in a sack an' drownin' her." Either was more than he had the heart to do ; yet he could not bear to think of his cat without a home. Would not Mrs. Norris take care of her, then ? " Oh yes, she'd *feed* her, but. . . . But Mrs. Norris can't *hear*, poor old soul. She bin a good ol' soul to me, though ; and so've Kid." Of course I did not tell Bettesworth how old Nanny had lately talked of him.

What to do about his cabbages puzzled him. He had paid old Carver Cook two shillings for digging the ground and planting them ; and now that he had given up the cottage, there was this value like to be lost ! He must get " whoever took the cot " to take to the cabbages too ; they ought to. He didn't like to cut 'em down—never liked to do anybody else a bad turn, but. . . . Ultimately I promised to get the price allowed, in settling with his landlord.

Through devious courses the conversation slid back to his nephew's family and household ways. Liz " don't sit down to dinner 'long o' the others." There are six boys besides her husband for her to wait upon, so that, were she to begin, " before she'd got a mouthful the others 'd be wantin' their second helpin'." The custom sounds barbarous—

or shall I say archaic ?—until one remembers that the husband and one or two of the boys must get home from work to dinner and back again within an hour. On Sunday afternoon " Jack was off to the town to this P.S.A. or whatever it is. He brought home another prize too. . . . A beautiful book—a foot by nine inches, and three or four inches thick ! Jack *can* read, no mistake !" Unfortunately he reads in a very loud voice, so that Bettesworth grows weary of it, in spite of his passion for being read to. On Saturday night Jack was reading the paper, and said, " ' Like any more ? ' " ' Not to-night, Jack ; I be tired.' All about this war " (in Manchuria). " Sunday he said, ' Shall I read ye the paper, uncle ? 'Tis nothin' but the war.' ' Then we won't have it to-day.' "

Bettesworth's opinions on the war were tedious to me ; he had so greatly misunderstood. He thought that, after Mukden, the Russians were retreating " right back into St. Petersburg," which would have been a retreat indeed ! " But it ought to be stopped now "; the other Powers should interfere and say, " You've had your go in, and now you must get back into your own bounds." For the Japanese, of course, Bettesworth was full of admiration : "fighting without food !" . . . He exclaimed at their pluck and their prowess.

Gradually his own memories of war were awaking, and at last, " The purtiest little soldiers I ever see was the Sardinians." He described their smartness ; their pretty tight-fitting uniform. " They camped 'longside o' we." Of their language " you could get to pick out a good many words " (I think he meant English words they used), " but it pestered 'em when they couldn't make ye understand. . . . But there, we was as bad. . . . Every nation has their own slang." The funniest Bettesworth ever heard was that of the Turks, " like a lot o' geese. . . . I remember once a lot of 'em come up over the hill by our camp, with about four hundred prisoners. They didn't let us have 'em, but was takin' 'em on to their own camp ; but they was so proud for us to see, an' they was caperin' and cuttin' and dancin' about, jest like a lot o' geese."

Something reminded him of George Bryant and his present job ; something else, of his own coal supply, now removed to Jack's ; and that brought up the coal merchant's receipt, which he had found in his waistcoat pocket. He had given it to Liz, with his wife's little box full of receipts for coal, groceries, tea, and so on, and had recommended Liz to " put 'em on the fire." " You *be* a careless old feller !" Liz retorted, and he repeated, laughing.

He had been here nearly an hour, and at last I stood up. Bettesworth took the hint. He was looking the better for his whisky as he went off. But all the time, while he sat dreamily talking, he had had a very mild, placid, old man's expression, and all my harsher thoughts of him had quite slipped away.

XXXVI

March 21, 1905.—There being no definite news of
Bettesworth since he crept away that day, this
afternoon I knocked at the door of Jack Bettesworth's cottage, where he is staying. Presently
the old man himself opened to me. His cheeks were
flushed and feverish. He led the way indoors,
saying that he was all alone ; and as we settled down
(he still wearing his cap) I remarked that he did not
seem to be " up to much," and he replied that I
was right ; " I got this here pleurisy, and armonium
or something 'long with it." He had got up from
bed, quite recently, to rest for an hour or two.

He had seen the club doctor—Jack had fetched
him on Sunday—" and you couldn't wish for a
pleasanter gentleman. He sounded me all over,"
and sent out a plaster which " I'm wearin' now,"
Bettesworth said, " like one o' they poor-man's
plasters." This reminded him of a similar one he
had once had, of which he said that he " wore 'n
for six months "; and truly the old-fashioned
" poor-man's plaster " was always alleged to be
unremovable. Once properly plastered, the patient
had to earn his name and wait until the thing should

wear or " rot off," as Bettesworth phrased it. How
this six-months' plaster—right round his waist, and
" wide as a leather belt "—had been " gored " by
his " old mother-in-law, or else 't'd ha' tore flesh
and all off," I will not spend time in relating.

Bettesworth had caught this new cold, he supposed, waiting for " they old women " to come and
pay him for his furniture ; who did not come to the
old cottage at the time appointed, and kept him
standing about. Nor have they yet paid all.

Not unhappily, but comfortably, he looked up
to the mantelpiece and said, " There's my old clock."
I recognized the dingy old gabled mahogany case ;
and the tick sounded familiar, reminding me of the
other rooms where I had heard it, and of the old
wife who had been alive then. " Mrs. Smith had
my other," said Bettesworth, " and she en't paid
for 't yet. I shall have 'n back, if she don't. Jack
persuaded me to go an' get 'n back last week.
' That's all right,' I says, ' only I can't get there.'
He wanted to go instead of me, but I wouldn't have
that. He might get sayin' more 'n what he ought.
But I shall have the clock back if she don't pay."

There also was his old mirror—he spoke of it—
looking homely over the mantelpiece ; and I heard
of a few pictures saved, which Jack had taken out
of their frames, to clean the glass, and had put back
again. It seemed to be comforting to the old man
to have these relics of his married life still about
him ; and in the midst of them he himself looked

very comfortable ; for, as his back was to the light (he sat in a Windsor chair with arms), I could not see the flush on his face. So pleasant was it to find him at last beside a clean hearth, warm and tidy and well cared-for, that I could not refrain from congratulating him. Yes, he acknowledged his good fortune ; he was swift to praise his niece. " She looks after me," he said warmly, " as well as if I was a child. I en't bin so comfortable since I dunno when." Perhaps never before in his life. " Before I was bad myself, there was the poor old gal. I went through something with she. When I was away at work, I was always wonderin' about her."

I had two shillings to hand over to him—the price obtained from his landlord for the cabbages left in the cottage garden ; and in answer to inquiries as to his finances, he said that he had enough money to keep him going for a fortnight or so. But he was paying Jack for his board and lodging, and seemed fully alive to the desirability of continuing to do so.

On Sunday morning there had come to see him his sister-in-law from Middlesham, to whom he complained of a brother-in-law's indifference. The complaints were reiterated to me. " Dick en't never bin near so much as to ask how I was gettin' on. I *told* her he never come even to his poor old sister, till the night afore the funeral. And after all I've done for 'n, whenever he was in any trouble or wanted help hisself, I was always the fust one he sent for, if there was anything the matter with he, same as that time when he fell off the hay-rick. Sent for me in the middle o' the night to go to the doctor's for 'n, when he'd got one of his own gals at home. It hurts me now, when I thinks of it sittin' here. . . . If he'd only jest come and say How do ! But no. . . ." We supposed that Dick feared lest he should be asked to give help in some way.

Pleurisy and pneumonia or not—it was hard to believe that he had suffered from either, yet he had got hold of the words somehow—Bettesworth was at no loss that afternoon for interesting sub-jects of conversation. An inquiry how his sister-in-law was faring led to a talk about her two sons, of whom one is out of work. The other, a basket-maker (blind or crippled, I do not know which) lives at home, and has just got a lot of work come in. " Mostly stock work," Bettesworth believed, "for some London firm he knows of." But besides this, he has a hundred stone jars from the brewery, to re-case with basket-work. The handles and bottoms are of cane, the rest " only skeleton work, as they calls it." Bettesworth always loved to know of technical things like this.

Odd it is, I suggested, how every trade has its own terms of speech. " Yes, and its own tools too," added Bettesworth ; and with deep interest he spoke of the tools this basket-maker uses for splitting his canes, dividing them " as fine !" And the tools are " sharp as lancets ; and every tool with a special name for it."

This reminded me to repeat to Bettesworth a similar account which a friend of mine had lately given me, and will publish, it may be hoped, of the Norfolk art of making rush collars. " Very nice smooth collars," Bettesworth murmured appreciatively. But when I proceeded to tell how the art is likely to die, because the few men who understand it keep their methods secret, this stirred him. " Same," he said, " as them Jeffreys over there t'other side o' Moorways, what used to make these little wooden bottles you remembers seein'. They'd never let nobody see how 'twas done. But I never heared tell of anybody else ever makin' 'em anywhere."

Yes, I remembered seeing these " bottles," like tiny barrels, slung at labouring men's backs when they trudged homewards, or lying with their clothes and baskets in the harvest-field or hop-garden. It was to the small bung-hole in the side that the thirsty labourer used to put his mouth, leaning back with the bottle above him. Whether the beer carried well and kept cool in these diminutive barrels I do not know ; but certainly to the eye they had a rustic charm. So I could agree with Bettesworth's praises : " *Purty* little bottles they got to be at last—even with glass ends to 'em, and white hoops. They used to boil 'em in a copper—whether that was so's to bend the wood I dunno.

Little ones from a pint up to three pints. . . . I had a three-pint one about somewheres, but I couldn't put my hand on 'n when I turned out t'other day. Eighteenpence was the price of a quart one—but they had iron hoops. . . . But they wouldn't let nobody see how they made 'em. . . . There was them blacksmiths over there, again—*they* wouldn't allow nobody to see how they finished a axe-head.

" These Jeffreys never done nothing else but make these bottles, and go mole-catchin'. Rare mole-catchers they was : earnt some good money at it, too. But they had to walk miles for it. You can understand, when the medders was bein' laid up for grass they had to cover some ground, to get all round in time. I've seen 'em come into a medder loaded up with a great bundle o' traps : an' then they'd begin putting' in the rods—'cause they was allowed to cut what rods they wanted for it, where-ever they was workin', and they knowed purty near where a mole 'd put his head up. 'Twas so much a field they got, from the farmer. I never knowed nobody else catch moles like they did, but they wouldn't show ye how they done it, or how they made their traps.

"There was a man name o' Murrell—Sonny Murrell we always used to call 'n—lived at Cashford. *He* was a very good mole-catcher. One time the moles started in down Culverley medders, right away from Old Mill to Culverley Mill—it looked as if they'd bin tippin' cart-loads o' rubbish all over the medders.

I never see such a slaughter as that was, done by moles, in all my creepin's." (I think " creepin's " was the word Bettesworth used, but his voice had sunk very low just here, and I could as easily hear the clock as him.) " But they sent for Sonny. He was a *clever* old cock, in moles ; they had to be purty 'cute to get round 'n—some did, though ; you'll see how they'll push round a trap—but after he'd bin there a fortnight you couldn't tell as there'd bin any moles at all."

One other topic which we briefly touched upon must not be omitted. Before my arrival Bettesworth had crept out to the gate by the road, he was saying, tempted by the loveliness of the sunshine ; and hearing of it, I warned him to have a care of getting out in this easterly wind. Ah, he said, we might expect east winds for the next three months now, for this was the 21st of March, and " where the wind is at twelve o'clock on the 21st of March, there she'll bide for three months afterwards." So he had once firmly held ; and he mentioned the theory now, though apparently with little faith in it. For when I laughed, he said, " I've noticed it a good many times, and sometimes it have come right and sometimes it haven't. But that old Dick Furlonger was the one. He said he'd noticed it hunderds o' times. We used to terrify 'n about that, afterwards—'cause he was a man not more 'n fifty ; and we used to tease 'n, so's he'd get up an' walk out o' the room."

XXXVII

DURING April I was away from home a good deal, and neither saw much of Bettesworth nor heard about him anything of importance. He seems to have recovered a little strength, to enable him to creep about the village when the weather was at all fit, but the drizzling rains and the raw chill winds of that spring-time were not favourable to the old man, who had almost certainly had a slight touch of pleurisy, if nothing worse, earlier in the year.

May, however, was not a week old before the weather brightened and grew splendid. The very sky seemed to lift in the serene warmth ; and now, if ever he was to do so, Bettesworth should show some improvement.

At first it almost looked as if he might rally. I remember passing through the village, in the dusk of a Sunday evening (the 7th of May), and there was Bettesworth, slowly toiling up the ascent to Jack's cottage, even at that late hour. It was too dark to distinguish his features, but by the lift of his chin and a suggestion of lateral curvature in his figure, I recognized him. He had been to the Swan, and was just going home, contented with his evening. The week that followed saw him here twice ; and again on the 15th he came, and, finding me in the garden, was glad enough to be invited to a seat where he might rest.

And then as we sat there together it became clear to me that he would never again be any better than he was now. The sunshine was soft and pleasant, where it alighted on his end of the seat, and the shade of the garden trees at my end was refreshing, but to him no summer day was to bring its gifts of renewed life any more. When he arrived, I had expected that presently, after a rest, it would be his wish to go farther into the garden and see how the crops promised ; but he made no offer to move. To get so far had been all that he could do. His thighs, as could be seen by the clinging of the trousers to them, were lamentably shrunken. His body was wasting : only his aged mind retained any of his former vigour.

A curious thing he told me, in connexion with the shrinking of his muscles. He had bared his thighs one evening, to show his " mates "—Bryant, George Stevens, and others—how thin they were ; and by his own account the men had solemnly looked on at the queer piteous exhibition, acknowledging themselves shocked, and wondering how he could creep about at all. Bryant, by the way, had already told me of the incident, speaking compassionately. He added that Bettesworth offered

to show his arms also, but that he had said, " No,
Fred, you no call to trouble.   I can take your word
for it without seein'."

Sitting there weary in the sunshine, Bettesworth
was in a melancholy humour.   " A gentleman on
the road," he said, had met him the previous day,
and remarked " to his wife what was with him,
' That old gentleman looks as if he bin ill.'   ' So he
have,' old George Stevens says, cause he was 'long
with me.   He " (the gentleman) " looked at my
hands and says, ' Why, your hands looks jest as
if they was dyin' off.'   I dunno what he meant ;
but he called his wife and said, ' Don't his hands
look jest as if they was dyin' off ?'   And she said
so they did. . . .   I dunno who he was : he was a
stranger to me.   But what should you think he
meant by that ?"

Mournfully the old man held out his knotted
hand for my opinion.   He was plainly worried by
the odd phrase, and fancied, I believe, that the
" gentleman " had seen some secret token of death
in his hands.

The instinctive will to live was still strong in him,
sustained by the conservatism of habit, and in opposition to his reason.   According to Bryant, he said
a day or two before this, " I prays for 'em to carry
me up Gravel Hill "; and that is the way from his
lodging to the churchyard.

May 17.—Once more, on the 17th of May, he found

his way here. Not obviously worse, he complained
of having coughed all night, and he was going to
try the remedy suggested by a neighbour : a drink
made by shredding a lemon, pouring boiling water
over it, adding sugar. . . . He was more cheerful,
however. He sat in the sunshine, and chatted in
his kindliest manner, chiefly about his neighbours.

There was Carver Cook, for instance. He was
seventy-seven years old, and fretting because he
was out of work. " I en't earnt a crown, not in
these last three weeks," he had told Bettesworth.
On the previous afternoon, just as it was beginning
to rain, the two old men had met near the public-
house, and gone in together out of the wet ; and
" Carver " standing a glass of ale, there they stayed
until the rain slackened, and had a very happy,
comfortable two hours. I asked what Bettesworth's
old friend had to live upon.

" Well," Bettesworth said, " he've got that cot ;
and he've saved money. Oh yes, he've got money
put by. But he says if it don't last out he shall sell
the cot. He shan't study nobody. None of his
sons an' daughters don't offer to help 'n, and never
gives 'n nothin'. His garden he does all hisself ; and when he wants any firin' or wood, he gets
a hoss an' gets it home hisself. But old Car'line,
he says, is jest as contented now as ever she was in
her life. ' Why don't ye look in and see her ? ' he
says. But I says, ' Well, Carver, I never was much

of a one for pokin' into other people's houses.' "
He paused, allowing me to suggest that perhaps he
preferred other people to come and see him. But
to that he demurred. ' No. . . . I likes to meet 'em
out ; an' then you can go in somewhere and have a
glass with 'em, if you mind to."

Thoroughly to Bettesworth's taste, again, as it
is to the groom's taste to talk of horses, or to the
architect's to discuss new buildings, was a little
narrative he had of another neighbour's work in the
fields. " Porter's brother," he said, " started down
there at Priestley's Friday mornin', and got the sack
dinner-time." How? Well, it was a job at hoeing
young " plants " in the field, at which the man got
on very well at first ; but presently he came to
" four rows o' cabbage and then four rows o'
turnips," and there the ground was so full with
weeds that to hoe it properly was impossible.
The hoe would strike into a tangle of " lily," or
bindweed, with tendrils trailing " as fur as from
here to that tree " (say four or five yards) ; and
when pulled at, the lily proved to have turned three
or four times round a plant, which came away with
it. " So when the foreman come and saw, he
says, ' I dunno, Porter—I almost thinks you better
leave off.' ' Well, I'd jest as soon,' Porter says,
' for I can't seem to satisfy *myself*.' " So he left
off, and the foreman supposed they would have to
plough the crop in and plant again.

It was pleasant enough to me to sit in the afternoon sunshine and hear this talk of village folk and outdoor doings, but after a little while I was called away, and did not see Bettesworth's departure. I should have watched it, if I had known the truth ; for, once he had got outside the gate, he had set foot for the last time in this garden.

XXXVIII

June 9, 1905.—Some three weeks later, not having in the interval seen anything of Bettesworth, I was on the point of starting to look him up, when his niece came to the door. She had called expressly to beg that I would go and visit him, because he seemed anxious to see me. He was considerably worse, in her opinion ; indeed, for the greater part of the week—in which there had been cold winds with rain—he had kept his bed and lain there dozing. Whenever he woke up, he had the impression either that it was early morning or else late evening ; and once or twice he had asked, quite early in the day, whether Jack was come home yet.

On reaching the cottage I found him in his bed upstairs. Certainly he had lost strength since I saw him. At first his voice was husky, and he was inclined to cry at his own feebleness ; soon, however, he recovered his habitual quick, quiet speech, though a touch of weariness and debility remained in it. Stripping back the sleeve of his bed-gown he exhibited his arm : the muscle had disappeared, and the arm was no bigger than a young boy's. He shed tears at the sight, himself. Nor was he without pain. As he lay there that morning his legs, he said, had felt " as if somebody was puttin' skewers into 'em, right up the shins "; but he had rubbed vaseline over them, and after about half an hour the pain diminished. The doctor, visiting, had said " Poor old gentleman "; and, to him, not much more. "Old age—worn out," was the simple diagnosis he had furnished downstairs, to Liz.

Another visitor had called—who but the owner of that cottage from which the Bettesworths had been compelled to turn out two years ago ? I do not think Mr. —— recognized Bettesworth. He had merely heard of an old man in bad plight—an old Crimean soldier, too—and he wished to be helpful. " And a very good friend to me he was !" Bettesworth said heartily, in a sort of emotional burst, losing control of his voice and crying again. Mr. —— had " come tearin' up the stairs—none o' they downstairs didn't know who he was," and had spoken compassionately. " ' What you wants,' he says, ' is feedin' up—port wine !—and you shall have it.' " He was told that the doctor had recommended whisky. " ' Very well. When I gets home I'll send ye over a bottle, the best that money can buy.' " Having left, " he come hollerin' back again : ' Here ! here's five shillin's for him !' " But, said Bettesworth to me, " I never spent it on jellies an' things ; I thought it might be put to better use than that."

Besides this unexpected friend, Bettesworth told

me that a Colonel resident in the parish was moving
on his behalf, endeavouring to get him a pension for
his services in the Crimea. " But that en't no use,"
the old man said ; " I en't got my papers," or at
any rate he had not the essential ones. He tried to
account for their disappearance : " Ye see, I've had
several moves, an' this last one there was lots o'
things missin' that I never knowed what become
of 'em."

He chatted long, and rationally enough, in his
customary vein, but saying nothing very striking
or particularly characteristic. There were some
pleasant remarks on one " Peachey " Phillips, a
coal-cart man. Peachey " looks after his old
mother at Lingfield," and is " a good chap to work "
(a " chap " of fifty years old, I should judge), but
has been hampered by want of education. According to Bettesworth, " he might have had some
good places if he'd had any schoolin'," and he had
regretfully confessed it to Bettesworth. " Cert'nly
he's better 'n he was. His little 'ns what goes to
school—he've made they learn him a little ; but
still. . . . Well, you can't get on without it. Nobody ever ought to be against schoolin'. . . . Yes,
a good many is, but nobody never ought to be
against it. I don't hold with all this drillin' and
soldierin' ; but readin', and summin', and writin',
and to know how to right yourself. . . ."

As Bettesworth lay in bed there upstairs, and
unable to see much but his bedroom walls and their

cheap pictures, for the window was rather high up and narrow, his mind was still out of doors. He inquired about several details in the garden ; and particularly he wanted to know if a young hedge was yet clipped, in which he had taken much interest. It chanced that a man was working on it that after-noon ; and Bettesworth's thought of it therefore struck me as somewhat remarkable. Evidently he was longing to see the garden ; and though we did not know then that the desire would never be gratified, still that was the probability, and per-haps he realized it. He was a little tearful, as the time came for me to leave him.

After this I tried to make a point of seeing him once a week. Friday afternoons were the times most convenient, and the following Sunday commonly afforded the leisure for recording the visits. I give the accounts of them pretty much as they stand in my book.

June 18, 1905 (*Sunday Morning*).—I saw Bettes-worth on Friday afternoon. His voice was husky, and feebler than I have before heard it ; but then in every way he was weaker, and seemed to have given up hope ; in fact, he said that he wished it was over, though not quite in those words. He complained of pain in his chest and about the diaphragm, and in his legs. I did not acknowledge to him that he seemed worse to me ; but visitors of his own sort practise no such reticence. He told me that Mrs.

Blackman, Mrs. Eggar and others had seen him, and they all said, " Oh dear, Fred, how bad you looks !" Carver Cook's observation was yet more pointed : " Every time I sees ye, you looks worse 'n you did the time afore." Bettesworth related all this almost as if talking of some third person.

The Vicar, lest the higher purpose of his visits should be overlooked if he went to Bettesworth as alms-giver too, had entrusted me with a few shillings for the old man, who received them gladly, but seemed equally pleased to have been remembered. When I handed the money over, and named the giver, " Oh ah !" he said, " he come to see me. I was layin' with my face to the wall, and Liz come up and says, ' Here's the Vicar come to see ye.' ' The Vicar !' I says, ' what do *he* want to see me for ?' I reckon he must have heard me say it. He set an' talked. . . ." But Bettesworth did not vouchsafe any information as to the interview. When well and strong, he had been suspicious of the clergy ; now, I believe, he was a little uncomfortable with a feeling that he had made a hole in his manners.

Feeble though he was, on the previous day he had crept downstairs, he said, and even out and to the corner of the road forty yards away. I think it must have been on some similar expedition that those women saw him, and uttered their discouraging exclamations upon his look of ill-health ; but the desire to be up and out was incurable in him.

Yesterday, however, he fell, and had to be helped
home, where he literally crawled upstairs on hands
and knees, exhausted and breathless. So now,
since the breathlessness troubled him, and since he
knew me to have had bronchitis, did I know, he
asked, " anything as 'd ease it "? Eagerly he asked
it, with a most pitiful reliance upon me ; but I had
to confess that I knew no cure ; and the poor old
man seemed as if a support he had clutched at had
disappeared. Drearily he spoke of his condition.
He couldn't eat : a pint of milk was all he had been
able to take yesterday ; the same that morning.
Liz had said, " ' We got a nice little bit o' hock—
couldn't ye eat a bit o' that ? ' " and had brought
him a piece, but he " couldn't face it." " But
what's goin' to become of ye ?" she exclaimed, " if
you don't eat nothing ?" But he couldn't. His
mouth was so dry ; he was unable to swallow anything solid. Was there anything I could get him,
that he would fancy ? He hesitated ; then, " Well,
. . . I *should* like a bit o' rhubarb They had some
here t'other day—little bits o' sticks no bigger 'n
your finger. And they boys set down to it. . . .
' En't ye goin' to spare me *none ?* ' I says." . . .
The story wilted away, leaving me with a belief
that none had been spared for him. So I promised
him some rhubarb, and the next day a small tart
was made and sent over to him. The bearer returned saying that Liz, seeing it, had laughed :
" We got plenty; and he's had several lots." If

this is true, as it probably is, Bettesworth's delusion
on the point is the first instance of senility attacking
his intellect.

For although on this Friday his usual garrulity
about other topics than his illness was noticeably
diminished, still in his handling of the subjects he
did touch upon his strong mental grip was no wise
impaired. From Alf Stevens, who helped him home,
he went on to Alf's father, old George, who " en't
so wonderful grand " in health, and to Alf's
brother, who " boozes a bit," being out of work and
unsettled, " or may wander off no tellin' where "
in search of a job. Being now quartered at home,
" he don't offer to pay his old father nothin'.
P'r'aps of a Sat'day he'll bring home a joint o'
meat . . . But a very good bricklayer." Bettesworth has the whole situation in all its details under
review before him. Moreover, this bricklayer out
of work led him to speak of a serious matter, not
previously known to me getting about the world,
but to him lying in bed very well known—the
alarming scarcity of work this summer. He named
a number of men unemployed in the parish. I
added another name to the list—that of a carpenter. " Ne'er a better tradesman in the district ;
but en't done nothin' for months," Bettesworth
murmured unhesitatingly in his enfeebled voice.
" And So-and-so" (he mentioned a local contractor)
" is goin' to sack a dozen of his carters to-morrow,
I'm told. . . ."

The old man lay there, aware of these things ; and as I write the thought crosses my mind that a valuable organizing force has been left undeveloped and lost in Bettesworth.

It looks more and more doubtful if he will linger on until the autumn.

June 25, 1905 (*Sunday*) —It did not occur to me at the time, but after I got away from seeing Bettesworth on Friday a resemblance struck me between his look of almost abject helplessness and that of poor old Hall, whom I saw at the infirmary and who is since dead.

In the morning, with extreme difficulty, and his niece helping him, Bettesworth had got into the front bedroom while his own bed was being made and his room cleaned. To that extent has he lost strength in the last few weeks. Sometimes his niece chides him (kindly, I feel sure) for being so cast-down, but he says, " I can't help it, and 'ten't no use for anybody to tell me not. It hurts me to think that a little while ago I was strong and ready to do anything for anybody else, and now I got to beg 'em to come an' do anything for me."

I suspect that he gives some trouble. Fancies and the unreason characteristic of old age appear— for instance, about his food. He cannot take solids : they go dry in his mouth and he is unable to swallow them ; yet he begged for some one to buy him a slice or two of ham the other day. He

" seemed to have had a fancy for it this fortnight."
All he takes, on his own evidence, is a little milk.

He confessed to being occasionally light-headed.
" I sees all the people I knows, in this room here.
After I got back into bed to-day, there was three
fellers leanin' over the foot o' the bed, lookin' at
me ; and one of 'em said, ' I reckon I shall get six
months if I don't quit the neighbourhood.' I
sprung forward—' I'll break your head if you don't
clear out of *here !*' and I was goin' to hit 'n, an' then
he was gone."

In telling this the old man suited his action to
the tale, and again sat upright, his thin grey hair
tumbled, his jaw fallen, his eyes hopeless for very
weakness. It was then that he looked so much like
old Hall.

He was wishing to be shaved, but could get
nobody to do it for him. A labourer across the
valley had been sent to : " He'd ha' come an' done
it right enough, only he has rheumatics so bad he
can't hold the razor."

There was not much talk of the old kind ; and for
the first time in my acquaintance with Bettesworth
I had to search for topics of conversation. One
subject was raised by my mention of a neighbouring
farmer who proposed to begin cutting his late hay
next week. " Ah, with a machine," said Bettesworth ; " he can't git the men. 'R else he used to
say he'd never have a machine so long as he could
git men to mow for him. Billy Norris and his

brother " (elder brother to Kid Norris) " mowed for
'n eighteen years " in succession. . . . " They'd
live in a fashion nobody else couldn't. Never no
trouble to they about their food. They'd just
gather a few old sticks an' bits o' rubbish, and make
a fire—nothin' but a little smoke an' flare—an'
stick a bloater or a rasher on a pointed stick and
hold it up again' the flare an' smoke jest to warm it,
and down he'd go, and they'd be up and on mowin'
again. Then there was a barrel o' beer tumbled
down into the medder—they used to roll 'n into one
o' they water-gripes and put a little o' the damp
grass over 'n, and the beer 'd keep as *cool*. . . . And
when he was empty then he'd be took away and
another brought in. . . . But 'twas tea—that's
what they drunk for breakfast. Jest have a drink
o' beer when they started mowin' ; then go on for
an hour or two. Then one of 'em 'd go back to
where their kit was, an' make the tea in the drum,
an' get a little flare an' smoke ; an' they'd jest hold
their bloater on a pinted stick again' the smoke—
I've laughed at 'em many's a time. Dick Harding
over here used to say 't'd starve he to work 'long
with 'em ; he could do the mowin' but he couldn't
put up with the food. That was their way, though.
If they was out with the ballast-train or the railway-
cuttin', they'd sit down on the bank—all they
wanted was a little smoky fire." Bettesworth
laughed a little, amused at these sturdy men, and
at his own description of their cooking.

I asked : " You never did much mowing yourself, did you ?"

He hesitated, yet scarcely two seconds, and then replied : " Not much. I helped mow Holt Park once. My father-in-law—*Foreman*, we used to call 'n—was at it—what lived where Mrs. Warner is, and I lived where Porter do. And the Foreman sent for me to go and help. I didn't want to go—'tis hard work ; anybody might have mowin' for me ; but at last I agreed to go. But law ! the second mornin' I was like that I didn't hardly know how to crawl down there·" the three miles. " It got better after an hour or two. . . . But if a feller goes mowin' for eight or nine weeks on end, it do give 'n a doin'.''

Thus for a little while Bettesworth chatted, in the vein that had first attracted me to him. Shall I ever hear him again, I wonder ? We tried other subjects : the washed-out state of our lane and the best way to remedy it, the garden, the celery, the position of this or that crop. It entertained him for a few minutes ; then he failed to seize some quite simple idea, and knew that he had failed, and said despondently, " I can't keep things in my mind like I used to."

July 2 (*Sunday*).—Perhaps Bettesworth would have been more like himself on Friday, if I had called at the usual afternoon hour, instead of in the morning. As it was, he seemed fretful and im-

patient, and his face was flushed. I did not perceive that he was noticeably weaker, but rather
that he was irritable. He had pain in his chest and
side ; and he said that at night, when he lies with his
hands clasped over his waist, his chest is full of
" such funny noises, enough to frighten ye to hear
'em." His temper was embittered and angry,
especially angry, when some reference was made
to his being in the infirmary in the spring. For he
affirmed, " If I hadn't ha' went there, I should ha'
bin a man, up and at work *now*. I told the doctor
there, ' If I was to bide here, you'd *starve* me to
death.' " Embittered he was against his acquaint-
ances, so that he almost wept. " It hurts me so,
to think how good I bin to 'em ; and now when I
be bad myself there en't none of 'em comes near
me." He instanced his sister and her two sons at
Middlesham ; and his brother-in-law too : " Look
what I done for him !" If only he could get about !
Get so that he could sit and feel the air ! But his
bedroom is upstairs, and he is too weak to leave
it. The previous night, trying to get out of bed,
he " almost broke his neck," falling backwards with
his head against the bedstead. " I thought I'd
split 'n open," he said, " but I never called nobody.
Jack said, ' Why hadn't ye called me ?' " . . . The
old man's talk was too incoherent, too rambling,
to be followed well at the time or remembered now.

We discussed a local beanfeast excursion to
Ramsgate, which was to take place the following

day ; and he brightened up to recall how he had joined a similar trip to Weymouth some years ago. It was his last holiday, in fact. Even now it made him laugh, to remember how old Bill Brixton had gone on that day ; and he laughed a little scornfully at the trouble they had taken to enjoy themselves, and the fatigues they endured. Then there came just a touch of his old manner : " I had a little bottle with me and filled it up with a quarte'n o' whisky ; and when we was comin' home it seemed to brighten ye up. I says to old Bill, ' Put that to your lips,' I says. So he tried. ' Why, it's whisky !' he says. But that little wouldn't hurt 'n. 'Tis a *lot* o' whisky you gets for fo'pence ! 'Twouldn't have hurt 'n, if he'd took it bottle and all."

These monster excursions had never really appealed to Bettesworth's old-fashioned taste. Rather than be cooped up in a train, I remember he used to say, give him a quiet journey on the open road, afoot or by waggon, so that a man may " see the course o' the country," and if he comes to anything interesting, stop and look at it. And now, on his bed, the ill-humour he was displaying that morning vented itself again, in reference to a project he had heard of for another excursion. The Oddfellows' annual fête was at hand ; and, he said, with a sneering intonation, " The secretary and some of they " (respectable new-fangled people, he meant) " wanted 'em to go to Portsmouth. So they called a full meetin', an' the meetin' "—ah, I have forgotten the turn of speech. It suggested that these officious persons, interfering to dictate how the working man should take his pleasure, had met with a well-deserved snub, since the excursion was voted down and the customary dinner was to be held. To myself, as to Bettesworth, this seemed the preferable course : " It's really better," I said. Then he, " So *'tis*, sir. It's the old, natural *way*. We *al*ways reckoned to have *one day* in the year, when we all had holiday. And then everybody could join in—the women with their little childern, and all. 'Tis *nice*. . . ."

Mentioning the endeavours of the Colonel and Mr. —— to get a pension for him, I said, " They're very interested in it." " More so than what I be," he answered. Still, I urged, it was worth trying for ; and as for the lost papers, duplicates of them might be obtained, if we knew the regiment. I was saying this, when with a sort of pride, though still irritably, the old man broke in, " I can tell ye *all* that : regiment, an' regimental number, and officers, and all." At that I asked what was his regiment ?

He stiffened his head and neck (was it just one last flicker of the so long forgotten soldier's smartness ?) and said, " Forty-eighth, and my number was three nought nought seven. . . . I could name twenty people that knowed about my service. There's old Crum Callingham. He used to work for Sanders then, the coal merchant. The day I came back, didn't we have a booze, too ! He was at work in

Sanders's hop-garden, and I found 'n out, and two more, and I kep' sendin' for half-gallons. . . . Yes, that was the same day as I got 'ome—from Portsmouth."

That afternoon I happened to meet old Beagley—the retired bricklayer, and recently Bettesworth's landlord. He spoke of Bettesworth with more than usual appreciation, saying that he had been a strong man, as if he meant unusually strong. His sight must have been bad "thirty or forty years," Beagley estimated. He (Beagley) remembered first noticing it when he dropped his trowel from a scaffold, and sent Bettesworth down the ladder for it. He observed that Bettesworth could not see the trowel, but groped for it, as one gropes in the dark, until his hand touched it. But, added Beagley, " he'd mix mortar as well as any man I ever knew. I've had him workin' for me, and noticed. I'd as soon have had him as anybody. He couldn't have *seen* the lumps of lime, but I suppose 'twas something in the *feel* of it on the shovel. At any rate, he always *done* it ; and I've often thought about it."

July 14 (*Friday*).—I saw Bettesworth this afternoon, and it looks as if I shall not see him many times more.

Since my last visit to him a fortnight ago, the change in him is very marked. His niece, downstairs, prepared me for it. He was very ill, she said, and so weak that now they have to hold him up to feed him. Of course he can take no solids ; not even a mouthful of sponge-cake for which he had had a fancy . His feet and the lower parts of his body are swelling : the doctor says it is dropsy setting in, and reports further that his heart is " wasting away." Hearing all this—yes, and how Mrs Cook thought he should be watched at night, for he could not last much longer—hearing this, I fancied when I got upstairs that there was a look as of death on the shrunken cheeks : they had a corpse-like colour. Possibly it was only my fancy, but it was not fancy that his flesh had fallen away more than ever.

It has been an afternoon of magnificent summer weather, not sultry, but sumptuous ; with vast blue sky, a few slow-sailing clouds, a luxuriant west wind tempering the splendid heat. The thermometer in my room stands at 80° while I am writing. So Bettesworth lay just covered as to his body and legs with a counterpane, showing his bare neck, while his sleeves falling back to the elbow displayed his arms. From between the tendons the flesh has gone ; and the skin lies fluted all up the forearm, all up the neck. But at the foot ot the bed his feet emerging could be seen swollen and tight-skinned. His ears look withered and dry, like thin biscuit.

He did not complain much of pain. Sometimes, " if anything touches the bottom o' my feet, it runs all up my legs as if 'twas tied up in knots." Again, " what puzzles the doctor is my belly bein'

like 'tis—puffed up and hard as a puddin' dish."
The doctor has not mentioned dropsy, to him.
Enough, perhaps, that he has told him that his heart
was "wasting away." "That's a bad sign," commented Bettesworth, to me. He said he had asked
the doctor, "'Is there any chance o' my gettin'
better?' 'Not but a very little,' he said. 'If
you do, it'll be a miracle.'" At that, Bettesworth
replied, "Then I wish you'd give me something to
help me away from here." "Why, where d'ye want
to go to?" the doctor asked; and was answered, "Up
top o' Gravel Hill" to the churchyard. "I told
him that, straight to his head," said the old man.

He lay there, thinking of his death. Door and
window were wide open, and a cooling air played
through the room. Through the window, from my
place by the bed, I could see all the sunny side of the
valley in the sweltering afternoon heat; could see
and feel the splendour of the summer; could watch,
right down in the hollow, a man hoeing in a tiny
mangold-field, and the sunshine glistening on his
light-coloured shirt. Bettesworth no doubt knew
that man; had worked like that himself on many
July afternoons; and now he lay thinking of his
approaching death. But I thought, too, of his life,
and spoke of it: how from the hill-top there across
the valley you could not look round upon the country
in any part of the landscape but you would everywhere see places where he had worked. "Yes: for
a hundred miles round," he assented.

It came up naturally enough, I remember, in the course of desultory talk, with many pauses. He had had " gentry " to see him, he was saying, and he named the Colonel, and Mr. ——. " Who'd have thought ever *he*'d ha' bin like that to me ?" he exclaimed gratefully. And each of these visitors had spoken of his " good character "; had " liked all they ever heared " about him, and so on ; and it was then that I remarked about the places where he had worked, as proof that his good character had been well earned. But as we talked of his life, all the time the thought of his death was present. I fancied once that he wished to thank me for standing by him, and could not bring it off, for he began telling how the Colonel had said, " ' You've got a very good friend to be thankful for.' " But it was easy to turn this. The Colonel too is a friend. He had left an order for a bottle of whisky to be bought when the last one sent by Mr. —— is empty ; and he has not given up yet the endeavour to get Bettesworth's Crimean service recognized with a pension.

I cannot recall all that passed ; indeed, it was incoherent and mumbling, and I did not catch all. He revived that imaginary grievance against his neighbour, for drawing money from me to pay his club when he went to the infirmary. It appeared that Jack had been going into the matter, and had satisfied Bettesworth that the payments had never been really owing ; so they hoped that, now I knew,

I should take steps to be righted. Bettesworth seemed to find much relief in the feeling that his own character was cleared from blame. " Some masters might have give me the sack for it," he said, " when I got back to work." To this he kept reverting, as if in the hope of urging me to have justice ; and then he would say, " There, I'm as glad it's all right as if anybody had give me five shillin's." To humour him I professed to be equally glad ; it was not worth while to trouble him with what I knew very well to be the truth—that Mrs. Eggar was in the right, and had really done him a service.

What more ? He said once, " I thinks I shall go off all in a moment. Widder Cook was here. . . . she was talkin' about her husband Cha'les. They'd bin tater-hoein', an' when they left off she said, ' a drop o' beer wouldn't hurt us.' ' No,' he said, ' a drop o' beer and a bit o' bread an' cheese, an' then git off to bed.' So they sent for the beer. And they hadn't bin in bed half an hour afore she woke, and he'd moved ; an' she put her arm across 'n an' there he was, dead." So the widow had told Bettesworth ; and now he repeated it to me—the last tale I shall ever hear from him, I fancy, and told all mumblingly with his poor old dried-up mouth. He added, almost crying, " I prays God to let me go like that." We agreed that it was a merciful way to be taken.

It still interested him to hear of the garden, and

he asked how the potatoes were coming up, and listened to my account of the peas and carrots, but said he was " never much of a one " for carrots. At home I had left George Bryant lawn-mowing. Well, Bettesworth too had mown my lawn in hot weather, and smiled happily at the reminiscence. He smiled again when, recalling how I had known him now for fourteen years, I reminded him of the great piece of trenching which had been his first job for me.

So presently I came away, out on to the sunny road, thinking, " I shall not see him many more times." From just there I caught a glimpse of Leith Hill, blue with twenty intervening miles of afternoon sunlight : twenty miles of the England Bettesworth has served.

Half-way down the hill the old road-mender, straightening up from his work as I passed, asked, " Can ye keep yerself warm, sir ? "   And I laughed, " Pretty nearly. How about you ? "   " It *boils* out," he said. The perspiration stood on his face while he spoke of motor-cars, and the dust they raised ; but to me dust and swift-travelling cars and all seemed to tell of summer afternoon. And though the reason is obscure, somehow it seems fit that possibly my last talk with Bettesworth should be associated with the blue distant English country, and the summer dust, and that sunburnt old folk jest which consists in asking, when it is so par- ticularly and exhilaratingly warm as to-day, " Can you keep yourself warm ? "

July 21.—The weather was as brilliantly hot this afternoon as a week ago ; and Bettesworth's bedroom looked just as before ; but the old man was changed. He lay with eyes looking glazed between the half-shut lids, and he was breathing hard. His niece accompanied me upstairs ; but he took no notice of our entry until she mentioned my name, upon which he turned a little and put up a feeble hand for me to take. He was in a sort of stupor, though he seemed to rouse a little, and to understand one or two remarks I ventured. But when he spoke it was as if utterly exhausted, and we could not always make out his meaning. In the hope of helping him to realize that I was with him, I told of the garden, and how Bryant was mowing again, though in this hot weather the lawn was " getting pretty brown, *you* know." " Yes," he said feebly, " and if you don't keep it cut middlin' short, it soon goes wrong." Next I reported on the potatoes —how well they were coming : " the same sort as you planted for me last year." " Ah—the *Victoria*, wa'n't they ?" The question was a mere murmur. " No, *Duke of York*. And don't you remember what a crop we had, when you planted 'em ?" There came the faintest of smiles, and " None of what I planted failed much, did they ?" Indeed, no. The shallots he had planted during his last day's work had just been harvested ; the beans which he sowed the same day had but now yielded their last picking. I told him they were over.

"You can't expect no other," he said, meaning at this time of year and in such dry weather. I mentioned the celery, reminding him, "you *have* sweated over watering celery, haven't you?" Again he just smiled, and I fancy this smile was the last sign of rational interest and pride in his labour.

For after this he became incoherent and wandering. Dimly we made out that he "wanted to put them four poles against the veranda," apparently meaning my veranda. "What for?" his niece asked. "To keep the wall up." Then I, "We won't trouble about that to-day," as if he had been consulting me about the work, and he seemed satisfied to have my decision. But I had stayed too long; so, grasping his hand, I said "Good-bye." He asked, "Are ye goin' to the club?" (He was thinking of the Oddfellows' fête arranged for to-morrow week, and had been wondering all day, his niece said, not to hear the band.) "It isn't till to-morrow week," we said. "How they do keep humbuggin' about," he muttered crossly. "Yes, but they've settled it now," we assured him.

I have promised to go again to see him—to-morrow or on Sunday, because, according to his niece, he had been counting on my visit, and asking for several days "if this was Friday."

The thought came to me on my way home, that he is dying without any suspicion that anyone could think of him with admiration and reverence.

July 25 (*Tuesday*).—Bettesworth died this evening at six o'clock.

July 28 (*Friday*).—This afternoon I went to the funeral.

A week earlier (almost to the hour) when I parted from him, he seemed too ill to take his money—too unconscious, I mean. I offered it to his niece, standing at the foot of the bed ; but she said, glancing meaningly towards him, " I think he'd like to take it, sir." So I turned to him and put the shillings into his hand, which he held up limply. " Your wages," I said.

For a moment he grasped the silver, then it dropped out on to his bare chest and slid under the bed-gown, whence I rescued it, and, finding his purse under the pillow, put his last wages away safely there.

On the Saturday I saw him, but I think he did not know me : and that was the last time. The thought of him keeps coming, wherever I go in the garden ; but I put it aside for fear of spoiling truer because more spontaneous memories of him in time to come.